A Kiss from
THERMOPYLAE

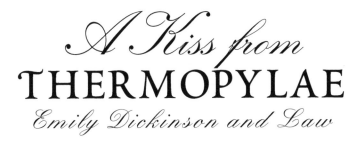

A Kiss from
THERMOPYLAE
Emily Dickinson and Law

JAMES R. GUTHRIE

University of Massachusetts Press
AMHERST AND BOSTON

ISBN 978-1-62534-113-6 (paper); 112-9 (hardcover)

Designed by Sally Nichols
Set in Adobe Garamond Pro
Printed and bound by Sheridan Books, Inc

Library of Congress Cataloging-in-Publication Data

Guthrie, James R. (James Robert)
  A kiss from Thermopylae : Emily Dickinson and law / James R.
Guthrie.
     pages cm
  Includes bibliographical references and index.
  ISBN 978-1-62534-113-6 (pbk. : alk. paper) — ISBN 978-1-62534-112-9
(hardcover : alk. paper) 1. Dickinson, Emily, 1830–1886—Criticism
and interpretation. 2. Dickinson, Emily, 1830–1886—Knowledge—
Law. 3. Law and literature. 4. Law in literature. I. Title.
  PS1541.Z5G885 2015
  811'.4—dc23
                              2014026027

British Library Cataloguing-in-Publication Data
A catalogue record for this book is available from the British Library.

For Rebecca

CONTENTS

ACKNOWLEDGMENTS

Many people's help and advice went into the making of this book.

A truncated version of my introduction appears in Cambridge University Press's *Emily Dickinson in Context,* edited by Eliza Richards. I am grateful for that press's permission to reuse the material, with special thanks to Eliza and to Ray Ryan at Cambridge University Press.

I thank Wright State University for granting me sabbatical funding and leave toward completing this project. I also owe a debt of gratitude to Cristanne Miller, Gary Stonum, Jane Eberwein, William and Nancy Pridgen, Jeff Morris, Charles Hallinan, Jed Deppman, Stephanie Tingley, Cindy MacKenzie, Cynthia Hallen, Paul Crumbley, and Roberta Engleman. At University of Massachusetts Press, thanks to Bruce Wilcox, Brian Halley, Carol Betsch, and especially Mary Bellino.

Most important, this project could not possibly have been completed without the advice and encouragement I received from my wife, Rebecca Cochran, professor of law at the University of Dayton School of Law.

A few notes about legal reference works: For contemporary definitions of legal terms, I have relied on *Black's Law Dictionary,* 8th edition, edited by Bryan A. Garner. For period definitions of legal terms, I have relied on the 1897 edition of *Bouvier's Law Dictionary.* Various editions of *Bouvier's,* first published in Philadelphia in 1839, served as essential reference works for American attorneys practicing during the nineteenth century.

A Kiss from
THERMOPYLAE

A CLIMATE OF LAW

orn into a family committed to the practice of law, Emily Dickinson became deeply engaged with legal language, legal topics, and legal thought. Remaining her entire life beneath her parents' roof, chiefly at the house the Dickinsons called the Homestead, the poet could observe at close hand what it meant to be an attorney. She must have listened, while seated at the dinner table, as her father explained issues of law affecting his clients' interests.[1] Edward Dickinson maintained his practice a scant quarter mile west of the Homestead in an office on the second floor of the Palmer Block, a brick commercial building constructed by his own father, "Squire" Samuel F. Dickinson. Eventually the poet's brother, William Austin Dickinson, followed suit, first by attending law school at Harvard College and then by becoming a partner in his father's firm. Amherst, small as it was and is, supported a comparatively large population of educated professionals, including attorneys. The town prided itself on being the site of Amherst College, which the Dickinson family helped establish. Amherst was an easy eight-mile ride from Northampton, county seat of Hampshire County; moreover, following the inauguration in 1853 of the Amherst & Belchertown Railroad, which Edward Dickinson helped bring to town, residents enjoyed convenient access to Boston, ninety miles distant. During the first half of the nineteenth century Amherst was a town on the rise, and a congenial location in which to practice law.

The poet's father made a good living, and so did Austin, particularly after his father's death in 1874 left a local legal vacuum. Both father and son represented clients, acted as treasurers for Amherst College, served on boards of trustees, were appointed to state court offices, and, in Edward's case, elected to positions in the state and national legislatures. The Dickinsons invested in real estate and bought shares of stock in successful and unsuccessful companies. In his politics, Edward Dickinson was a staunch Whig who identified the prosperity of the business community with the welfare of the country overall. He disliked abolitionists and disapproved of fellow Whigs who bolted to the newly founded Republican Party. He threw himself into civic projects, and, when he died, he was trying to expedite the funding and construction of the Hoosac Tunnel in northwestern Massachusetts, the longest railroad tunnel in the world. Austin, less conservative in his politics, his religion, and his artistic tastes than his father, nevertheless emulated him by immersing himself in the business affairs of Amherst College, in the construction of the First Congregational Church, and in various public and private landscaping projects throughout the area. When Austin died in 1895, his obituary in the *Springfield Republican* called him Amherst's "most influential citizen." The Dickinson legal dynasty spanned virtually the entire nineteenth century.

The emergence of a poet of talent from such a family background may come as something of a surprise. Yet a continuity existed between Emily Dickinson's practice of writing and the male Dickinsons' practice of law. A review of Emily Dickinson's correspondence reveals that the poet's attitude toward her grandfather's, father's, and brother's professional lives was marked customarily by loyalty, sympathy, and curiosity.[2] She shared their pride in the family's reputation for civic-mindedness, as well as their shame over the financial ruin of the family patriarch, Samuel F. Dickinson, who, having risen to become one of the county's most successful attorneys,[3] tumbled into financial failure, largely as a result of his contributions to founding Amherst College. Because the Dickinsons were preoccupied with law, it, rather than literature, would have constituted the poet's primary linguistic context, as well as one of the more important cultural bases for her thought. The reading and writing of literature, while seen by Edward Dickinson and his wife, Emily Norcross Dickinson, as desirable cultural embellishments to be encouraged in their children, were ordinarily subordinated to what the poet's father called "real life."[4]

Among the family certain psychological and behavioral traits predominated. As Richard Sewall points out, despite their devotion to civic projects the Dickinsons tended to be home centered, inward looking, and emotionally volatile.[5] On both sides of the family, the poet had relatives judged by neighbors to have been out of the ordinary, if not downright eccentric. In exchange for remaining close by to the rest of the clan, Dickinson family members were suffered, albeit within limits, to pursue their individual bents.[6] Edward Dickinson's relationship with his literarily inclined daughter was respectful, without being necessarily comprehending or sympathetic. For her part, she probably realized that his hard-headed approach to life made her life of the mind possible, as well as the entire family's comfortable upper-middle-class existence.

Father and daughter were affiliated not just by blood, but also by a mutual interest in language. Without showing a marked talent for writing himself, as a young man Edward Dickinson, a graduate of Yale College, enjoyed reading a variety of books, and he recommended individual titles to his fiancée, Emily Norcross. He was not immune to the beauties of poetry, quoting Shakespeare occasionally, or the somber verses of Edward Young.[7] Still, Edward Dickinson never lost sight of the fact that his chosen profession required a less fanciful approach to language. His daughter, on the other hand, gloried in poetry, savoring the sounds and rhythms of words as well as the disquieting power of metaphor. Not unexpectedly, many of her images and figures of speech draw on the law directly or indirectly. She imported legal terms as part of a far-ranging diction that integrated brief, pungent Anglo-Saxon words with polysyllabic Latinate terms drawn from science, business, and the professions.[8] Occasionally, as lawyers have ever been prone to do in writing and in speech, she also employed specific Latin words and phrases.[9] At Amherst Academy she took classes in Latin as part of a more rigorous "Classical" track of instruction roughly equivalent to a modern college-prep curriculum, and indeed, Dickinson belonged to the first cohort of American women to attend college. At Mary Lyon's Mount Holyoke Female Seminary, she exhibited aptitude in the areas of chemistry, physiology, music, and writing.[10]

In her own fashion, Dickinson's practice of writing and recopying pencil drafts, and of editing her poems and marking variant words for possible future consideration, demonstrated an approach to composition as utilitarian as her father's drafting of his legal briefs. She often assembled fair copies of her work into packets and fascicles carefully sewn together with thread, a method of self-publication that lent to an intensely private pursuit an air of professionalism. Then too, the vocation of law requires sophisticated interpersonal skills, and, despite her notoriously reclusive habits and a reluctance to submit her work for publication, Dickinson was not an isolated writer. She often made presents of poems to friends, and she initiated a long-standing correspondence with the prominent literary critic Thomas Wentworth Higginson. The world of getting and spending, of which the business of writing and publishing books formed a part, was not alien to Emily Dickinson, nor did she ignore or disdain it. While writing, she would have been compelled, even involuntarily, to turn her thoughts at least occasionally to matters of law and business, if only because some of her poem and letter drafts were composed on scrap paper torn from Edward Dickinson's legal form books, providing a sort of physical link between father's and daughter's contrasting, yet conjoined, modes of thinking and writing.[11] She did not regard her vocation as a vehicle for parodying or impugning her father's profession, or his speaking and writing style; instead, she usually held in high regard all legal professionals, whether they worked as judges, attorneys, police officers, or lowly bailiffs. Moreover, Emily Dickinson respected—even loved—the law itself.

Thus within the Dickinson household an atmosphere of law likely prevailed. Yet in my examination of Emily Dickinson's relation to the law, I also want to consider the wider cultural environment of contemporary American attitudes toward the legal profession. During the first half of the century, particular areas of the law, notably bankruptcy, equity, and criminal law, were undergoing major reforms, even as the profession of law itself was enjoying a sort of Golden Age. Later, as the poet grew older, the nation's mood as expressed through discussions about law shifted radically again from the optimism, idealism, and reformist energy marking the antebellum era to an anxiety rooted in the reunited republic's effort to contain forces of social upheaval unleashed by the war.[12] Especially after her father's death in 1874, Dickinson's poems and letters display an increasing uneasiness over the dangers posed by a perceived spread of lawlessness.

In her late friendship and romance with Otis Lord, a distinguished jurist of her father's generation, Dickinson discovered both a renewed connection to legal philosophies fashionable before the war and an emotional sanctuary during the turbulent years coinciding with the end of Reconstruction. This period was made even more difficult for the poet both by a series of deaths and by her brother's adulterous affair with Mabel Loomis Todd, the wife of Professor David Peck Todd and the future editor of Dickinson's poems. That liaison, which instigated a period of intrafamily enmity called the "war between the houses," overlapped her affair with Judge Lord. Despite being her senior by eighteen years, Lord made a suitable candidate for the poet's affections not least because he combined a taste for literature with a passionate interest in the law. Drafts of letters evidently intended for him, and late poems written by Dickinson with him probably in mind, are especially rich in legal references and terminology. Thus to the end of her life the poet dwelled within a self-willed climate of law that helped determine what she wrote about, her attitude toward her native land, and whom she loved.

Dickinson's deployment of legal terms, images, and metaphors in her poems and letters reflects indirectly her inheritance of a family and regional culture with a complex and at times contentious relation to law. The Puritan settlers of New England, among whom her ancestors were numbered, brought with them from Britain the language of covenant theology, which emphasized a contractual, legalistic relation between humankind and God. At the same time, however, the Puritans, some of whom had fled abuses associated with the juryless Star Chamber, harbored a deep distrust of laws conceived and enforced by figures in entrenched positions of authority. In America as a whole, citizens dwelling both east and west of the Alleghenies increasingly resisted (often vainly) the proliferation of laws accompanying the raw republic's national maturation as a larger polity dwelling under the rule of law.

Initially, at least, Americans also inherited from their British cousins a deep-seated antipathy toward lawyers and the profession of law, a sentiment that has never really gone away on either side of the Atlantic. Above all, laymen have tended to distrust lawyers' professional ethics and business practices. Criminal law attorneys are often accused of defending clients whom they know or believe to be guilty.[13] Not infrequently, by indulging in "pettifogging, sophistry, and cavil" (Miller, *Legal Mind* 205), lawyers have also been charged with inflating their fees by deliberately introducing needless complexity into simple matters of litigation. By 1788 the phrase "Philadelphia lawyer," coined initially as a term of praise, had become instead one of opprobrium for attorneys who knew how to split legal hairs to an exceedingly fine degree. The entire process of going to law was infamous for delay and expense; then too, juries were widely held to be so capricious that one important measure of an attorney's effectiveness lay in keeping his client *out* of court. Thus it is all the more ironic that Americans in general and New Englanders in particular were proverbial among foreign observers for an eagerness to litigate, particularly against their neighbors.[14] Often, those professing greatest hostility toward the law were not reluctant to invoke it when they determined that their rights—especially their property rights—had been infringed.

By the time Edward Dickinson became an attorney in the 1820s, Americans' attitudes about lawyers and the law had begun undergoing a sea change. As Perry Miller observes, during the early decades of the nineteenth century public opinion shifted from despising lawyers and the law to seeing them as important safeguards of personal liberties and national values. "A phenomenon of fundamental importance for both the social and intellectual history of America," he writes, "is the amazing rise, within three or four decades, of the legal profession from its chaotic condition of around 1790 to a position of political and intellectual domination" (*Life of the Mind* 109). In 1835 Toqueville observed that in America, lawyers "form the highest political class and the most cultivated portion of society" (qtd. in Miller, *Life of the Mind* 114).

This retrieval of attorneys', and the law's, reputations in America was achieved partially through the appearance during the republic's early years of an unusually gifted and innovative group of legal thinkers that included James Kent, Joseph Story, David Hoffman, and John Marshall. Kent's, Story's, and Hoffman's treatises became required reading for apprenticing attorneys, and Marshall's career on the bench of the Supreme Court—a virtually unprecedented legal venue, in comparison to Europe's higher courts—inspired respect and emulation. Kent and Story helped persuade their countrymen that the English common law provided a solid foundation for American law. They rendered Blackstone more palatable to Americans, while nevertheless remaining conscious of intrinsic differences separating legal priorities of the mother country from those of the new nation. Attorneys also earned the admiration of their colleagues and the public at large with displays of eloquence and learning. When Daniel Webster argued a case he drew crowds, and his address to the Supreme

Court in *Dartmouth College v. Woodward* was held up as a model of forensic excellence. Webster's progress from the courtroom to the Senate chamber exemplified a national trend of attorneys winning public office, a trajectory Edward Dickinson himself would follow by being elected first to the Massachusetts legislature and subsequently to Congress.

As a young attorney, Edward could take some satisfaction in knowing that Massachusetts was a bellwether among the states in confronting contemporary legal quandaries and developing stellar judicial talent. Lemuel Shaw, a distinguished judge and Herman Melville's father-in-law, was viewed as an exemplar of personal rectitude and legal sophistication. Other courtroom luminaries included Story himself, Rufus Choate (against whom Edward Dickinson argued on at least one occasion), and Robert Rantoul. Massachusetts generated some of the antebellum era's more important cases: *Charles River Bridge v. Warren Bridge* (1837), *Farwell v. Boston & Worcester R.R. Corp.* (1842), and the Anthony Burns case testing the Fugitive Slave Act (1854). When he proposed marriage to Emily Norcross, Edward Dickinson could reasonably expect the establishment of his own legal practice to presage financial security, respectability, and perhaps even a national reputation. His subsequent ascent to becoming the most prominent attorney in Amherst, and perhaps in all of Hampshire County, represents an impressive personal achievement.[15]

As the profession's reputation changed, so too did the path to becoming an attorney. In the eighteenth century, young men aspiring to become lawyers "read" law in established practices as informal apprentices. Thus Samuel F. Dickinson read law in the office of Simeon Strong, as Abraham Lincoln later read law on the rustic Illinois frontier. But the professionalization of law in America resulted largely from a proliferation of law schools. Beginning with the founding of a law school at the College of William and Mary in 1779, and then Tapping Reeve's school in Litchfield, Connecticut, established in 1784, academies began offering formal curricula and instruction by distinguished faculty members. Harvard College established a law school in 1817, followed by Yale's in the 1820s. Edward studied law locally at Northampton Law School, also attended by Franklin Pierce. Samuel Fowler Dickinson, confronting financial ruin in 1828, briefly proposed opening a law school himself in Amherst, a project that never got off the ground (Habegger, "How the Dickinsons Lost Their Homes" 180).

By the time Austin Dickinson attended Harvard law during the early

1850s, legal education in America was well on its way to becoming thoroughly standardized and professionalized. At Harvard, Austin applied himself to a rigorous academic program that included reading Blackstone's and Kent's *Commentaries* and taking required courses in Property, Commercial Law, Civil Law, Constitutional Law, Criminal Law, and Equity.[16] While Austin was boarding in Cambridge, he and his sister maintained a lively correspondence in which they often joked about the law and about his future legal career, a brand of sibling humor that probably did not always please their sober-sided father. Although he was proud his son had followed in his footsteps, Edward Dickinson evidently questioned whether Harvard could produce young men up to the challenge of practicing law on a daily basis, year in and year out. In a letter the poet wrote to Austin in April 1853, when he had just commenced his legal studies, she reported their father's reactions to letters he had been sending home: "You cant think how delighted father was, with the account you gave of northerners and southerners, and the electioneering – he seemed to feel so happy to have you interested in what was going on at Cambridge – he said he 'knew all about it – he'd been thro' the whole, it was only a little specimen of what you'd meet in life, if you lived to enter it.' I could'nt hardly help telling him that I thought his idea of life rather a boisterous one, but I kept perfectly still" (L116).

Although the poet evidently enjoyed learning about the law vicariously from her father and brother, little evidence exists to suggest she envied them or wished that women, too, could attend law school and enter practice. (Women would not begin being admitted to the bar until the late 1870s, just about a decade before Dickinson died.) She did complain occasionally, and facetiously, that she should be granted the same freedom of action in law and politics granted to men. In a comically melodramatic letter (L94) sent to her friend and future sister-in-law, Susan Gilbert, in 1852, a year before Austin entered law school, Dickinson said,

> Why cant *I* be a Delegate to the great Whig Convention? – don't I know all about Daniel Webster, and the Tariff, and the Law? Then, Susie I could see you, during a pause in the session – but I don't like this country at all, and I shant stay here any longer! "Delenda est" America, Massachusetts and all!
>
> open me carefully

Dickinson's hyperbole mimics the flights of oratory then so popular in American politics, while simultaneously removing herself from that arena, literally so as she threatens either to leave the country completely or to destroy it, as Cato had recommended his fellow senators should eradicate Carthage ("delenda est"). Her subscript even seems to suggest that the entire letter be treated gingerly, as if it were a bomb—although of course if it had been, Sue, in breaking the seal, would have been blown to bits. Edward Dickinson, a delegate to this same Whig convention held in Baltimore on June 16, 1852, probably discussed with his family his fellow New Englanders' support for Webster as a potential presidential candidate. While visiting Baltimore, Edward delivered this letter from his daughter to Susan, then teaching mathematics at a local school (Johnson, *Letters* 212). Knowing her father is bearing her news, Emily Dickinson lampoons the male-dominated, rhetorically aggressive realm of American politics while signaling indirectly that she misses him and her best friend, together without her in distant Maryland. That Emily Dickinson did indeed comprehend something about "the Law" Susan Gilbert would have understood, yet it is unlikely that Susan would have interpreted this particular paragraph as an expression of thwarted ambition or smoldering resentment over male political and professional prerogatives.[17]

Dickinson's stated willingness to make the trip to Baltimore and attend the convention is not meant to be taken seriously. Ordinarily, the poet was content to remain at home in Amherst, a town that offered a developing writer several advantages: an intimate scale; a familiarity founded on the fact that several generations of Dickinsons had lived in the area; proximity to nature; and access to the larger world, chiefly through Amherst College and its faculty. The college, besides representing a source of civic pride for the family deriving from Samuel F. Dickinson's role in helping found it, opened a window to the world for Dickinson and other Amherst residents.

Another distinguished cofounder of Amherst College was Noah Webster, renowned patriot, veteran of the Revolution, attorney (as well as cousin to Daniel Webster), and compiler of the *American Dictionary of the English Language*. The 1844 edition of Webster's work became Dickinson's "lexicon," from which she drew both inspiration and reading pleasure. Webster approached language with a lawyer's keen eye for discerning shades of meaning, and his phonetically logical and consistent orthography became, and remains, the standard for written American English.

Within the limits of its at times shaky financial resources, Amherst College strove to attract the best and the brightest, especially from among New England's younger teachers. Thus, for example, the college hired Nathan Welby Fiske, professor of Greek, Latin, and philosophy, as well as father of the noted author Helen Hunt Jackson, who became Emily Dickinson's friend in adulthood. Other local luminaries in the fields of law and literature included Charles Bartlett Andrews, a near-contemporary of the poet and a graduate of Amherst who studied law in Connecticut before going on to become governor of that state. Osmyn Baker progressed from Amherst Academy and Yale College to practicing law before being elected to Congress. During Emily Dickinson's youth, the town of Amherst constituted a small, yet intense, confluence of knowledge, language, and law, an auspicious environment for the maturation of a poet.

Dickinson's diction, metaphors, and poetic personae all owe a great deal to the legal environment in which she was nurtured. Legal references are comparatively easy to spot in her writings: the attorney and Dickinson scholar Robert Lambert cites nearly one hundred different legally related words in her poems, leaving aside those found in her letters.[18] Her poetic diction is also characterized by many not necessarily legalistic terms which nevertheless have commonly understood legal meanings. She developed a practice of substituting legally inflected words for those having more generic denotations, as in using "arraign" to mean "stop"; "adjourn" to mean "leave"; "abrogate" to mean "prevent"; "perjure" to mean "lie." More broadly, law's influence may be reflected in her rational, logical approach to her subject matter, in her habit of conciseness (a quality in legal writing championed by judges with crowded dockets, and, as practiced by attorneys, often more honored in the breach than the observance), and perhaps even in her custom of capitalizing significant words at will.[19] Thematically, Dickinson gravitated toward issues involving personal rights and responsibilities, liberties and liabilities, trespasses and defenses of property, petitions and denials. Like her Puritan forebears, she tended to view the universe legalistically, taking pains to distinguish, for example, what belonged to her as opposed to what fell within the province of a monitoring and occasionally covetous God.

But it is Dickinson's figural language that makes richest use of legal terms and concepts. My aim in this volume is to unpack some of Dickinson's legally inflected metaphors to show how, in many instances, comprehending their legal content may open up readings of her poems. Conversely, readings that ignore or underestimate her poems' legal content may seriously diminish their intellectual and affective impact. Moreover, in her letters and poems Dickinson often showed herself to be acutely aware of topical issues pertaining to law as it was then being practiced in Massachusetts and in the country at large. Not unexpectedly, poems and letters addressed to recipients she knew to be conversant in matters of law—for example, her brother, her sister-in-law, Elizabeth Holland, and Otis Lord—are apt to contain a greater concentration of legal references and terms. Ironically, Dickinson's obscurity as a writer permitted her the freedom to use legal and professional language to a degree not commonly observable in the works of more conventional and widely known women poets, such as those written by her friend Helen Hunt Jackson. Dickinson was comfortable writing about what she knew, to people whom she knew.

Even in her most casual correspondence, Dickinson was apt to resort to a legal idiom. Cynthia MacKenzie's concordance to Dickinson's letters lists twenty-one occurrences of the word "law." But beyond these, references to law in her letters suggest she applied a legal perspective to everyday events.[20] Writing to her cousins Fanny and Louise (Loo) Norcross concerning the probably accidental removal from their house of a spool of thread, she confesses, "I defrauded Loo of 1 spool of thread; we will 'settle,' however –" (L267). She concluded one letter to Mrs. Holland, wife of Josiah Holland, the editor of *Scribner's,* by observing, "Blossoms belong to the bee, if needs be by *habeas corpus*," and in another, wondering whether Mrs. Holland was the mysterious donor of a box of candy, "Jacob versus Esau, was a trifle in Litigation, compared to the Skirmish in my Mind –" (L227, L743).[21] Two of Dickinson's enigmatic "Master" letters refer to feeling as if she lived in a jail, immured like Byron's prisoner of Chillon (L233), or a "culprit" who pleads paradoxically to be "punish[ed]" by her unknown correspondent through being incarcerated, rather than "banish[ed]" from his presence (L248).

The poet's knowledge of law also contributed to some of her keenest displays of wit, and not always in ways complimentary to legal professionals, or to humanity in general. Yet even by writing in this vein Dickinson could have been emulating legal practitioners. Seasoned attorneys who, in their offices or in the courtroom, may witness a generous sampling of human folly are sometimes accused of conceiving a cynical or jaundiced view of their fellow man. Although Dickinson respected optimists such as Emerson and Thoreau, a latent strain of Calvinistic thought peculiarly hospitable to an attorney's or a judge's gimlet-eyed view of human nature often informs her writings. Perhaps as a consequence, Dickinson became something of a moralist, reverting to the neoclassical manner of thinking and writing natural to her more conservative father—but with a twist. The distinctly human element of practicing law appealed to Dickinson, and the personae in her poems, drawn from the several human types to be encountered in virtually any county court, speak in dialogic, nearly novelistic, voices. Many of her writings concerning law exhibit a satirical edge, and she took special delight in what attorneys call their "war stories": narratives involving trials gone awry, witnesses who had perjured themselves on the stand, runaway juries.[22]

A few quick examples may serve to demonstrate the law's importance to Dickinson's poetic practice. In "A prompt – executive Bird is the Jay –" (F1022 B), Dickinson compares a bluejay to three human figures, two of whom would commonly be encountered in courtrooms:

A prompt – executive Bird is the Jay –
Bold as a Bailiff's Hymn –
Brittle and Brief in quality –
Warrant in every line – | Warrant / Business –
Sitting a Bough like a Brigadier
Confident and straight –
Much is the mien of him in March
As a Magistrate.

Dickinson characterizes the bluejay first as a bailiff and brigadier, and then as a magistrate, that is, a high-ranking local judicial officer, such as a judge. Bailiffs are empowered to carry out the court's will bodily, delivering subpoenas in person, serving summonses, and maintaining order in the court. Typically, bailiffs were (and are) physically imposing, and during the nineteenth century some were equipped with truncheons. In delivering a summons, a bailiff would get right to the point: his address is "Bold," "Brittle," and "Brief." As if to indicate her

adjectives' interdependence, Dickinson's alliteration links them phonetically and conceptually, so that to be "bold" is to be "brief," and vice versa.
The bailiff's formal, nearly ceremonial speech betokens his "Warrant,"
that is, his authorization to compel someone to provide testimony or
present himself at court.[23] After delivering his message, the bailiff might
conclude, "You have been served," signifying both that his task is completed and that a legal process had just been enacted. He might also add,
"Disobey at your peril."

In the courtroom a bailiff would stand ramrod straight, reflecting his
responsibility for maintaining decorum during the proceedings. As Judy
Jo Small has suggested (43), Dickinson's comparison of the bailiff's terse
manner of speaking, his "Hymn," to a bluejay's raucous call may allude to
the bailiff's cry showing that court was in session, "Oyez, oyez, oyez!"—an
utterance also resembling a line from a hymn in its brevity, its refrain,
and its ritualistic significance. The other two figures in Dickinson's trio
of human analogues are similarly distinguished by a martial bearing. In
likening the bluejay to a "brigadier," the poet may have had in mind the
markings on that bird's wing, which resemble the chevrons on an officer's
uniform, like that worn by a brigadier general; Dickinson also compares
the jay to a brigadier in F1596, "No Brigadier throughout the Year." Finally,
the jay's erect posture also reminds the poet of the magistrate sitting stiffly
at his bench. By appearing "Confident" and "straight," the judge asserts the
power of the state, invested as well in the bailiff, and in the soldier.

The contours of Dickinson's poetic speech also reflect power relations
within the courtroom. An executive sits highest in administrative authority, as would a magistrate or a brigadier general who directs subordinates
in the courtroom or on the battlefield, yet Dickinson's adjective "executive" also reminds us that in law, language itself may be *executory*. Wills,
deeds, and contracts are executed by the application of a signature, or a
seal, or both. Even capital punishment may be administered in the *execution* of a convicted felon, a sanctioned form of killing that fulfills written
or verbal commands issued by a court. In the terminology of speech act
theory, legal language is frequently performative, in that words authorize
the taking of an action, often without delay.

In particular, as Dennis Kurzon points out, the word "hereby" signals
this rhetorical and linguistic function, as in the sentence "It is *hereby*
declared that the office of Lord Chancellor is and shall be tenable by an

adherent of the Roman Catholic faith" (6–7, 10).[24] The language of the entire legal apparatus is replete with words and expressions conveying a sense of enactment not present in virtually any other mode of discourse. Even the *sentence* handed down by the court does not quite resemble sentences uttered or written under other circumstances, such as by writers of fiction. At the very moment such legal formulae are said or inscribed, the very fabric of reality may be altered, not just for the adjudged, but also for the rest of society, which in delegating power to officials, implicitly authorizes and consents to such acts.[25]

Attorneys must also remain cognizant of the executory power of language whenever affidavits or depositions are signed. These signatures may be those of the principals in a legal transaction, or of attorneys, judges, witnesses. Witnessing, the activity often being attested to by the provision of a signature, was a matter attorneys did not, and do not, take lightly. Many attorneys certify themselves as notaries so that they may take statements under oath from witnesses or attest to the authenticity of signatures, even of individuals who are not their clients. Edward and Austin Dickinson were both notaries, and evidence within the poems suggests that Emily Dickinson was mindful of the symbolic and legal importance of confirmatory signatures and seals. Her father often assigned to the poet a defined legal function as witness and signatory. Alfred Habegger has determined that the poet's signature appears in a witnessing role on legal documents generated by her father much more frequently than those of other family members.[26] While it is true that a stay-at-home daughter could be depended on to be available for such responsibilities, the same would have been true of her younger sister, Lavinia. The frequency with which her father turned to Emily suggests his selection of his older daughter was deliberate. Witnesses to legal transactions were expected to be of age, competent, and aware of the general import of the papers they were signing.[27] Within the Dickinson family, Emily was known from an early age to be especially adept at reading and writing, and perhaps her father credited her as well with a sophistication about business and personal affairs.

An exposure to legal language may also have influenced the formal and rhetorical architectures of Dickinson's poems. Compression and brevity have long been recognized as hallmarks of her writing style. Few of her poems exceed sixteen lines, and her succinct tetrameter packs a good deal of meaning into a very small space. In "A prompt – executive Bird is the Jay –," brevity is intrinsic to the executory success of the bailiff's message, whether delivered in court or on a doorstep. That he speaks with authority is signified not just by his tone of voice, but also by the bailiff's austere demeanor, his "Warrant" showing in every line of his bearing, as the magistrate's authority is reflected in every line of his writ. The word "brief" would also have been familiar to Dickinson, of course, from having encountered it in a specifically legal context: the briefs her father was continually writing in performance of his professional capacity. *Black's Law Dictionary* defines "brief" as "A written statement setting out the legal contentions of a party in litigation, esp. on appeal; a document prepared by counsel as the basis for arguing a case, consisting of legal and factual arguments and the authorities in support of them" (204).[28] In a letter to Thomas Wentworth Higginson, the poet described her family's general indifference to literature, saying that her mother "does not care for thought" and that Edward Dickinson was "too busy with his Briefs – to notice what we do –" (L261). Between these parental extremes the poet staked out her own imaginative terrain, and Dickinson's poems often resemble "briefs" in their own right, "Bulletins . . . From Immortality" presenting concise statements of fact, marshaled evidence, and grounds for argument.[29]

An essentially forensic approach to language and to thought may be discerned in F1435, written probably to her brother Austin around 1877. The poem states its case as concisely as would a lawyer's brief, while hinting simultaneously at a possible source of friction between the poet's argumentative nature and her Calvinistic religious heritage:

> The Fact that Earth is Heaven –
> Whether Heaven is Heaven or not
> If not an Affidavit
> Of that specific Spot
> Not only must confirm us
> That it is not for us
> But that it would affront us
> To dwell in such a place –

The presence of the words "Fact," "Affidavit," and "confirm," as well as the speaker's scrupulously logical presentation of her argument, emphasizes this epistle-poem's foundation in law. Dickinson's theological *jeu* seems to have been designed specifically to entertain Austin, by 1877 a seasoned attorney nearly fifty years old. Dickinson could have relied on her brother's legal background to provide a context for understanding the poem's figural foundation in property law.

The speaker begins by distinguishing between facts provable in court, as attested to by a witness who submits a signed affidavit, and facts anyone may ascertain empirically. Thematically, the poem makes the somewhat conventional point that a bird in hand is worth two in the bush: although the New Testament promises us heaven after we die, our prior experience of a terrestrial, edenic paradise impels us to reject conventional Christianity's promise of eternal life, represented here as a sort of proposal, such as one might find in a real estate prospectus. The pronoun "it" in line 6 refers to the allegedly superior parcel of property being submitted to the collective "us" of all Christians, or, alternatively, the two siblings who act in concert in considering and then rejecting what heaven offers. Despite stipulating that no affidavit attesting to the reality that earth is indeed heaven exists, the offerees, for whom the poem's persona implicitly serves as spokeswoman, decline the conventional heaven because they are prevented from seeing it beforehand, at first hand. The poem's language is drawn from the bargaining preliminary to negotiating a land contract, which, like all contracts, necessarily entailed potential benefits and disadvantages for buyer and seller alike. Accepting earth as heaven, rather than heaven as heaven, does present an element of risk to would-be buyers or believers, whose heresy might disqualify them from ever attaining the conventional heaven subsequently.

Yet from a legal point of view, assessing the hazards involved in purchasing either of two offered parcels of land is relatively straightforward: buyers would be prudent not to subscribe money for a lot they were prevented from inspecting. The empirically ascertainable "fact" that earth *is* heaven, whether certified as such or not, makes it the more desirable property. Austin would have savored the legal connotations of his sister's use of the word "fact," just as he would the poem's implicit religious skepticism. Shorn of its legal content, the philosophical, metaphysical, and intellectual impact of this poem would be seriously diminished.

In the chapters that follow I discuss ways in which Dickinson's poems and letters address specific areas of law—bankruptcy, equity, contractual law, wills and estates, property law, and criminal law.[30] These topics possessed some urgency for the legal minds of her day, and her reactions to them, transmuted indirectly through the medium of poetry, reflect concerns shared by her countrymen and countrywomen. Reading her poems with a consciousness of her commitment to law may also shed new light on her thinking about broader subjects such as authoritarianism and individuality, social responsibility and the rights of citizens, religion and reason, fairness and obedience. What finally emerges is a portrait of a writer who, rather than being a sheltered recluse, was deeply immersed in the national intellectual culture. We may also *witness*—in the literary and legal significances of that particular verb—a ferocious display of intelligence, verbal facility, wit, and passion.

1

DELINQUENT PALACES
Bankruptcy

Although she couldn't possibly have known it, bankruptcy was the primary legal issue confronting the Dickinsons when the poet was born. Her grandfather, Samuel Fowler Dickinson, had recently become insolvent, in large part as a result of his involvement in helping to found Amherst College. Her father, Edward Dickinson, was still absorbing the news about Squire Dickinson's imminent financial ruin during the years when he was just embarking (with some trepidation) on his own legal career. Like many other eastern debtors, Samuel F. Dickinson finally left Massachusetts to reinvent himself financially and professionally west of the Alleghenies, in Ohio.[1] Back in Amherst, Edward Dickinson, his new wife, Emily Norcross Dickinson, and their young children, Austin and the infant Emily, were compelled by debts left in the patriarch's wake to move out of the Homestead, which Samuel had built during better times, not to return until 1855, when the poet was twenty-five years old.

But the threat of financial disaster continued to loom over the family: the poet's uncle Loring Norcross went bankrupt in 1851, and in 1857 the railway company Edward Dickinson helped establish, the Amherst & Belchertown, went into receivership. Emily Dickinson could hardly have avoided being affected by these financial exigencies. In a letter written to Austin in 1847 she describes a nightmare in which she dreamed their father had failed, compelling the family to mortgage the rye field she and her mother had planted (L16). In the poems, homesteads are apt to prove unsteady structures vulnerable to a range of disasters. They may be threatened by lightning ("The wind begun to knead") or battered by blizzards ("Like Brooms of Steel"), or the roof over one's head might even vanish ("I felt a funeral").[2] Certainty and security are greatly to be desired, yet also apt to prove elusive, even delusory. Narrators are haunted by a sense of deprivation, but often without quite comprehending what, exactly, they had lost, or how.

Among American property owners and businessmen, Samuel Fowler Dickinson's financial predicament was not unusual. According to at least one historian, in the early years of the nineteenth century "one out of every five householders experienced actual business failure" (Coleman 287). Since its founding, the nation periodically experienced severe economic contractions rendering millions of previously prosperous individuals and businesses insolvent and bankrupt, often with little legal recourse available for them or for their creditors in state or federal courts.

The short-lived first federal Bankruptcy Act, passed in 1800, was repealed after only three years. A second national law would not be passed until 1841, so that during the better part of the Jacksonian era the country lacked comprehensive bankruptcy legislation. Attempts to model bankruptcy laws on those of Britain proved largely failures, because, for one thing, the mother country's laws continued to emphasize harsh punishments for debtors while upholding the rights of creditors—Britain did not cease imprisoning debtors until 1869, decades after the policy had been abolished in America—and also because the American economy was so unlike Britain's: more volatile, more subject to booms and busts, and spread out across a vast geographic expanse in which each state possessed a nearly sovereign authority to make and enforce its own laws. Then too, the frequency with which individuals entered into bankruptcy removed some of the stigma it retained in Britain. De Toqueville was astonished by the willingness Americans displayed to cheat their creditors by falsely claiming to be insolvent: "There is no American legislation against fraudulent bankruptcies. Is that because there are no bankrupts? No, on the contrary, it is because there are many. In the mind of the majority the fear of being prosecuted as a bankrupt is greater than the apprehension of being ruined by other bankrupts, and so the public conscience has a sort of guilty tolerance for an offense which everyone individually condemns" (224–25).

At the time Samuel Fowler Dickinson failed, no comprehensive national law addressing bankruptcy applied in the United States,[3] and among the states themselves, Massachusetts courts possessed a reputation for being especially tough on debtors. Massachusetts was one of the last states to cease enforcing imprisonment for debt, ending the practice in 1842, four years after Samuel Dickinson died in Ohio, still indebted. Yet back in his home state, the financial failure of Samuel Dickinson was undoubtedly viewed with considerable sympathy, and we are probably mistaken in thinking very much opprobrium attached to the family name as a result of Samuel's fall. He had exhausted his resources in the service of a worthy cause, and he did make a good-faith effort to pay back his creditors, some of whom were his relatives.[4] Thus although Squire Dickinson left a trail of worthless paper behind him, it is unlikely that his lifelong friends, business associates, and family members would have found it in their hearts to consider him a dishonored man.

The words "redeem" and "redemption" came to possess a special weight for Squire Dickinson's granddaughter, two of several terms in her poems that productively merge legal or financial meanings and religious meanings. Jesus *redeems* humankind, through his sacrifice, from Original Sin; in matters legal and financial, bonds and promissory notes are *redeemed* when they are paid off. At least some evidence would seem to indicate that the poet came to associate her grandfather, whom she never met as an adult, with Adam, the first sinner, whose fall was remembered by his progeny with a mixture of shame and pride. Like Adam, Samuel was forced to leave his native soil and to labor by the sweat of his brow. In a campaign to reclaim solvency, Samuel Dickinson accepted a position at yet another new, religiously affiliated educational institution, Lane Seminary, in Cincinnati. At Lane, he was put in charge of the school's department of manual labor, where students were taught vocational skills such as printing.[5] Also, like Adam the gardener, Samuel was known in Amherst for his appreciation of landscaping, manifested in his contributions to laying out the college campus and beautifying local public roadways.[6] This affinity for plants and planting would be passed down to his descendents—first Edward, and then Emily and Austin. If Squire Dickinson could be considered a sort of Adamic figure, his financial ruin and subsequent efforts to salvage his own reputation and that of the family may be construed as elements of an ongoing, evolving mythopoesis for his granddaughter involving human origins, temptation, and redemption.

Samuel Dickinson's move to the West left his son to face the consequences of his father's folly. For Edward, Squire Dickinson's failure generated a morass of local disgrace, long-term debt, and friction between his own family and the Norcrosses, the business-minded family from Monson, Massachusetts, he married into. At the beginning of his courtship with Emily Norcross, Edward Dickinson may have flattered himself somewhat by thinking he was condescending, to a small degree, in associating the locally distinguished Dickinson name with that of the mercantile, farming Norcrosses, yet, as Vivian Pollak has shown in *A Poet's Parents*, Edward was actually marrying *up*. Joel Norcross, Emily's father, substituted for the father Edward must have occasionally wished he had had: although not well educated, Joel was wise in business matters in ways that Samuel Fowler Dickinson emphatically was not. Joel could also offer sage advice to a son-in-law just then trying to establish himself as lawyer and businessman. A merger of the Dickinson and Norcross families thus turned out to have emotional and financial repercussions that revealed themselves over time to Edward, as the contrast with Samuel's imprudence brought them into sharper relief.

Just before Samuel Dickinson's financial affairs began unraveling in the late 1820s, Edward Dickinson tried to persuade Emily Norcross that he was responsible enough, and solvent enough, to offer a secure future to her. He proposed to her on June 4, 1826, in a letter emphasizing his prospects and industriousness. At this time he probably did not know the magnitude of the debts his father was incurring, the totality of which would push Samuel over the fiscal brink two years later. Arguing his case in lawyerlike fashion, Edward described to Emily the nobility of law as a profession:

> I have said thus much upon this topic, because, notwithstanding my settled desire to form a permanent connection with you, & my full conviction of your merits & your virtues, I do not wish you to risk yourself on my protection without you are satisfied of a reasonable expectation of having your happiness secured – and however strong my attachment may be for you, if you have good reason to believe that you expose yourself to unhappiness, thro' your life, certainly you ought to decline my addresses. It would be a source of unceasing regret

to me, if I should persuade you to join yourself with me, & too late you should discover faults, or traits of character which were inconsistent with your enjoyment. . . . My life must be a life of business – of laborious application to the study of my profession – for no profession requires such continual devotedness & such untiring perseverance as ours. The whole course of practice & the new works on different branches of the Law are undergoing such changes & receiving such additions, that, to attain any thing like eminence, a man must be industrious & patient & persevering & constant in his attention to his professional duties. And notwithstanding the great number of Lawyers, there are comparatively few who can claim anything like a moderate title to distinction, & never was true merit better rewarded – & never was there a time, when men of solid acquirements, were more high regarded, & more needed, than the present. (qtd. in Pollack, *A Poet's Parents* 18–19)

Edward, in referring repeatedly and pointedly to Emily Norcross's future happiness, emphasizes his ability to support her financially. He understands that she might have qualms about allying herself with a man who could turn out, after they had married, to be incapable of fulfilling his material promises to her, or who might even suffer, through his own mistakes, financial reverses. Edward Dickinson professes himself willing to do his part by putting in long hours and keeping himself abreast of developments in the law, while subtly warning her that, should she accept his offer, they would sometimes be compelled to spend time apart, when she would have to manage without him. It is ironic that even as Edward tries to convince his intended fiancée of his own financial trustworthiness, he almost certainly did not know that his own father was spiraling into insolvency, mortgaging property after property in a frantic effort to keep himself financially afloat.[7]

Alfred Habegger has argued Edward was unaware that even the house into which he intended to move his bride would be swept up in his father's ruin ("How the Dickinsons Lost Their Homes" 181). Edward planned for them to live in the Montague house in Amherst, one of several properties included in his father's fatally overleveraged real estate portfolio, and Edward expended considerable expense and energy fixing up the half of the house he intended he and his bride should occupy. In reality, Samuel Fowler Dickinson had already surrendered control of the Montague property to his own brother-in-law and sometime business partner Oliver Smith, and through him to John Leland and Nathan Dickinson. That Edward Dickinson did, in fact, work so hard to fix up the property would seem to indicate he was unaware of the gravity of his father's situation. Perhaps Samuel intended to keep Edward in the dark until after his son had celebrated his marriage, because only a few months after Edward and Emily's wedding on May 6, 1828, Samuel Fowler Dickinson's financial failure became public knowledge in Hampshire County. It is doubtful whether Emily Norcross would have agreed to marry someone she knew to be a member of a financially irresponsible family, and it is equally doubtful whether Joel Norcross would have endorsed such a match.

After the nuptials were concluded, Edward and Emily Norcross Dickinson did indeed occupy half of the Montague house, but it probably soon became quite clear to Edward that the long-term benefit he had expected to reap from living in a family-owned property would not be realized. He then turned his attention to another property putatively owned by his father, the Homestead, a large brick house reputed to be among the best properties in town, built by Samuel Dickinson in 1813. By 1825, however, Squire Dickinson's financial situation had become so dire that he had taken out two mortgages on the house, and, even though his name continued to show up on the town tax rolls as the property's owner, control of it, according to Habegger, had actually passed to the same buyers of other properties Samuel had sold, namely John Leland and Nathan Dickinson ("How the Dickinsons Lost Their Homes" 172).

In April 1830, with one child in tow and another on the way, Edward agreed to purchase half of the Homestead from Leland and Nathan Dickinson. As Habegger points out, Samuel F. Dickinson and Edward were evidently able to hash out some sort of tacit agreement with the Homestead's co-owners to the effect that grandparents, parents, and grandson could all live together in the house's western half. These cramped quarters, which reflect indirectly the extended Dickinson family's straitened finances, soon became even more crowded in December 1830, when Emily Elizabeth Dickinson was born. It is worth remarking that the poet's birth coincided rather closely with Edward Dickinson's purchase of one half of the Homestead, the house which, in better times, his family had once owned outright.

When the poet was two, her grandfather left the Homestead, the village of Amherst, and the state of Massachusetts for his new position in Cincinnati, seven hundred miles distant. Samuel may have moved to avoid potential imprisonment for debt, but more likely because his business prospects in Amherst, once so promising for an ambitious and civic-minded attorney, had reached a dead end. Nearly contemporaneously with his departure, his son entered into a complex real estate deal with Leland and Nathan Dickinson to sell the entire Homestead to General David Mack. As part of the arrangement, Edward Dickinson and his family, along with his mother, Lucretia Dickinson, and two of Edward's sisters, at first reoccupied the entire house as tenants, but then, after the Macks moved in and assumed possession of the western half of the property, Edward Dickinson consolidated his own family and his relatives in the house's eastern half.

Following a year's delay, in spring 1834 Lucretia and Edward's siblings moved out of the Homestead to rejoin Samuel Dickinson in Cincinnati; they later followed him to Hudson, Ohio, where Samuel accepted a new position in the service of yet another fledgling educational institution, Western Reserve College (a forerunner of today's Case Western Reserve University). The dispossessed Dickinsons all remained in Hudson with Samuel until he died in 1838, "disillusioned, neglected, and forgotten" (Sewall 306n33). Squire Dickinson's timing was especially unlucky: in that same year, Massachusetts passed its first bankruptcy law, which could potentially have permitted Samuel to continue living in Massachusetts. Back in Amherst, Edward Dickinson and his family continued to occupy half of the Homestead as Mack's tenants until 1840, when they were finally able to buy an entire house of their own on North Pleasant Street, on the strength of Edward Dickinson's increasingly profitable law practice with his partner, Elbridge Bowdoin.[8]

Having seen his own father overwhelmed by debt, Edward Dickinson preached thrift at home, with the perhaps unsurprising consequence that Austin, as he grew older, showed an inclination to profligacy in his taste for domestic art, architecture, and landscaping. To the end of his life, Edward maintained a careful annual account of his own debits and credits, reconciling them on the first day of each new year.[9] It also stands to reason that Edward would subsequently have followed with a partisan's eye the erratic course of bankruptcy statutes enacted nationally and in Massachusetts. Then too, as a Whig committed to improving the nation's business climate, Edward Dickinson probably would have fallen into line with the party platform when it addressed wider concerns about bankruptcy. In the wake of the Panic of 1837, Whig figureheads such as Daniel Webster and Rufus Choate agitated for passage of the second federal Bankruptcy Act, passed in 1841, which offered millions of debtors relief while also helping to keep in circulation the intellectual capital represented by failed businessmen, who could apply existing entrepreneurial skills to new enterprises. The question of whether Edward discussed these various developments with the rest of his family remains unanswerable, yet it is difficult to believe that the subject of bankruptcy would not have arisen frequently in the Dickinson household. In 1841 the future poet was eleven, old enough to understand some of her father's political enthusiasms and some of the family lore concerning her grandfather, once so prominent a citizen in Amherst, yet a man who had effectively vanished from her family circle and from the town's ongoing civic projects.[10]

For the poet, her family's experience of having been uprooted repeatedly, and their remaining uncertainty about staying where they were, was transmuted enduringly into poems describing exile, banishment, and a lost Eden—the lost home, or rather, *Homestead*. Consider, for example, "The Bible is an antique Volume" (F1577), written in the early 1880s, only a few years before she died. There, Dickinson treats the Bible jokingly as a primitive serial novel, a sort of early "three-decker" in which one plotline describes the loss of "Eden – the ancient Homestead." Dickinson evidently wrote that poem specifically for her nephew, Ned, then twenty-one years old and resident nearly his entire life at the Evergreens, the house next door to the Homestead. Ned would have savored his Aunt Emily's sly reference to the primary site of Dickinson family identity, and to its by-then antiquated architecture, which made it seem "ancient" in comparison to the more fashionable Italianate style of the Evergreens. Knowing her audience, Dickinson did not even bother to describe in the poem how the "Eden" of the "Homestead" had been *lost;* for Ned, an awareness of who was responsible for the loss of the Dickinson house was as familiar as the attribution of Eden's loss to Adam. For the poet, then, bankruptcy considered as a legal concept was subordinated to one of bankruptcy's potential consequences, the forfeiture of a house, itself a surrogate for Eden or paradise.[11]

Yet the sense of shame that might be expected to oppress someone closely related to a bankrupt is generally missing from Dickinson's references to the topic in her letters and poems—a reflection, perhaps, of the entire nation's nonchalance about the matter in comparison to the British legal tradition of viewing the bankrupt as a dishonored man. On the contrary: in America, and specifically within the Dickinson family, the bankrupt could be seen as *honorable*. As Dickinson wrote in one of her very earliest poems, a comic valentine (F2 B):

> Mortality is fatal –
> Gentility is fine,
> Rascality, heroic,
> *Insolvency, sublime!*

The first two lines are silly redundancies, but the third line points to an only seeming contradiction familiar to readers of novels with scamps as protagonists: How could a rascal be a hero? Then Dickinson puts to work a romantic term, the *sublime,* associating it with a topic that, at least ostensibly, could hardly be more prosaic or *non*-sublime, insolvency. One frame of reference here may be Dickens's rascal hero Micawber, locked up in debtor's prison; *David Copperfield* was first published as a novel in 1850, only two years before Dickinson penned this valentine.[12] (I will have more to say about the term "rascal" in chapter 7.) Dickinson's references to literary terms and to insolvency, paired with the convolutions of her logic, appear designed to cater to a literate, legally minded reader, and such may indeed have been the case when she wrote her valentine. As would be true three decades later when Dickinson would give "The Bible is an antique Volume" to her nephew, Ned, the poet is likely addressing in her valentine someone who knows her, and her family, well: William Howland, a tutor at Amherst College who studied law with Edward Dickinson before being admitted to the Massachusetts bar.

Howland, as someone trained to be alert to the relation of logic to language, may have been particularly amused by the poet's semantic play (and he would also have appreciated the schoolbook Latin phrases of the valentine's first two stanzas).[13] But as someone who knew at least the essentials of the Dickinson family's financial history, he may also have scanned the phrase "*Insolvency, sublime!*" with a knowing eye. As printed in the *Springfield Republican,* to which Howland forwarded the valentine, those words are italicized, as if for particular emphasis, perhaps as a subtle hint from the author to the reader that the line should be understood in light of a shared private knowledge, and a shared awareness that rascals *could* be heroes.[14] Then too, the poem's fifth stanza addresses the reader facetiously,

> Put down the apple, Adam,
> And come away with me,
> So shalt thou have a *pippin*
> From off my father's tree![15]

Here Dickinson, as a sort of alternative temptress supplanting Eve, proffers the reader a different apple, a "pippin," that is, an especially succulent fruit. Her father's ownership of the apple tree suggests that, as the writer is another Eve, her father is another Jehovah, and that the original version of the fall described by Genesis may be only one version of what had actually taken place in Eden. All this is said tongue in cheek, of course, but the young poet's suggested association of her father, who was Howland's legal mentor and patron, with Jehovah may, for a knowing reader, again resituate the story of the fall within the Dickinson family circle.

By accepting bankruptcy as a topic falling legitimately within the scope of her poetic expression, Dickinson could also hope to remove some of its sting. Conflating the allied subjects of homelessness, loss, and a mysterious, enduring shame sometimes intermingled with pride may indicate she wanted to enlist her art in sorting out her own reactions to the Dickinsons' collective trauma. Despite her occasional celebration of insolvency as being paradoxically honorable, in her poems Dickinson was equally apt to employ narrators who concede that bankruptcy has consequences: a decline in status, a forfeiture of confidence in the future, and a consequent nearly existential vulnerability to external and internal forces understood only dimly. Such, I think, is the case in "A loss of something ever felt I —" (F1072), a poem about the loss of a home in which the speaker contrasts her childish and adult sensibilities about having been, in a sense, evicted or banished. Employing diction designed to encourage a reading inflected by the literary genre of the fairy tale, the poem ends on a note of rueful, emphatically adult, self-recognition:

A loss of something ever felt I –
The first that I could recollect
Bereft I was – of what I knew not
Too young that any should suspect

A Mourner walked among the children | walked / lurked
I notwithstanding went about | went / stole
As one bemoaning a Dominion
Itself the only Prince cast out –

Elder, Today, a Session wiser
And fainter, too, as Wiseness is –
I find myself still softly searching
For my Delinquent Palaces –

And a Suspicion, like a Finger
Touches my Forehead now and then
That I am looking oppositely
For the Site of the Kingdom of Heaven –

The speaker, whom I see as being representative of the poet, says that
even while a child she was aware of a sense of loss, but for what, she did
not grasp. If this poem is indeed even partially autobiographical, the poet
may be remembering the family's loss of the Homestead, a "palace" in
comparison to their modest, yet still relatively comfortable, lodgings on
North Pleasant Street, the house in which she chiefly grew up. This personal loss resonates with a literary metaplot in which a princess or prince
has been disenfranchised of a royal residence, while, simultaneously, the
emphatically sophisticated diction steers the poem away from childish
fantasy to hard-won wisdom, the words "Session" and "Delinquent"
shifting the child's fairy-tale story of loss to the adult legal milieu of
courtrooms, lawsuits, and mortgage payments. The word "Delinquent,"
in particular, connotes the late, or entirely neglected, payments that had
led to the speaker's eviction, and "Session" suggests that the matter of late
payments culminated in a court appearance, as in a judicial *session,* the
speaker having been arraigned by her creditors. The speaker's complicity,
even guilt, in the entire matter is suggested by two alternative words in
the second stanza, "lurked" for "walked," and "stole" for "went." These
two terms, which may also have legal nuances, help reinforce the poem's
presentation of the speaker as feeling at least partially responsible for
what had happened, and we may recall that Edward Dickinson signed

the deed to one half of the Homestead on March 30, 1830, nine months before Emily Dickinson was born.

Edward Dickinson ultimately surrendered ownership of the Homestead when the poet was two years old, a toddler too young yet to walk very competently among other children. The image in the final stanza of being touched by a possibly admonitory or accusatory finger on one's forehead is at once emblematic of the speaker's earlier childlike and subordinate status, of the public nature of virtually all legal proceedings, and of a conviction of personal culpability. The phrase "juvenile delinquent" is an invention of a later age, but even so, the imputation of blame conveyed in this poem attaches as freely to the child as it does to the adult.[16] The word "Delinquent" even extends a sense of blame to the structure itself: that adjective is not a synonym for "missing," but rather a reference to a legally defined responsibility. The failure of its previous owners to fulfill a duty is thus displaced onto the forfeited property.

Despite the final stanza's emphasizing of perplexity and guilt, the inclusion of "Prince," a term simultaneously indicative of social status and hereditary right, could suggest an alternative happy ending for this ironized fairy tale. Although she may have lost title to the missing palace, the narrator may yet be *entitled* to it, by royal right of succession. As the poem's penultimate stanza states, the speaker is "still softly searching" for her lost home, and in the final stanza, the "Suspicion" that she was at least partially responsible for its loss may also connote that she suspects her previous search strategy had been flawed, so she may yet prevail by looking "oppositely." As "Prince," she confronts an imaginative quest consisting of the recovery of the "Palace" from which she had been banished. The poem's final phrase, "Kingdom of Heaven," appropriates the ritualistic language of prayer (perhaps specifically of the Lord's Prayer) and imports it into the poem's secular fairy tale exploring the psychological effects of disenfranchisement.

Although this poem does, I would agree, support various more religiously determined readings focusing on Emily Dickinson's state of belief, qualified belief, or unbelief, I suggest that we also read the final stanza's description of exclusion from "Heaven" within the context of the poet's revisionistic and imaginative retelling of how her family had surrendered the Homestead. Whether as an "Eden" forfeited by the progenitor, Adam, or as a "Heaven" previously enjoyed but subsequently relinquished, home is rendered figurally in Dickinson's poems as a Paradise Lost. Exiled for

their own imprudence, the erstwhile occupants of this domestic paradise might yet hope to regain it through deserving and sheer effort. In a
conventional fairy-tale plot, a banished prince may return to his rightful
estate upon the death of the old king. As princes or as "Queens," dispossessed nobility are entitled to the property, even after being compelled to
renounce it temporarily following a precipitous decline in status. Edward
Dickinson's repurchase of the Homestead in 1855 represented a personal
and familial redemption of sorts, a recovery from the financial excesses
that had ruined Samuel Dickinson.

A presentation of heaven specifically as a house, a *mansion* to which
one may aspire, appears in the fragmentary F1144, which could be a
playful commentary on Jesus's claim in John 14:2, "In my Father's house
are many mansions":

> Paradise is that old mansion
> Many owned before –
> Occupied by each an instant
> Then reversed the Door –
> Bliss is frugal of her Leases
> Adam taught her Thrift
> Bankrupt once through his excesses –

The equating of paradise with a house signals that Dickinson's primary
concern here is Eden, a primitive, terrestrial state of bliss rendered not as
a garden but as a secure residence, rather than the conventional Christian
heaven or the afterlife. Adam is the profligate whose spendthrift ways
robbed his progeny of their inheritance in happiness, his "excesses"
having cost a feminized "Bliss" her birthright. Notably, the mansion of
"Paradise" may only be rented, or leased, rather than owned, and God,
like an indignant landlord, shows Adam the door after his disobedience.[17]
But the experience of being expelled from paradise has its compensa-
tions: Adam, the original exile, has passed down to his descendant, a
personified Bliss, the hard-won quality of having expectations that are
economical rather than grandiose. And even the "old mansion" may not
merit prolonged mourning. The phrase "Many owned before" signifies
that the state of bliss is briefly enjoyed by many, and within the figure's
parameters, the house of paradise may look a bit run down, having been
occupied by successive tenants.

The Homestead itself, built around 1813 by Samuel F. Dickinson as a seat for the Dickinson family, had come to be occupied by other owners, namely the Macks. General Mack was the proprietor of a nearby hat factory, a prominent citizen of Amherst, and, as a prosperous business owner, a competitor for the same rung of the town's social ladder the Dickinsons had occupied. Although the Dickinson family's memories of the Macks, their erstwhile landlords, were favorable, it could hardly have escaped their attention that they had been supplanted by an arriviste.[18] At the risk of reading this poem too reductively and autobiographically, I think it is worth remembering that Emily Dickinson was not entirely sanguine about moving from the North Pleasant Street house back to the redeemed Homestead. In that sense, Dickinson lost *two* houses, the one in which she had been born, and the one in which she was raised.[19] In packing up their belongings to make the move, Dickinson wrote in a November 1855 letter (L182) that she experienced a "*gone-to-Kansas feeling*," that is, a sense of being deracinated and sent on to a new home in a distant metaphorical West.

Family discussions during the years succeeding her grandfather's bankruptcy may have turned the poet's thoughts to the topic of the lost home. Yet for Edward Dickinson, any grief prompted by the loss of the Homestead may have been tempered with a hope that once his fortunes improved he could think more realistically about buying the house back from the Macks, thereby returning the family to their symbolic position of civic prominence and dispelling the ignominy that had attached to the family name. The similar spellings of "hope" and "home" probably did not escape the attention of his verbally precocious daughter. In a letter draft evidently written late in life to her lover Judge Otis Lord, the poet said, "You spoke of 'Hope' surpassing 'Home' – I thought that Hope *was* Home – a misapprehension of Architecture –" (L600). The preservation of hope and a determination to redeem the past inform another poem, F1125 B, written near in time to "Paradise is that old mansion" and also concerning Adam, his excesses, and a lost paradise:

> Paradise is of the Option –
> Whosoever will
> Own in Eden notwithstanding | Own / Dwell
> Adam, and Repeal.

Despite the poem's elided punctuation, Dickinson's message here is clear: a state of paradise lies within everyone's grasp, despite God's banishment of Adam from the original paradise of Eden, a rescinding or "Repeal" of God's fiat granting him implicit dominion over the rest of the creatures of Eden. The poet's use of language drawn from real estate offers and transactions—"will / Own in Eden," "of the option,"—operates simultaneously to frame the topic with an ironizing humor and to validate the poem's opening assertion, in language characteristic of deeds and guarantees.[20]

Moreover, when read in the historical context of the Dickinsons' own experience with debt underwritten by oversubscribed mortgages, the poem's estimated date of composition becomes suggestive. Thomas Johnson assigns a date of about 1866, when the poet was thirty-six years old and had been living at the Homestead for a decade. In 1867, only a year later, the third federal Bankruptcy Act was passed. Its predecessor, the act of 1841, had been lambasted by critics inside and outside of Congress for being too lax in permitting debtors to escape their obligations to creditors. The third act inaugurated the bringing of *involuntary* bankruptcy suits against individual debtors: that is, creditors could force debtors into court against their will.[21] The policy of invoking involuntary bankruptcy against individuals (as opposed to corporations) was controversial, and, as the nation's economy suffered yet another downturn, even this new act grew increasingly unpopular, with President Grant himself urging its repeal. Debate within the legal community over the desirability of rescinding the Bankruptcy Act of 1867 would have been raging during the year in which Dickinson likely wrote "Paradise is of the Option."

If discussion of repeal was in the air in 1866, Dickinson may have been reminded of an earlier repeal of a national bankruptcy statute, John Tyler's in 1843 of the 1841 act, enacted three years after Samuel Dickinson had died. If we interpret Emily Dickinson's poem "Paradise is of the Option" as referring, as least tangentially, to her grandfather's situation, the phrase "notwithstanding / Adam and Repeal" may be seen as saying that the Dickinsons could hope to recoup the family's reputation by repurchasing the Homestead, despite both the excesses of their progenitor and President Tyler's *repeal* of laws that would have provided considerable relief to debtors like Samuel Dickinson. Dickinson's figure of speech involving Adam serves to mitigate her family's awkward financial history by associating it with the entire history of humankind, demonstrating that despite set-backs including the excesses of the fathers and the periodic passage and rescission of legislation that would potentially have helped "involuntary" bankrupts, the Dickinson family could still hope to "Own in Eden." The existence of an alternative for "Own," "Dwell," indicates that Dickinson is considering the differences between being the owner of a property and being merely an occupant.[22] In that sense, "Own" is superior to "Dwell," because the owner of a property cannot be compelled to leave it. The imminent passage of the 1867 act, with its renewed imputation of individual failure to debtors in the form of involuntary bankruptcy, may have provided the writer with an ironic reminder of Samuel Dickinson's collapse. Read thus, Dickinson's brief poem defends her Adamic ancestor, laments the disgrace of insolvency, and endorses the wisdom of persistence in seeking absolution. In its deployment of language consciously emulating that found in real estate contracts, the poem imitates a developer's pitch inviting potential purchasers of paradise to make an offer on a parcel they had considered as being priced beyond their means, thus reenacting the moment when the Dickinsons had prevailed in their effort to repurchase the Homestead and salvage their collective reputation.

Dickinson also represented voluntary bankruptcy as sexual desire, a giving up of oneself, bodily and emotionally. In a letter draft written probably around 1878 to Judge Otis Lord, she invokes a phrase with which, as a jurist, Lord would have been entirely familiar from having witnessed the vexed history of successive federal bankruptcy acts. Replying, evidently, to an accusation that her passion for him had overwhelmed her better judgment, she asks, flirtatiously and facetiously, "Will you punish me? 'Involuntary Bankruptcy,' how could that be Crime?" A kind of voluntary sexual bankruptcy is also enacted in an early poem, F426 (written around 1862), which predates their affair by at least a decade:

I gave Myself to Him – | Myself to Him – / Him all Myself –
And took Himself, for Pay,
The solemn contract of a Life
Was ratified, this way –

The Wealth might disappoint –
Myself a poorer prove
Than this great Purchaser suspect,
The Daily Own – of Love

Depreciate the Vision –
But till the Merchant buy –
Still Fable – in the Isles of Spice –
The subtle Cargoes – lie –

At least – 'tis Mutual – Risk –
Some – found it – Mutual Gain –
Sweet Debt of Life – Each Night to owe –
Insolvent – every Noon –

I will take the liberty of identifying the speaker of this poem overtly as another avatar of the poet herself, who imagines how she might feel after having slept with a lover. The speaker begins by construing the phrase connoting sexual surrender, "I gave myself to him" both literally and legally. An alternative in the manuscript, "I gave Him all myself," gets a near-rhyme with "Life," yet without drawing quite so frankly on the commonly used expression for sexual capitulation, "giving oneself." The phrase establishes a foundation for the rest of the poem's conceit, which treats sexual intercourse, love, and marriage as risky financial transactions in which both partners must hazard all they have, and are.

Although the first line refers secondarily to the marriage contract partially solemnized when the bride's party is asked, "Who *gives* this woman to be wedded to this man?," the poem emphasizes sex more than matrimony. Making love each night, the pair gives everything they have to each other, achieving a state the next day of sexual satiety and emotional "insolvency" that is also replenished daily, so that the cycle of renewed lovemaking may commence again. Dickinson's larger metaphor implicitly treats bankruptcy and insolvency as noble rather than shameful, in the same way that sexual surrender is to be considered a virtue rather than a vice, and the poem's contractual language emphasizes that enamored bankrupts generally enter into hazardous transactions not with a business partner but with a lover, who may then share in their failures or successes. The poem literalizes romantic relationships as partnerships in the sense that such unions resemble the formation of joint corporations, while treating the lovers' emotions as a form of capital, which may be invested for a return, or oversubscribed to the point of failure.

The second stanza continues literalizing the mutual and contractual basis of lovemaking by inventorying the speaker's emotional assets. She worries that she may prove to be worth a good deal less than her lover had realized when their relationship began. Another danger is that he might grow weary of her, and the phrase "Daily Own," a linguistic invention, conflates "own" and "owe" in a fashion peculiarly appropriate for describing a lover's simultaneous claim on and debt to the beloved.[23] So proprietary an attitude may itself become cloying or tiresome over time, if a lover begins to resent the hold exerted on him or her. Then too, there is the simple fatigue of love: as her lover becomes bored, the speaker's own value as a *commodity* depreciates, so that the "Vision" her lover had once had of her, like a flashy prospectus touting a business opportunity, would become diminished, over time, by routine and dull reality.[24]

Yet unless her lover is willing to take a chance on her, he cannot realize a "profit" on the goods he has acquired. The narrator's troping of her own sexuality—perhaps even her own genitalia—as "Isles of Spice" and "subtle Cargoes" is fairly conventional, yet her historicizing of her own desirability as a commodity imported from the distant Indies constitutes an implicit rebuttal of her previous concern about coming to seem too quotidian or too pedestrian. Forcefully, she makes a case for her own exoticness and rarity, which are to be discovered by a lover who can see her in her proper light. Such a romanticizing projection of herself to her lover is a "Vision" in its own right, and Dickinson emphasizes the necessity that the speaker's lover, troped as business partner, reciprocate by suspending disbelief, assessing her true worth accurately, and subscribing himself to their joint enterprise. One virtue of Dickinson's underlying conceit in this poem is that she presents the imagination itself as an asset that may be risked, overstated, or overspent, in its evaluation of a potential lover. Yet unlike committed business partners, lovers embarking on a new relationship must make an imaginative leap of faith by not withholding themselves emotionally from each other; they must be willing to risk all, sexually and emotionally, rather than hedging their bets, or holding back a reserve.

The poem's tone is passionate, humorous, ironic. Dickinson's legal and commercial terms, and her focus on measurable amounts, prices, and return on investment, contrast with the absolute, all-or-nothing commitment required by love. Part of the poem's message is that one cannot, should not, think about love in terms of quid pro quo, because the mutuality and reciprocity of love cannot be so minutely quantified. The speaker gives herself to her lover freely, not for pay as a prostitute would. Yet the irony implicit in considering passion and profitability in the same breath is underlined by Dickinson's logical contradiction in the poem's first two lines—if the speaker *gives* herself to her lover, logically she receives no dividend, unless that gain is "Himself." An important difference between voluntary and involuntary bankruptcy is that an involuntary bankrupt is haled into court, an imposition that grated on Americans' conceptions of liberty and their distrust of unilateral authority. Voluntary bankruptcy, on the other hand, signifies a bankruptcy declared by the debtor, an exposure of present assets before the court so that creditors will plainly perceive what they may, or may not, recover.

Dickinson was well aware, I would argue, of the irony inherent to her poetic treatment of love affairs, not business affairs, as a "balancing of the books." The equality between lovers, which resisted the implicitly desired achievement of profit in matters of business, furnished an underlying figural opportunity similar to that which Thoreau exploited in writing about his sojourn at Walden Pond, where his "business" enterprise succeeded most when it generated no profit whatsoever. In that sense, bankruptcy may be "sublime" because it indicates a wholehearted commitment to a worthy cause or a love affair for which all must be risked, voluntarily. In "I think To Live – may be a Bliss" (F757), the beloved is figured as a sort of entry in the speaker's emotional ledger, one that corrects an earlier mathematical "mistake":

> I think To Live – may be a Bliss
> To those who dare to try –
> Beyond my limit to conceive –
> My lip – to testify –
>
> I think the Heart I former wore
> Could widen – till to me
> The Other, like the little Bank
> Appear – unto the Sea –
>
> I think the Days – could every one
> In Ordination stand –
> And Majesty – be easier –
> Than an inferior kind –
>
> No numb alarm – lest Difference come –
> No Goblin – on the Bloom –
> No start in Apprehension's Ear,
> No Bankruptcy – no Doom – | Bankruptcy / Sepulchre – / Wilderness

But Certainties of sun –
Midsummer – in the Mind –
A steadfast South – upon the Soul –
Her Polar time – behind –

The Vision – pondered long –
So plausible becomes
That I esteem the fiction – real –
The Real – fictitious seems –

How bountiful the Dream –
What Plenty – it would be –
Had all my Life but been Mistake
Just rectified – in Thee

The "Bank" on which the speaker of this poem imagines herself standing while still living a constrained emotional life is implicitly a riverbank, not a savings bank, so that the contrast between her past and present perspectives is tied to differences in perspective achieved by the side of a river, or by the sea. When a river overflows its banks or breaks through a levee, another kind of "rupturing" has taken place, and, as I have argued elsewhere, Dickinson literalizes the meanings of the two constituent morphemes in the tem "bankrupt."[25] Indirect references to daily expenses and balance sheets weave in and out of the poem. Ordinary days may stand in "Ordination," another word that productively intermixes legal and business language with religious terminology. Her new emotional perspective reminds the speaker of a candidate for the ministry being ordained, while simultaneously the word suggests numbers, or days, arranged ordinately, that is, in rows or columns.

Taken altogether, the poem's individual tropes suggest to mind a deponent or a defendant presenting financial evidence during a trial. Such a reading is solicited early on by the presence of "testify" in the first stanza's last line, and even though the speaker professes her own inability to represent accurately the *value* of what has happened to her, the rest of the poem is concerned with doing just that. The tangential, indirect reference in her metaphor to banks being ruptured to admit swelling waters also suggests that the party speaking in this poem is refuting a charge of malfeasance: she has been challenged, we may imagine, to make her figures (in a double sense) stand up in court, as a bulwark against accusations ranged against her. Her overriding concern is that a "Difference" will be found between her figures, made either through miscalculation or intentionally. Then an accusatory voice could shock her by telling her to her face that her numbers don't add up, promising a "Doom" of "Bankruptcy." Variants for "Bankruptcy," "Sepulchre" and "Wilderness" reemphasize the poet's equation of insolvency with a kind of death, as well as with exile from paradise into the hinterlands east of Eden.

But the deponent narrating this poem reassures herself that her assessment of her past and present emotional states is indeed accurate, that her testimony is "steadfast." The "Polar time" of emotional deprivation (expressed in zeroes, as if to the bone?) is gone, and she has grown emotionally solvent. Although her testimony in court had been challenged so aggressively that even she had begun to question her ability to separate fact from fiction, "Real" from "fictitious," she has emerged triumphant, "bountiful" with "Plenty," so that, at least within the poem's overarching figure, her financial reputation remains intact. The poem's last word comes as only something of a surprise: the "Bliss" that the speaker had achieved, the reason why her "Heart" had become enlarged by her new romantic perspective, is revealed to be "Thee," which becomes not just a pronoun identifying her lover, but also a sum, or a balance. Characteristically, Dickinson denies the quantifiability of emotion, even as her language and metaphors direct readers to the highly concrete domains of numbers, dollars, and units of measure. Consequently her confessed love promises at the poem's end to "rectify," or make right, her mathematical "Mistake," while simultaneously permitting her to reconcile desire and its fulfillment in her economy.

Dickinson's employment of legal, accounting, and business or financial terminologies to describe states of emotional security and insecurity both replicates and interrogates Edward Dickinson's ceremonial toting up of gains and losses at the end of every year. Lawyer Dickinson, conscious of his own father's improvidence, was evidently determined not to repeat Squire Dickinson's mistakes; in addition, he was undoubtedly aware that his business success hinged, to a large degree, on building and maintaining his own reputation for personal rectitude, discretion, and diligence. His daughter, even as she praised those willing to accept risk—especially in matters of the heart—grew to prize emotional security, confidence about the future, and immunity to sudden reverses. In connoting states of assurance she recurred often to language she heard her father use, words like "indemnity," "surety," "guaranty." Her integration of financial terms to represent the search for certainty in an uncertain world is exemplified by an elegy (F897 B) written around 1865:[26]

> She sped as Petals of a Rose
> Offended by the Wind –
> A frail Aristocrat of Time
> Indemnity to find –
> Leaving on nature – a Default | a Default / an attitude on Time / a magnitude
> As Cricket or as Bee – | Cricket / Monad   Bee / Fly
> But Andes, in the Bosoms where
> She had begun to lie –

Dickinson evidently wrote this poem for Susan Gilbert in sympathy for the loss of a two-year-old niece, named for her aunt.[27] Although the speaker characterizes the deceased in terms denoting high social standing ("frail Aristocrat"), the poem associates the dead child as well with the humblest representatives of nature, "Cricket" and "Bee," creatures that emulate, in their diminutive size, a toddler's stature. "Aristocrat" though she may have been, one consolation accessible to mourners is that the dead child will no longer be subject to uncertainty, once shielded by heaven's "Indemnity"; similarly, "frail" as she was in life, in eternity she will no longer be subject physically to time's depredations.

Virtually the entire poem conforms to a figural dynamic organized around visual orientation, moving abruptly from high to low, large to small, adult to child. Variants for "Cricket" and "Bee," "Monad" and "Fly," diminish the size of the departed child even further, and another variant, for the phrase "on nature – a Default" in the fifth line, "a magnitude on Time," confirms an impression that Dickinson intended that her poem focus on perspectival shifts in stature, physical and temporal. Simply stated, the poem expresses wonder that losing such a small person could cause such tremendous grief. Yet emotional loss, in this fair copy version of the poem, is also associated with *financial* loss, in its grouping of "Aristocrat," "Indemnity," and "Default." In the ledger of the emotions, the child's loss leaves a deficit that may be counted, objectively, as seemingly negligible in financial terms, as the bodies of crickets or bees seem insignificantly small, yet in an alternative, affective economy, the child's death acquires a worth large as the "Andes"—another example from nature intended, I think we may assume, to be understood as the antithesis of the tiny (and therefore also implicitly childlike) insects. The "indemnity" the child seeks, in dying, is also financial in the sense that she will no longer be subject to sudden reverses, or, as Dickinson put it in "I think to Live – may be a Bliss," "No start in Apprehension's Ear, / No Bankruptcy – no Doom –." Certainty is denoted by "Indemnity," an immunity to chance, disaster, and mortality that may be realizable only in an ideal, unreal, world.

"Indemnity," used as poetic shorthand for both protection from anxiety and a state of equilibrium achieved in the midst of life's alternating currents of bliss and bereavement, reappears in the fragmentary F1202, written around 1871, when Dickinson was in middle age. It portrays the speaker as being in the very act of reviewing a ledger recording life's various gains and losses:

> Of so divine a Loss
> We enter but the Gain,
> Indemnity for Loneliness
> That such a Bliss has been.

Here, by entering a Gain as a Loss, the speaker essentially "cooks the books," misrepresenting a debit as a credit. Yet in the alternative economy of the emotions, she has achieved a state of fiscal neutrality, a Thoreauvian "zeroing out" of the values in her personal inventory. Dickinson's term "Indemnity" emphatically locates the poem in the figural realm of accountancy, insurance, and law, although the poet once again transfers the language of getting and spending to that of emotional capital. Thus "Bliss," in Dickinson's poems, is apt to describe a condition of absolute solvency, the dialectical opposite of deprivation, emotional naïveté, or self-denial.

To know that bliss exists negates the threat of "Loneliness," and Dickinson's emphasis here is again both epistemological and emotional, or rather, it's an emotional epistemology. Written late in life, this poem likely describes another loss of someone she had loved (quite possibly Samuel Bowles). At midlife the poet assesses the deaths that had begun to accumulate in her life, here expressing her confidence that she will be protected, *insured* against grief or loneliness by the knowledge that such a person as her friend had once existed. Yet the word she uses to signify that protection, "Indemnity," may also be understood here in light of her father's reaction to the family's brush with financial disaster. The speaker of this poem has just committed, we may imagine, an act of fraud by entering a loss as gain, but has she also committed a sort of crime against her friend's memory by seeking to resign herself to his death? She exculpates herself by declaring loss and gain as being effectively equals, rather than opposites. She "pays" to purchase the "indemnity," or future peace of mind by accepting the loss of her friend—*he* is the price she pays. Simultaneously, she absolves herself from blame for computing this new system of emotional equivalencies—and thus she can close her own ledger.

In his biographical scholarship concerning Dickinson, Alfred Habegger adduces the family's history of bankruptcy as part of an effort to show that "contrary to what has often been imagined, the family into which the poet was born could not take for granted a privileged gentry status" ("How the Dickinsons Lost Their Homes" 189). Habegger's statement acknowledges indirectly that during the previous decade's worth of Dickinson studies, the social and financial standing of the family had furnished grist for several critical arguments concerning the poet's supposed sense of entitlement to being a member of Amherst's, and America's, rough-hewn aristocracy—as when, for example, she characterizes herself in her poems as a "Queen." But the fact is that the Dickinsons attained financial security and an improved social status during a nationally tumultuous period that saw rapid shifts in the solvency of many American families. In that context, a considerable portion of what Dickinson wrote concerning her own or her family's claim to high status may be thought of as a species of wish fulfillment, after her family had come very close to falling out of Amherst's upper middle class.

In the volatile economy of antebellum America, shifts in social status could occur at a jarring pace, and properties once thought secure could be taken away with the stroke of a pen. Although Emily Dickinson may have been a lawyer's daughter, and thus potentially the beneficiary of what would ordinarily be considered a privileged and secure social status in nineteenth-century New England, she was also the heir of a distinctly legal habit of mind that insisted on staring facts in the face, even—or perhaps especially—when those facts proved unpleasant to contemplate. In that sense, the practice of law represents, as much as any school of philosophy, a habit of thinking aimed at seeing life straight and true, despite intervening curtains of deception woven by society, by one's family, or even by one's own mind.

2
NOR HERE NOR THERE
Equity

*I*n law, equity means much more than simple fairness or equality. Equity constitutes a body of law almost entirely distinct from that of common law. In Britain, courts of equity, or chancery, date from the fifteenth century, and the history of equity, both in Britain and in America, influenced how Dickinson deployed that word. Yet during her lifetime, the legal doctrine of equity was also rapidly becoming a relic, an outdated conception of law as it had once been practiced. Consequently, an air of antiquity often clings to her references to equity, particularly in the related context of her discussions of justice. Although Dickinson was necessarily familiar with biblical narratives concerning justice, another historical-literary source available to her for associating equity with justice was *The Merchant of Venice*. In Shakespeare's tragicomedy, Shylock, while pursuing what he perceives to be justice in his suit against Antonio, is finally compelled by Portia, dressed as the young legal scholar Balthasar, to conform to other notions of justice endorsed by the powerful Venetian state. This chapter will examine how Dickinson treated the idea of equity ambivalently, respecting its historic value as a means of dispensing justice while also critiquing it, as an American and as a daughter of Massachusetts, where courts of equity had a turbulent legal history. I will also devote a large portion of this chapter to analyzing a poem that has lately received considerable critical attention, "Alone and in a Circumstance."

Modern American jurisprudence has largely shunted equity aside, a process that was already well under way during the poet's adulthood. During the latter half of the nineteenth century, most state courts merged equity with common-law courts, so that today, few discrete state courts of equity remain. But equity as an area of legal thought persists vestigially in such contemporary legal concepts and instruments as trespass, class action suits, and injunctions, especially in the widely used temporary restraining order. Britain abolished formal courts of chancery in 1875, but before that time, chancery had a long-standing reputation in British law as a legal resource for those who considered the pursuit of other remedies to have met a dead end. Two primary differences between ordinary common-law courts and equity courts rested in the sorts of remedies afforded to plaintiffs, and in the fact that deliberative power was invested in judges rather than in juries, a departure from the hallowed jury-trial system.

Damages assessed under common law were generally monetary, while equity courts ruling in favor of plaintiffs often required defendants to perform specific actions, such as rendering services, returning objects, or following through with an offer or promise. In that sense, rulings handed down by courts of equity or chancery may be considered as altering more palpably the subjectively experienced realities of both plaintiff and defendant than would be true of judgments rendered by common-law courts. Equity also intruded itself more forcefully in matters of morality than did the law, seeking—even while recognizing its own limitations—to repair damaged relationships between litigants. In this sense chancery remained true to its roots in the church. Rather than operating philosophically from a purely materialistic point of view, courts of chancery interposed themselves between parties in an effort to promote an ideal, one-on-one, implicitly Christian basis for the way individuals should treat one another, and, more broadly, in the way society as a whole should operate by moral principles not exclusively defined under common law.

In Britain, courts of chancery were overseen by the Lord Chancellor, a member of the King's Council. The practice arose because, since ancient times, British subjects had been allowed the liberty of appealing common-law decisions they considered unfair directly to the sovereign. Over time, because the chancellor was both moral counselor and confessor to the sovereign, he was delegated to hear these petitions on behalf of the king, acting as the "King's conscience."[1]

Because chancellors were usually clergymen, they were also considered as representing the interests of the church, and many chancellors had prior experience with canon law. Chancellors (and later, chancery judges) came to be regarded as exponents of political and ecclesiastic domains of authority that complemented, exceeded, or superseded the collective will of the citizenry embodied in common-law courts and in the twelve members of the traditional English jury. Chancery judges were empowered to rule unilaterally on the merits of cases brought before them, and considerable power came to be vested in the office—so much so, at times, that complaints were lodged against the government for allowing excessive latitude to chancery courts, as well as to other special courts circumventing the jury system. In English law, perhaps the most notorious example of such perceived abuses of judicial authority was the Star Chamber, which was particularly active during the reign of Charles I, when charges of sedition were sometimes brought covertly against nobles who dared oppose Crown policies. Such practices rankled in the breasts of many Britons, and not a few of those arraigned by the Star Chamber were Puritans, some of whom, when they emigrated to the New World, brought with them an ingrained distrust of juryless, privately conducted trials.[2]

Yet resentments of chancery courts came to be stored up for other reasons as well. In part because they did not depend strictly on *stare decisis,* or a system of precedent, relying instead on the conscience and judgment of a seasoned, often virtually autonomous jurist, chancery courts were thought more likely than common-law courts to become bogged down by the caprices of whoever occupied the office of chancellor at any given time, by complexities generated by the necessarily idiosyncratic nature of equity appeals, and by delay. As a result, courts of chancery acquired a reputation for dilatoriness, obfuscation, and expense, qualities that Charles Dickens satirized in *Bleak House,* which Dickinson read (see Capps 95). For literate audiences on either side of the Atlantic, *Jarndyce v. Jarndyce* came to represent a particular sort of legal quagmire.

In the colonies, courts of chancery and equity, despite being championed by such venerated figures as Benjamin Franklin and Joseph Story, generally did not prosper, especially in New England, where memories of Star Chamber outrages lingered. Massachusetts, as a state in which anti-British sentiment ran high both before and after the Revolution, proved especially hostile. As Perry Miller writes, one reason Bay Staters balked at establishing a court of equity was a fear of potential abuse by governmental authorities: "In Massachusetts, the Constitution of 1821 did allow for a court of Chancery, but in spite of the urging of Story and other judges, 'the terrors of the court'—which to the public were 'terrors of the unknown'—restrained the General Court from establishing Chancery until 1877" (*Life of the Mind* 173). Even after its establishment only a decade before Emily Dickinson died, chancery was promptly absorbed by Massachusetts common-law courts, as had already been done in New York, under that state's adoption of the Field Code (named after its originator, the legal reformer David Field).

Thus poems in which Dickinson mentions equity may treat the subject as being largely historical, philosophical, perhaps even a bit fusty. Yet during her lifetime the laws of Massachusetts nevertheless continued to address concerns that had lain traditionally within the precincts of equity rather than the common law: trespass, marriage, divorce, wills and estates, patents, the guardianship of minors. Even as courts and judges dedicated to equity gradually disappeared from the poet's local legal landscape, it survived as a set of principles embedded within the law. The rich history of courts of chancery in British literature, and equity's traditional identification as an alternative court for litigants seeking a remedy unavailable under common law, would have been sufficient to attract the poet's attention. Then too, textual evidence suggests Dickinson was drawn emotionally to the primary, all-important encounter between suitor and judge without the interceding presence of a jury. Such a direct plea for mercy or justice harked back to a British subject's ancient right of petitioning the sovereign directly, sometimes in person. Despite her ancestors' distaste for it, the elemental courtroom experience enacted within chancery sometimes boiled down for Dickinson to personal need pleading for assistance from executive power.

From its inception, equity differentiated itself from the older common law, yet without contesting its preexistent authority. In Britain, chancery courts always considered themselves an adjunct to common-law courts, not a substitute. For example, chancery did not impose prison sentences or decree capital punishment, although it could, and did, remand defendants to the tender mercies of the common-law courts, sometimes after offering its own opinion on what would constitute condign punishment for moral, as well as criminal, offenses. Indeed, for centuries, equity deferred on the question of whether any decision handed down by its courts was law at all in a technical sense, since equity decisions were not strongly rooted in precedent, or even codified. Cases coming before the chancellor were, almost by definition, sui generis, and remedies could be tailored to fit particular situations. The intensely personal nature of equity law virtually guaranteed that a high degree of variability existed between courts and between judges. For litigants, as I have said, much depended on the conscience (some said *whim*) of whichever judge happened to occupy the bench.[3] The chancellor did not rule upon the law, but instead issued orders or granted injunctions according to his evaluation of the legal problem set before him.[4] This latitude in constructing legal remedies ultimately grated on Americans, for an injunction could compel an individual to perform specific acts against his will in seeming violation of the country's foundational philosophic emphasis on personal liberty and freedom of action.

For all these reasons, equity may be considered as being somewhat akin to law while not yet being identical to law. Rather than relying on communal wisdom or history, equity obeyed its own set of philosophic principles and guidelines. Lawrence Friedman writes, "Equity became, in short, almost a system of antilaw" (xviii). Many of these principles-not-precedents are enshrined in the so-called maxims of equity, which law students have long been expected to con by heart. Translated from the original Latin, many of them possess a nearly Mosaic tone that is in keeping with chancery's origins in canon law: "Equity regards as done that which ought to be done." "One who seeks equity must do equity." "Equity aids the vigilant, not those who slumber on their rights." "Equity acts *in personam*" (that is, equity acts upon the person, not their property). "One who comes into equity must come with clean hands." "Equity delights to do justice and not by halves." "Equity follows the law" (that is, common law retains priority; equity supplements it). "Equity will not allow a trust to fail for want of a trustee."

Because it is rooted in the possible personal intercession of authority via the king's conscience or the church, equity has tended to be considered roughly synonymous not with *law,* but rather with *justice* and *mercy.* Both concepts underlie Portia's famous speech in *The Merchant of Venice,* a play Dickinson knew well (and to which she refers directly in the poem "What would I give to see his face?," which I will discuss in the next chapter).[5] An examination of legal concepts Shakespeare employed in that speech provides contexts for both how equity has been perceived historically and how Dickinson herself understood the term, especially in what was, for her, the especially congenial intellectual grounds of literature melded with law.

In addressing the court, where the Duke of Venice, in concert with the Magnificoes, sits in judgment, Portia (disguised as Balthasar) emphasizes the emblematic Christian quality of mercy, which she contrasts with the Jew Shylock's Old Testament definition of justice. In his efforts to avenge himself upon Antonio by exacting the flesh bond, Shylock would inevitably call to mind for Shakespearean audiences the *lex talionis,* a more "primitive" basis for law than that followed by late-Renaissance European courts. Portia addresses Shylock directly, while speaking simultaneously to the duke, who might yet intercede unilaterally in excusing Antonio from the consequences of failing to meet his pledge:

> The quality of mercy is not strain'd,
> It droppeth as the gentle rain from heaven
> Upon the place beneath: it is twice blest,
> It blesseth him that gives and him that takes,
> 'Tis mightiest in the mightiest, it becomes
> The throned monarch better than his crown.
> His sceptre shows the force of temporal power,
> The attribute to awe and majesty,
> Wherein doth sit the dread and fear of kings:
> But mercy is above this sceptred sway,
> It is enthroned in the hearts of kings,
> It is an attribute to God himself;
> And earthly power doth then show likest God's
> When mercy seasons justice: therefore Jew,
> Though justice be thy plea, consider this,
> That in the course of justice, none of us
> Should see salvation: we do pray for mercy,
> And that same prayer, doth teach us all to render
> The deeds of mercy. I have spoke thus much
> To mitigate the justice of thy plea,
> Which if thou follow, this strict court of Venice
> Must needs give sentence 'gainst the merchant there. (4.1.180–201)

Several concepts in this speech are closely akin to interests specific to equity. For example, Portia focuses on the *deeds* of mercy, rather than merely a merciful attitude; equity courts, in handing down injunctions, seek to affect relationships between individuals concretely and lastingly. In this emphasis on their tangibility, acts of mercy also resemble acts of nature, which may be known empirically as phenomena, like rain. Shylock himself is made to feel palpably the reality of mercy when he is finally compelled to beg for his life on his knees before the duke. Portia's simile comparing mercy to rain also emphasizes, of course, the valueless-ness, in monetary terms, of the rain, thus making a subtle distinction between those things for which a value may be assessed, and those for which it cannot, or between common law and equity. The fact that rain falls from on high reinforces the Christian organization of space between heavenly and sublunary domains and between ruler and subjects, so that the descending rain also endorses condescension, when justice stoops to aid the needy. Finally, Portia's observation that "mercy *seasons* justice" employs a pun to remind the play's auditors that mercy, like a spice, sup-plements or complements a basic diet of justice, and that it is natural for man to feel an impulse to show mercy, which is also "seasonal" in being connected to the real world, through the annual cycle. The "natural" origin of mercy serves as testamentary evidence (in a legal *and* in a New Testament sense) of God's endorsement of mercy in the same way that the Pentateuch offered documentary evidence of Moses having received the Decalogue from God on Mount Sinai, in the form of tablets. Finally, in implicitly comparing God's offer of mercy to poor sinners—that is, all humankind—to Shylock's bond with Antonio, Portia emphasizes the contractual nature of the relationship between divinity and humanity, replicated, ideally, in equitable contractual relationships struck between men.[6]

Dickinson understood the concept of *justice* in a multilayered cultural context deriving from English literary tradition, from her Protestant heri-tage, and from her own observations of how the courts of Massachusetts, and of Hampshire County, administered justice. In "It always felt to me – a wrong" (F521), the word "equity" appears to be roughly synony-mous with "justice," as the speaker ponders the situation of Moses him-self, after he is permitted to see Canaan without being allowed to enter it. The poet may also be attempting here to make, like Shakespeare in *The Merchant of Venice*, a distinction between Old Testament and New Testament concepts of justice:

It always felt to me – a wrong
To that Old Moses – done –
To let him see – the Canaan –
Without the entering –

And tho' in soberer moments –
No Moses there can be
I'm satisfied – the Romance
In point of injury –

Surpasses sharper stated –
Of Stephen – or of Paul –
For these – were only put to death –
While God's adroiter will

On Moses – seemed to fasten
With tantalizing Play
As Boy – should deal with lesser Boy –
To prove ability – | prove ability / show supremacy

The fault – was doubtless Israel's –
Myself – had banned the Tribes –
And ushered Grand Old Moses
In Pentateuchal Robes

Upon the Broad Possession | Broad Possession / Lawful Manor –
'Twas little – He should see – | He should see – / But titled Him – to see –
Old Man on Nebo! Late as this –
My justice bleeds – for Thee!

Several terms possessing legal nuances signal Dickinson's intent to
identify the law itself as her subject: "wrong," "point of injury," "fault,"
"Possession," "titled," "Lawful Manor." Like an attorney offering to
represent a client whose interests she considers to have been frustrated
within the ordinary processes of law, Dickinson's narrator here constructs
a legal argument, virtually a brief, about dispossession and trespass, with
Moses as plaintiff and God as defendant. God, in prohibiting a rightful
owner, Moses, who has "title" to Canaan, from entering his own "Lawful
Manor," has broken the law, in an act that is implicitly ironic because
it involves the eponymous provider of Mosaic law. The underlying issue
of trespass includes not just unlawful entry but also the prohibiting of a

rightful owner access to his lands. That Moses possesses "title" to Canaan proves that the land properly belongs to him, and Dickinson's phrase "Lawful Manor" reinforces the validity of Moses's claim. "Manor," in law, signifies not just a house, but also the surrounding lands, a meaning emphasized by Dickinson's variant "Broad Possession," which also nods to the encompassing view of Canaan achieved from Mount Nebo. Moreover, "Manor" is indicative of the status of the landholder, because in English law the term particularly referred to demesnes granted to a loyal noble servitor who in feudal times enjoyed near-total legal power over lands deeded to him.[7] The words "wrong," "justice," and "injury" suggest that this legal issue should be located within the jurisprudence exercised by equity courts rather than common-law courts. Dickinson's legally inflected terms construct Moses as a disenfranchised nobleman suffering from the ingratitude of his sovereign, that is, God considered as king. From a historical perspective, such a case might indeed reasonably be expected to fall within the purview of a court of equity, even though the defendant, God, would, ironically, be the very voice and source of absolute authority vested in the power of a chancery court, translated either through the aims of the church or the promptings of the king's conscience.

Searching for a precedent, the lawyerly narrator compares her client's situation with that of Stephen and Paul, who suffered martyrdom, presumably again with God's complicity. Yet Moses endures a fate even harsher than theirs, one that, to the poet, smacks of an almost childish willfulness on the part of God; alternatively, God represents a figure of authority who has overstepped the limits of his power, like a sovereign who has interposed himself improperly by flaunting his own omnipotence rather than extending mercy and kindness to his servant Moses. That patriarch of the church seems to have been dealt with by God in conformance with a more "primitive" system of justice, at least as considered from the point of view of a Christian such as Dickinson, for whom the New Testament functioned legally as a sort of extension of precedent, or reinterpretation, of the Old Testament. Her comparison of Moses with the New Testament figures Stephen and Paul implies that they, like he, were made to suffer martyrdom for the sake of an overweening monarch.

Boldly and presumptuously, the narrator substitutes herself for Jehovah, retrospectively and retroactively permitting Moses entry into the Promised Land rather than teasing him in a wanton, nearly sadistic fashion. A concept of justice that permits a display of power for its own sake, and which ignores essential human pain and suffering, must undergo a kind of judicial revision, as the narrator of this poem proposes. Implicitly, Dickinson even interrogates the term "Promised Land" from a legal standpoint, since God's assurances to Moses that the Jews would dwell in Canaan may be considered as an ambivalently drafted contract, so that the word "Promised" is shown to have lost virtually all legal meaning. Had Moses, after leading his people out of the wilderness, been defrauded? "My" justice, the narrator says, "bleeds – for Thee!" as she volunteers to take on his case and seek an injunction permitting him to enter Canaan. Implicitly, she suggests that this New Testament perspective, available in the poem's implicit coupling of Moses's suffering with that of Stephen and Paul, would supplement the Old Testament with the same Christian virtues of mercy and compassion endorsed by Portia in *The Merchant of Venice.*

The speaker also makes clear that whatever shortcoming among the Israelites God was condemning, her putative client was not to blame. "The fault – was doubtless Israel's –," she says, distinguishing between the Jews and their spokesman, Moses, her imputation of "fault" pointing directly to the question of liability. Yet the question of "fault" is not in itself entirely sufficient for determining whether elemental justice has been done in this situation. Speaking as attorney, the narrator seeks a shift of jurisdiction from common law to equity: her client has been dealt with unfairly, and questions of "fault" or material recompense are themselves immaterial in the context of the case. Because Moses's remedy at law has proven inadequate, he should seek the extraordinary remedy of *performance,* by being permitted to live on and to enter Canaan, rather than being allowed merely to *see* it before dying. According to "My" justice, the speaker says, Moses should seek performance of a contract previously negotiated with God, perhaps implicitly on Mount Sinai, when he first received the commandments. Moreover, Dickinson's possessive pronoun signifies not only her own preferences about how justice should be meted out but also the exclusive, nearly godlike judicial authority she is arrogating to herself, as if she were a chancery judge whose power rivaled that of a sovereign.

The word "remedy" possesses special significance in equity, for it connotes considerations that augment or replace pecuniary damages. The underlying principle of equity law is that money isn't everything—a plaintiff seeking relief in such a court wants an action done. In this sense, equity simulates a somewhat utopian model of fairness and equality in human relations that is as exacting, in a moral sense, as a common-law court's precise assessment of damages in round dollar figures. In this way, as I have said, equity, as a body of law, hewed to its ancestral roots in the church and the office of chancellor. Two of the maxims of equity are "Equity will not suffer a wrong to be without a remedy," and "Equity delights to do justice and not by halves," sayings that impute to the law an almost personal moral satisfaction in the balancing of competing legal interests. Yet such a view relies, implicitly, on a confidence that moral justice can be distributed accurately and fairly, an attitude eschewed by modern courts, which tend to gravitate toward a judicial relativism. Contemporary jurisprudence is more likely to concede that wrongs *do* exist for which there can be no remedy, in monetary damages or in performance, and that an ideal state of equitable relations between human beings is more achievable within the precincts of religion than in law; heaven may be perfect, but life on earth decidedly is not. Such an attitude may have helped erode the prestige of courts of equity virtually from their inception. In *The Merchant of Venice,* Portia may affect to discern a similarity between heaven and earth, but what happens to Shylock in the rest of act IV shows that justice may be shaped to suit the needs of the powerful after all, so that fairness, ostensibly a desideratum of the universal law, is reduced to a matter of personal subjectivity. Shakespeare's Jewish moneylender is penalized for seeking revenge in the guise of justice, yet what is done to Shylock by the court looks very much like revenge in its own right. Antonio is provided by the play's plot with an ingenious (and not entirely plausible, from a legal standpoint)[8] remedy to save him from death, yet Shylock receives virtually no relief, save his own life. The play denies the validity of the *lex talionis* while at the same time inflicting it, virtually point for point, upon the antagonist.

Considered from a literary rather than legal perspective, the word "remedy" also offers several obvious advantages in the construction of metaphors. In this sense, the "wrongs" of a plaintiff resemble a "disease" that the court, as "physician," attempts to ameliorate, if not cure. In F1692 Dickinson may be capitalizing on these manifold meanings:

> Of this is Day composed
> A morning and a noon
> A Revelry unspeakable
> And then a gay unknown
> Whose Pomps allure and spurn
> And dower and deprive
> And penury for Glory
> Remedilessly leave

The word "Remedilessly," although virtually impossible to scan, synthesizes here both the medical and legal connotations of "remedy." One of Dickinson's many definition poems,[9] "Of this is Day composed" describes the diurnal cycle, beginning with morning, passing to the brilliant light of noon ("A Revelry unspeakable"), to gaudy sunset ("a gay unknown / Whose Pomps allure and spurn," etc.), and finally the chromatic deprivation of darkest night. Dickinson's terms "Revelry" and "Pomps" suggest to mind a boisterous party, glittering to behold and marked by flirtations ("allure and spurn"), and that party's aftermath.

The terms "dower" and "deprive," and then "penury" and "Glory," are two sets of dialectical opposites, signifying absolute poverty and absolute wealth—an all-or-nothing equation. "Dower" has a specific legal significance crucial to the poem's meaning, and one I will examine at greater length in the next chapter. That term means "to make a gift," as in the word "endowment," yet in common law, as practiced during Dickinson's lifetime, the word specified a *feminine* gift—both in the sense that a dower is the portion of a man's estate left to his widow (in ancient parlance, the "widow's third"), and in "dowry": "The money, goods, or property that a woman brings to her husband in marriage" (*Black's* 530). Thus the *wealth*—particularly in the sense of display, or outward show— of daylight hours is expressly feminized. In that sense, the individual left penurious at the poem's end is implicitly a man, who has flirted with an attractive woman during a party and realized subsequently that she has disappeared, rather like Cinderella, after the ball is over. The adjective "Remedilessly," particularly in concert with the legal term "dower" and with words drawn from terminology associated with net worth, "deprive" and "penury," would seem to imply that for someone witnessing day's end, a gaudy sunset represents a display of sensory "wealth" that cannot be recovered either under common law or in courts of equity. As such, the loss of daylight does indeed constitute a wrong for which no remedy exists, or an emotional or sensory malady for which there is no cure.

The subject of power relations between lovers occupies Dickinson's attention in several poems, yet she often also conflates emotional coercion with authority exercised institutionally, as in the court system, or existentially, in an individual's encounters with deity. Equity's consolidation of power within the figure of the chancellor may be seen as distilling the experiential reality of confronting absolute, or near-absolute, authority. Symbolically, the role of equity or chancery judge combined judicial, royal, and ecclesiastic powers. One might reasonably expect the consolidation of judicial and moral authority within the single figure of the chancery judge to have seemed abhorrent to a Protestant such as Dickinson. But not so. The absolutist judicial model of equity appealed to the poet in representing, analogically, the emotive power lovers wielded over each other. This emphasis is visible in a handful of legally inflected poems in which prisoners are reprieved at the last moment by executive clemency; alternatively, at the last minute authority might refuse to save a victim's neck from the headsman's block.[10] In "Elizabeth told Essex" (F1336), for example, the Virgin Queen assents to the execution of the Earl of Essex for treason despite the fact that he had once been her favorite at court:

> Elizabeth told Essex
> That she could not forgive
> The clemency of Deity
> However – might survive –
> That secondary succor
> We trust that she partook
> When suing – like her Essex
> For a reprieving Look –

Plainly the poet's sympathy rests here with Essex. By the poem's logic, Queen Elizabeth should have subordinated even the interests of the realm to her own romantic instincts. Also, the poem's suggestion that Elizabeth, after her own death, would have to submit herself in turn for judgment before God, who might condemn her for having killed a man professing love for her, implies that heaven, too, would endorse a privileging of love over country.[11] "Suing" connotes both defendants' pleas to a superior authority for mercy, but that word also reminds readers that Essex had *sued* for Elizabeth's love, and the possessive pronoun "her" in the same line simultaneously establishes the earl's status as both potential lover and royal subject. The "secondary succor" Elizabeth recommends to Essex refers obliquely either to an appeals court or to chancery, yet in this particular legal drama, the conscience of the sovereign may not be awakened until too late, when she herself had died.[12]

Dickinson remained deeply impressed by the power vested in the judiciary, and, late in life, she could witness at first hand the effects wrought by a forceful personality occupying the bench. In letters to Otis Lord, who was a justice on the Massachusetts Supreme Court, Dickinson refers to the virtually godlike power of his position, from which he might choose to show mercy or send the condemned to the penitentiary or the gallows. The poet and her family had implicit faith in Judge Lord's rectitude and wisdom. But the near-absolute power entrusted generally to the office of judges of any kind, and more immediately and unilaterally in the office of equity court judges, did raise questions and problems of which Dickinson seems to have been well aware. The judge-made law of equity courts posed a risk to petitioners in that it was based on the discretion, or whim, of a single person, on a single occasion. In that sense, as I have said, courts of equity emulated the relation between sovereign and subject, as opposed to the jury system's broader and more egalitarian treatment of plaintiffs and defendants as fellow citizens judged by their peers. In F1409, Dickinson appears to be meditating on the problem of judicial caprice:

> Death warrants are supposed to be
> An enginery of Equity
> A merciful mistake | merciful / hazardous
> A pencil in an Idol's Hand
> A Devotee has oft consigned
> To Crucifix or Block | Block / stake

The passive verb in this poem's first line generates a basic interpretive quandary. Does "supposed to be" signify "ought to be," or "imagined as"? I read this poem as a critique of the ancient practice in chancery courts of recommending (sometimes, virtually ensuring) capital punishment for those it found against, while keeping its own hands comparatively clean.

Such decisions are "Merciful mistake[s]," that is, mistakes of mercy, miscarriages of justice in which mercy has gone awry, resulting in the issuing of death warrants by the ruling sovereign.[13] The poem's syntax may be clarified by adding punctuation: a comma after "equity" in the second line, and a period after "mistake" in the third. Dickinson's reference to "equity" strongly suggests she has in mind here courts of chancery, or even the courts of the Inquisition, which may also be indicated by the variant "stake," signifying the death by burning reserved for victims of the Inquisition who were intended to feel, in the manner of their deaths, a premonitory indication of their souls' consignment to hellfire.[14] The word "enginery" is especially apt, for it suggests simultaneously fiendish "engines" of torture, and "machination," that is, a bureaucratic plot directed at the accused.

In "Death warrants are supposed to be," the locus of authority is designated as an "Idol," in the sense that a chancery judge implicitly acts for the interests of the physical, actual church, in which *idols*—according to Dissenter critics of the Roman, or even the Anglican, church—may be found. The poem could be a meditation on the improper exercise of power by ecclesiastic rather than civil authority. A monarch such as Elizabeth could sentence Essex to death because she is his sovereign, yet the chancellor, in arrogating for himself both ecclesiastic and judicial domains of authority, may overreach himself, the poem's speaker would seem to imply, by authorizing a death warrant despite the fact that equity courts lacked the power to authorize capital punishment. Hand-in-glove arrangements made between chancery and common-law courts to get rid of perceived troublemakers might seem to undermine the concept of essential justice. The word "pencil" emphasizes both the arbitrariness and the banality of such bureaucratic shuffling. In that sense, it is the pencil itself which is a *device* resembling the "engine[s] of Equity" resulting in the execution of a man or a woman, a "Devotee." In combination with the first line's passive-voice deletion of agency, and the pejorative term "Idol," this imputation of responsibility to an implement rather than to a human conscience emphasizes the impersonality, even depersonalization, of absolute authority acting both unilaterally and mindlessly.

In the poems we have seen thus far, equity is aligned with challenges to power that could result potentially in disastrous consequences for a legal supplicant. But Dickinson was also entirely capable of employing the concept of equity to make fun of *powerlessness,* as she does in F1174, one of the more intensively legalistic of all her literary creations:

Alone and in a Circumstance	|in / of
Reluctant to be told	
A spider on my reticence	
Assiduously crawled	|deliberately / determinately / impertinently
And so much more at Home than I	
Immediately grew	
I felt myself a visitor	|a / the
And hurriedly withdrew	|hurriedly / hastily
Revisiting my late abode	
With articles of claim	
I found it quietly assumed	
As a Gymnasium	|As / for
Where Tax asleep and Title off	
The inmates of the Air	|inmates / Peasants
Perpetual presumption took	|presumption / complacence
As each were special Heir –	|special: lawful / only
If any strike me on the street	
I can return the Blow –	
If any take my property	|take / seize
According to the Law	
The Statute is my Learned friend	
But what redress can be	
For an offense nor here nor there	|"not anywhere" crossed out
So not in Equity –	
That Larceny of time and mind	
The marrow of the Day	
By spider, or forbid it Lord	
That I should specify.	

Before discussing these lines in detail, I think it important to emphasize the poem's humor—both sophisticated legal satire and low comedy. I agree with David Porter's reading that identifies the setting as a privy.[15] Very likely written in the spring of 1870 when Dickinson was forty years old, "Alone and in a Circumstance" combines stereotypically unsophisticated rustic humor in its description of events transpiring in an outhouse with a comparatively technical legal discussion. For reasons

I will develop, I think Dickinson intended for this poem to be read by someone in her own family who could appreciate an elaborate legal burlesque.[16]

"Alone and in a Circumstance" is constructed around a series of humorous legal dilemmas confronting the narrator, a property owner trying to reassert her rights before a presumably legally empowered authority, such as a judge or magistrate. The narration simulates testimony, moving from personal experience, to a complaint, and then to a more abstract discussion of the various legal principles applying to her situation. She was alone in the privy, the narrator says, when she was rudely interrupted. Her language studiously avoiding describing either her posture (sitting) or her activity (relieving herself), the narrator hints that an intruder came into direct contact with her person. The phrase "Reluctant to be told" parodies the euphemistic language and passive-voice construction employed by a prudish witness providing testimony during the very public circumstances of making a complaint, filing a deposition, or attending a court hearing. Here the plaintiff's "circumstances" are indelicate, and therefore "Reluctant to be told." The narrator's squeamishness about discussing spiders and her implicit embarrassment about describing her situation in public allow the presumption that she is to be understood as being female.

Her reluctance to be more specific about her "Circumstance" is reinforced by the word "reticence," which does more than simply comment on her evident shyness. As readers we are quite justified, I think, in regarding "reticence" as a pun, perhaps also a malapropism, for "residence." The entire poem concerns a "residence," which is what an outbuilding is—for spiders, however, rather than for human beings, who visit it only intermittently. But because the poem's language treats "reticence" as a concrete object upon which a spider crawls, rather than as an abstract concept, that word may also be read as a euphemism for "leg," a word sometimes proscribed in polite Victorian-era conversation, or even for "derriere." That the narrator was so shocked as to leave *hurriedly* suggests that her encounter with the spider was intimate, in the sense that it had touched her. In the poem overall, Dickinson may be constructing a funny and ingenious legal argument about property considered as an extension of the self, especially of the corporeal self. In this sense, her presentation in the poem of a leg or other part of her body as a "reticence" / "residence" functions as part of a larger legal metaphor in which the body, considered in light of all its various functions (including excretion) is regarded as a domicile, with ramifications both public and private.

Dickinson's legal and verbal jokes keep up a rapid pace in the poem's middle stanzas. Her phrase "at Home" capitalizes on the reader's familiarity with that cliché, as in the phrase "Please inform callers that I am not at home," while simultaneously implying that the outhouse may be a home for *someone*. The spiders, by maintaining a residence there—spinning webs, swinging from their strands of silk, and refusing to leave—threaten to present a legally defensible claim to ownership of the building. In implicit confirmation that the spiders have established not just residency, but ownership, the narrator confesses that she had felt *herself* to be a "visitor" or trespasser, and fled.[17] She returned with "articles of claim," presumably broom and dustpan, but Dickinson's joke, of course, is that the word "article" also signifies a legal instrument, such as a land title or deed of claim. The term "article" participates within an overall rhetorical campaign waged by the narrator to impress her projected auditor, a legal authority of some sort. Consequently she refers to the privy self-importantly and euphemistically as an "abode," although this is also a transparent lie, since she does not actually live within the outhouse, as the spiders do. She uses the word to bolster her legal argument that the outhouse is *her* house. From a legal standpoint, she has tried to repossess her property by wielding "articles of claim," yet the spiders refuse to leave, we may infer, and the narrator rather sheepishly and indirectly admits that her own rights to the property may rest on shaky legal ground. If she is indeed approaching a judge in an effort to persuade him to issue an injunction against the alleged trespassers, she seems to realize she will be facing several daunting legal obstacles.

As I mentioned earlier, one of the ancient jurisdictions in equity was trespass. A property owner alleging that an intruder had entered and occupied his lands—sometimes *vi et armis,* with force and arms, as legal language has it—could go first to the King's Bench, and then, monetary damages alone having proved insufficient, to the chancellor, to request a writ of ejectment that could both debar the trespasser and authorize the owner to reenter his own lands. Originally, so many such petitions began to be made to the Crown that judicial responsibility for them was shifted to courts of chancery. For plaintiffs alleging trespass, the advantage of winning a ruling in chancery was that an equity court could hand down an injunction, even in the absence of the trespasser from the court, ordering him to leave and authorizing the landowner's legitimate reoccupation of his property.

The spiders, to press their case, must refute an accusation of trespass, alleging instead that they are rightful and lawful occupants of the premises. Their challenges to the narrator's claim of ownership are really threefold. First, the spiders and their ilk have staked a claim to the privy through *adverse possession.* That is, by occupying a property openly and over a lengthy period, they assert a right to title, especially if the owner of record has been absent or has displayed no evident interest in maintaining the property.[18] An important component of making an argument for adverse possession is that the claimants should be "notorious and open" about living there, so that the public at large is acquainted with the fact of their residency. While the spiders have "assumed" the property "quietly," the figure that follows, "As a Gymnasium," would seem to contradict that adverb, gymnasiums being by definition places reserved for sports and physical training. Although it is true that the spiders make little or no noise (an aspect of behavior Dickinson emphasizes in other poems about them),[19] they weave their webs like rope ladders or trampolines hanging in mid-air, climbing and riding them like children knocking about a gym.[20] Such behavior is hardly furtive or inconspicuous. The narrator's tone here may even be construed as sarcastic: their occupation was about as quiet as a schoolyard at recess. If so, however, the spiders' case for claiming adverse possession is only strengthened, for their occupation of the building is patently obvious. Moreover, the character of these anthropomorphized spiders is tacitly admitted to be comparatively benign. The initial spider crawls "Assiduously," that is, industriously, upon the narrator's body, and this kinetic activity is reinforced by fellow spiders' mid-air acrobatics.[21] Claimants to land may also stipulate in court that they should be considered rightful owners because they have made improvements to the land, and the spiders in the poem are implicitly admirable for their activities as athletes, builders, and explorers.

A second challenge the narrator faces in her campaign to retain legal control over her property is her failure to maintain it or occupy it continuously. Privies are, of course, occupied only occasionally, as necessity dictates. Further, the very presence of spiderwebs is a clear indication that she has failed to maintain the structure conscientiously, and her indolence suffers by contrast with the spiders' industriousness. Worse, the narrator has evidently failed to make tax payments on the property, putting it at risk of foreclosure. The poem suggests this may have already happened, for "Title [is] off," meaning that her title to the privy is in jeopardy. Taxes owed on the property have been left "asleep," or unpaid, and soon the question of who actually does hold title to the structure may be submitted for a court to determine. One of the maxims of equity is "Equity aids the vigilant, not those who slumber on their rights," and the narrator of this poem has "slumbered" on her rights as property owner. Considered in a broader legal context, her inaction may be construed as *laches:* "Unreasonable delay in pursuing a right or claim—almost always an equitable one—in a way that prejudices the party against whom relief is sought. —Also termed *sleeping on rights*" (*Black's* 891). The narrator has neglected both her property and her rights, rendering her vulnerable to contesting claims of ownership.

A third problem is the implicit suggestion that the spiders might allege a family relation to the narrator, and thus be eligible to inherit her property. They behave "As each were special Heir," a term with specific meaning in law. An estate left in fee-tail can descend only to the "heirs of the body" of the testator, that is, his or her direct issue or progeny: "An estate-tail may be general, *i.e.* limited to the heirs of the body merely: or special, *i.e.* limited to a special class of such heirs, *e.g.* heirs male or heirs female, or those begotten of a certain wife named" (*Bouvier's* 2: 766). The potential attribution to the spiders of a masculine identity—as *heirs,* not heiresses—may also raise the slightly titillating suggestion that the invasive, putatively male spiders are behaving voyeuristically in encroaching on an outhouse occupied by a female. By taking such liberties with the narrator, including crawling on her, the invading spider also conducts himself as if he were a near relative, that is, someone entitled to touch her person in a somewhat ambiguous display of affection. In some ways, the spiders are portrayed in the rest of the poem as rambunctious juveniles obscurely related to the narrator. If not her own actual offspring, they at least resemble minors, whose rights courts of both law and equity have historically been at pains to protect.

The spiders' effrontery in claiming to be her relations, and, presumably, in touching her, constitutes a "presumption" from her point of view, although the only explicitly identified way in which the spiders show such presumptuousness is to occupy the privy "Perpetual[ly]," that is, by staying there indefinitely, like tiresome visiting relatives who refuse to leave. For the narrator, any such claim of consanguinity would probably be both disgusting and ridiculous. Rather, she characterizes the spiders as "inmates of the Air," a felicitously chosen phrase that recognizes spiders' acrobatic talents while suggesting simultaneously that they are lunatics confined to an asylum, where exercise may be prescribed as a form of therapy.[22] Correspondingly, a court should dismiss any claim the spiders might make about being her relations as outright nonsense.

Next, the narrator turns to the nature of her complaint. Did the spiders' perhaps physical contact with her constitute *battery*, defined as the harmful or offensive touching by another? If so, the law entitles her to defend herself. And yet she makes an important distinction between the incident in the outhouse and battery that may occur in public: "If any strike me on the street / I can return the Blow –." Within her own home—of which the outhouse is an extension—she would have difficulty bringing charges against alleged batterers already resident there (and who may also claim to be distant relations), since the authorities might dismiss the incident as a domestic fracas. Conversely, if she were assaulted in the street, a public place, she could more easily bring criminal charges of battery against an assailant, because the law has an interest in maintaining peace and order in public places; then, the "Statute"—that is, the criminal law statute— would indeed be her "Learned friend," for her attacker would likely be arrested, charged, and prosecuted. But she is not on the street, or in any similarly public place: she is sitting in a privy, by definition a very *non-public* place.

Well, then, had the spiders committed theft of any sort? If so, the narrator asserts, she would have a probable cause of action, and a reason to eject them. But the only theft of which she may reasonably accuse them is "Larceny of time and mind," evidently a stock phrase used by plaintiffs to indicate nonmaterial losses, including anxiety, incurred through the dereliction of others.[23] Like "pain and suffering," that phrase was probably used to describe nonquantifiable losses in complaints plaintiffs brought before courts of equity in hopes of reinforcing their claims against defendants. Plaintiffs making such allegations represented themselves as having been required to devote considerable time and energy to the matter, at the "cost," implicitly or explicitly, of other, perhaps more profitable, business matters to which they might have been attending. These intangible losses do not, by definition, fall under the rubric of *larceny*, a legal category pertaining exclusively to the theft of material chattels.[24] In speaking of the time she has lost, the narrator laments missing "The marrow of the Day," which I can only speculate signified to Dickinson's contemporaries the most productive hours of the day, so that the time taken from the narrator represents a substantial, not just trivial, injury. She reidentifies the spider as chief culprit, yet she hesitates once again to spell out precisely what she thinks has been taken from her, as part of her overall reluctance to describe either her physical circumstances or the legal status of her claim to ownership: "By spider, *or*" she says, "forbid it Lord," a perhaps intentionally ambiguous expression she uses in requesting the court both to forestall, perhaps by injunction, the spiders' further intrusion as well as any further humiliation she might suffer by being compelled to offer testimony. Her appellation "Lord" may also hint that a putatively British court of chancery is where her complaint has finally washed up, every common-law alternative having been exhausted.

The narrator's reluctance to describe what had happened, where it had happened, and who had done something to her represents a potentially fatal flaw in her legal argument, not least because her testimonial "reticence" makes it more difficult for the court to determine jurisdiction. Her complaint is neither "here nor there," neither in law, nor in equity. Still, the law provides, as the narrator says, powerful safeguards for property owners. "The Statute is my Learned friend," she declares, boasting of the law's protection, codified in black-letter law. Yet "my learned friend" was a euphemism frequently employed condescendingly by American and British attorneys to describe opposing counsel. The narrator's decorous, patronizing language may indicate that she has been reduced to casting aspersions on her legal opposition; moreover, her scorn stands in stark contrast to her portrayal of herself elsewhere in the poem as legally naive, prudish, and obsequious. If the spiders' treatment of the narrator is neither assault nor theft, how can she accuse them of being felons, and, even if she could, what sort of remedy could she possibly seek: "what redress can be[?]" The word "redress," legally synonymous with "remedy," also suggests a double-entendre, especially since it is being deployed to describe the flight of a panic-stricken, half-undressed woman from a privy. We may legitimately imagine, I think, the intended legally minded reader of this poem as smiling at Dickinson's joke.[25]

But the narrator's reference to "redress" also helps signal the poem's emphasis on the legal question of jurisdiction. If no assault, theft, or fraud had been committed, the narrator will have difficulty finding standing in a common-law court. A plaintiff might then still hope to find legal relief in a court of equity and seek an injunction against the spiders (such as, for instance, compelling them to vacate the premises). But, as the narrator admits (perhaps under oath?), the spiders' offense was "nor here nor there," neither a crime, like assault, nor a tort, like trespass—an ambiguity that applies in more than one way to her legal predicament. An outhouse, being an outbuilding, like a barn, and not a permanent residence (for human beings, at least) or a rental property, could have an uncertain status in considerations of property law. Also, Dickinson may well be referring to the linguistic paradox of saying the unsayable, as was true in "Of this is Day composed," which described "A Revelry *unspeakable.*" The narrator cannot name the *place* where she was, or *what* she was doing there, and her euphemistic description of her encounter with the spider as having transpired "nor here nor there" both literalizes the unmentionable reality of her "Circumstance" while inevitably and ironically trivializing the status of her complaint at law. To say that something is "neither here nor there" signifies, idiomatically, that the subject is not germane to the matter at hand, a dismissal of it from the realm of pertinent discourse. Further, the offense committed against the narrator is more philosophical than physical, an affright instead of a fight, so that her legal complaint is truly neither here nor there, falling into a sort of jurisdictional limbo between crime, civil law, and equity. She can barely bring herself to describe her own circumstances ("Reluctant to be told"), or what the spiders did to her, where they did it, or on which body part of hers that they did it ("on my reticence /. . . crawled").

In the poem's final line, she begs the court not to press her any more closely to describe precisely what had happened. Thus the narrator's own excessive modesty provides yet another example of legal self-sabotage, her testimony serving to conceal more than it reveals. Unable to formulate a protest about how she has been injured, the narrator effectively admits that she has no actionable complaint in equity, which would ordinarily be the court of last resort for a plaintiff who could not find a remedy in the common law. She cannot herself categorize what has happened to her, so that, we may speculate, the legal authority to whom she is speaking will be charged with the responsibility of providing his best professional advice about what alternative legal avenue she might pursue. The complainant's testimony, which is illogical, inarticulate, fawning, and self-serving, may do more to damage her interests than it will to advance them.

"Alone and in a Circumstance" effectively creates a sort of legal "hypo," a legal fact pattern expressly constructed to test the legal acumen of law students, or any other legally trained mind. But the poem also portrays a legal debacle, a specimen of the "war stories" attorneys like to tell. Contemporary readers might legitimately ask, for whom could such a comic legal tour-de-force have been written? We know that Dickinson, who usually did not seek publication, often addressed her poems to particular ears, at particular times. In 1870, which of her friends or family, we might ask, could appreciate this poem's legal jokes and exuberant wordplay, and yet not be offended by its bawdy humor? Physical details in the original, autograph manuscript indicate, I suggest, that she wrote it for the edification and amusement of her brother, who, by 1870, was firmly established in his own legal practice.

One clue that she may have had Austin in mind is the poem's manuscript appearance, which is unusual, to say the least. As Thomas Johnson describes it, "Pasted onto the center of the front half of the half-sheet of notepaper on which the poem is written there is an unused three-cent postage stamp of the issue of 1869. Beneath one side of the stamp are two small strips clipped from *Harper's Magazine* for May 1870. One bears the name 'George Sand' and the other 'Mauprat'—the title of the novel by George Sand published in 1836. The poem was written after the stamp and strips were pasted onto the sheet, for the lines accommodate themselves to the occupied space" (*Poems* 2: 816). Two details Johnson does not mention here are also significant, I think: the postage stamp affixed to the manuscript depicts a locomotive, in blue, and the two strips of paper taken from *Harper's* are arranged so as to converge upon the stamp, which rests at the apex of the sideways V they create. The three interpolated items effectually constitute an arrow, with the engine at its tip. As Johnson says, the text of Dickinson's poem is written right around this mini-collage, fitting itself into the spaces created by it. The pasted items are therefore intrinsic to the body and text of the poem. Certainly, if she had wished, Dickinson could have written "Alone and in a Circumstance" on a different, completely blank piece of paper. Why might she have chosen such a highly idiosyncratic visual and textual format for this particular poem?[26]

I speculate that the postage stamp is a pictorial, almost cartoon-ish,[27] reference to Edward Dickinson, for whom the engine is a visual metonym. His presidency of the Amherst & Belchertown Railroad served for a while to elevate his civic prominence, and to local citizens he served as figurehead for that road's very existence. Edward Dickinson took particular pride in having brought the cars to Amherst in 1853; indeed, he remained active to the end of this life in promoting the construction of railway lines in Massachusetts. So inextricable was Edward Dickinson's identity as man, attorney, and congressman from the town's efforts to construct the railway that a locomotive was renamed in his honor, and the "Edward Dickinson" hauled passengers and freight for a couple of years until the line went bankrupt in 1857 (see Leyda 2: 71). Despite the Amherst & Belchertown's failure as a business venture, Emily Dickinson took considerable pride in her father's achievement, and she too identified the man with the machine.[28] In a letter penned to her cousin Louise Norcross in 1871, perhaps one year after she had written "Alone and in a Circumstance," Dickinson said, "Father was very sick. . . . I hope I am mistaken, but I think his physical life don't want to live any longer. You know he never played, and the straightest engine has its leaning hour" (L360). As early as 1851, the poet wrote to Austin, "Fathers real life and *mine* sometimes come into collision, but as yet, escape unhurt!" (L65). This figure of speech describing their father may have had a long history within Emily and Austin's sibling relationship.

In the "illustration" for her poem, the engine indeed does not go straight—or perhaps it does. The strips of script converge on the image of the engine like lines of perspective, and the engine faces outwards, away from the strips, as if receding into the distance.[29] For a person like Emily Dickinson, who possessed some talents as a graphic artist, but for whom creating drawings depicting objects in their proper perspective likely exceeded her skills, the pasted pieces of paper create a next-best alternative. The image, then, is of an engine speeding down the tracks—a visual surrogate for Edward Dickinson. If the creation of the image did precede the writing of the poem, we may speculate that such a sequence implies intent of a sort: after pasting together a graphic equivalent of her father, Dickinson wrote the poem as a humorous homage to the man.

Yet although Edward Dickinson makes a viable candidate for being the poem's deflected subject, it remains unlikely that he was its intended audience or recipient. He certainly could have understood the poem's various legal references, but it is doubtful he would have appreciated his daughter's artfulness, much less her grafting of outhouse humor onto the dignified practice of law.[30] If this poem did, in fact, have a projected intended audience, Austin Dickinson remains, I think, the most logical candidate. Austin knew as well as his sister the effort their father had expended in bringing a railway line to Amherst; he would also have understood all of her legal terms and references; and he would have appreciated a few innocuous jokes made at their father's expense.

References to George Sand on the strips may also suggest Austin's complicity. Although Edward Dickinson approved, generally, of his older daughter's habit of reading novels, he apparently did not share her interest in fiction.[31] Austin, on the other hand, besides being a lawyer, sympathized with his sister's tastes in art and in literature. To fantasize a bit, then, we may imagine the collage of the original manuscript as depicting an engine traveling on rails composed of references to European literature (Sand's novel), surmounting those guides, while nonetheless continuing to be guided by them. Or perhaps the engine named "Edward Dickinson" is riding roughshod over sensibilities finer than its own—who can tell? But the poem feels like a family in-joke written for Austin's amusement: the legal witticisms, the low-comedy references to a woman making a hurried exit from an outhouse, the appended graphic reference to a hard-charging, somewhat narrow-minded legal sensibility that would have been exasperated by the poem's meandering legal narrative. The poem is so contrived as to make a literarily minded lawyer laugh, and Austin fills the bill.[32]

By 1870, the estimated time of composition for this poem, even though the Amherst & Belchertown Railroad Company continued to represent a personal accomplishment for Edward Dickinson within his immediate family, the line itself had proved a financial disaster. In 1857 the company was reorganized, with the result that stockholders lost almost $200,000, a huge sum.[33] Evidently Edward Dickinson himself emerged comparatively unscathed from the collapse, having concentrated his own investment in bonds rather than in stock. But the specter of suits potentially brought against the company by investors could have helped keep the topic of equity at the forefront of the Dickinson family's collective legal strategizing, for the very concept of receivership owes its existence to courts of equity. Lawrence Friedman discusses New England's gradual realization that equity could be used as a means of preserving industrial capital and limiting liability, helping to explain why equity, once loathed in post-Revolutionary times, tended, ironically, to survive in New England longer than it did in states that had adopted it more readily:

> Those New England states that had never given their courts full equity powers—Maine, New Hampshire, Massachusetts—expanded equitable remedies after the Civil War. In fact, many striking legal developments, between 1850 and 1900, depended on creative use of tools of equity. Courts put bankrupt railroads into (equity) receivership and virtually ran them; they forged out of the injunction a terrible sword to use in industrial disputes. Injunction and receivership were both old tricks of equity, rapidly and vigorously reshaped. Equity, free from the whims of a jury, was made to order for a judge with a taste for power. (298)

Thus equity may have been a legal matter of considerable professional and personal interest to Edward Dickinson and his family at the time "Alone and in a Circumstance" was written, and the exercise of power, whether judicially or extrajudicially, may have lain at the root of their interest. In its references to the general concept of equity, and in its cartoonish presentation of a railroad engine at its center (at its very heart), the poem distills the importance of equity to the individual in the outhouse, and perhaps even to corporations.

"Alone and in a Circumstance" finally provides a subversive commentary about the limits of authority, and the poem generates a subnarrative describing relations between commoner spiders and patrician human beings. Sand's novel *Mauprat* treats that very subject overtly, in contrasting the somewhat dissolute nobleman Bernard Mauprat to the peasant philosopher Patience.[34] A variant Dickinson contemplated using in the poem's fourteenth line for "inmates" was, in fact, "Peasants," suggesting that she may have intended all along for the poem's narrator to be understood as a type along the lines of the aristocratic Bernard Mauprat, narrator of Sand's novel, a man with a sufficiently liberal education to regard the interests of his social inferior, Patience, dispassionately and objectively.[35]

Another variant in line 4, "impertinently" for "Assiduously," reinforces the notion that, at some point in its composition, Dickinson considered framing the narrative in the poem as a specimen of class conflict. If so, a visual allusion to her father would again have been entirely appropriate. As leading citizen of Amherst, local champion of law and order, and "engine" of local economic development, Edward Dickinson exemplified, as much as any citizen in egalitarian America could, a consolidation of moral, legal, and class power. Dickinson's raucous poem gives a tweak to such legal hubris, and, accordingly, her manuscript text dances around the onrushing engine, escaping unscathed. Dickinson's references to equity may also have appealed to Austin as someone who had received a liberal education in law at Harvard. Versed not just in the technicalities of law but also in the wider humanistic and novelistic interests of European writers such as George Sand, Austin would have grasped his sister's references to aristocracy and to plebes, the letter and the spirit of the law. To her brother, then, Dickinson may have presented herself in "Alone and in a Circumstance" not just as an antiquarian of the law, but also as a literarily informed legal and social critic. The poem nods knowingly at forces that uphold the law, even while caricaturing them as a form of power that could sometimes be rendered powerless.

SEALS, SIGNS, AND RINGS

Contracts

ontracts formalize relationships between people, typically in matters of business. They may be as informal as an oral promise, or as elaborate as a witnessed and sealed property deed. During the nineteenth century, comparatively few women would have entered into commercial contracts. Although a wife's right to portions of her deceased husband's estate enjoyed some legal protection, ordinarily a wife with a living husband was considered an extension of his own legal interests. Yet contract law also pertained to noncommercial transactions of crucial importance to women, especially betrothal and marriage. Marriage itself was interpreted legally as an agreement struck between partners; thus, for example, *Bouvier's* defined "marriage" as "A contract made in due form of law, by which a man and woman reciprocally engage to live with each other during their joint lives, and to discharge towards each other the duties imposed by law on the relation of husband and wife" (2: 318). A betrothed woman, on the other hand, lived in a sort of legal limbo, not yet attached to the property interests of a husband, yet potentially entitled to some legal remedy should the engagement fall through. In this chapter I will examine the poet's overall figural treatment of contracts, focusing on issues of particular importance to women, such as breach of promise, marriage, and dowries. I will also look at three legally significant means of certifying contracts Dickinson employed symbolically in her poems: seals, signs, and rings. In seeking once again to provide a simultaneously legal and literary context for Dickinson's thinking and writing, I will revisit *The Merchant of Venice*.

Dickinson demonstrates herself to be well aware that a woman's marriageability and reproductive potential were assets that could be negotiated in contractual terms which were either specifically legal or metaphorically so within a legally determined context. We have already seen Dickinson's representation of the sexual potential of a putatively female narrator in the poem "I gave myself to Him." There, the "solemn contract of a Life" is "ratified," yet in terms that remain insistently (and ironically) quantifiable, as the speaker surrenders up her own body as a kind of collateral for the emotional bargain she seeks to negotiate. Here is another poem (F266) in which the narrator behaves as if she is offering a contract based, indirectly, on her own sexuality. As in the previous chapter, Dickinson's references to *The Merchant of Venice* may help clarify the poem's philosophical stance:

What would I give to see his face?
I'd give – I'd give my life – of course –
But *that* is not enough!
Stop just a minute – let me think!
I'd give my biggest Bobolink!
That makes *two* – *Him* – and *Life*!
You know who "*June*" is –
I'd give *her* –
Roses a day from Zinzebar –
And Lily tubes – like Wells –
Bees – by the furlong –
Straits of Blue
Navies of Butterflies – sailed thro' –
And dappled Cowslip Dells –

Then I have "shares" in Primrose "Banks" –
Daffodil Dowries – spicy "Stocks" –
Dominions – broad as Dew –
Bags of Doubloons – adventurous Bees
Brought me – from firmamental seas –
And Purple – from Peru –

Now – have I bought it –
"Shylock"? Say!
Sign me the Bond!
"I vow to pay
To Her – who pledges *this* –

One hour – of her Sovereign's face"!
Exstatic Contract!
Niggard Grace!
My *Kingdom's worth* of Bliss!

This poem simulates the bargaining going on before the signing of virtually any contract, with the narrator to be understood as addressing her potential contractual, not romantic, partner. Dickinson's punctuation and her sparse, intermittent rhyme help generate a temporal illusion that these negotiations are going on in real time. The narrator even provides specific contractual language in the final stanza for the other party, as if she were drafting a legal document to be submitted to "Shylock." The terms of value set forth by the narrator are explicit: for the privilege of seeing her beloved's face for a single hour, she will offer all the things in the world that give her happiness, that is, which possess hedonic value. Such a contract would itself be "Ecstatic," yet really this agreement redefines the experience of happiness itself, which is subordinate to the state of ecstasy to be realized in reunion with the beloved. Ostensibly, the deal the narrator seeks would transfer satisfactions to be derived from appreciating the natural world to the contractual partner, yet her figures emphasize a continuity between nature and another repository of subjective, affective value: sexuality and reproductive potential.

The poem's focus on birds, bees, and flowers gestures stereotypically toward fertilization and fecundity. In describing lilies, for example, the narrator draws attention to the lily bloom's "tube," its "Well" that a bee must plumb in order to gather pollen, an image that emphasizes flowers' morphologic equivalency to genitalia. The narrator professes a willingness to trade emblems of generalized sexuality in nature for the specific sexually and emotively charged experience of seeing the face of her "Sovereign," a designation for her lover. Overall, by suggesting that such an exchange could be negotiated within two separate systems of value, nature and property, the poem subtly equates nonhuman, botanical sexuality with human sexuality. The narrative voice in this poem is presented as impulsive, unsophisticated, and overwrought, as if belonging to the very sort of person who might be cheated by an unscrupulous bargainer. Yet the narrator's suggested naïveté, in offering the terms that she does, may be only superficial. The possibility, raised at the end of the poem, of seeing the beloved's face again introduces an adult pathos that contrasts with the poem's earlier, almost childish, personifications of nature. The speaker of the poem is to be understood as knowing what she is doing, and trying to drive the best bargain she can get.

The reciprocal party is denoted "Shylock." By referring specifically to Shakespeare's usurious moneylender, the narrator implies that her bargain *seems*, at least, to be one-sided in favor of the other negotiator. Yet like Antonio, who agrees to surrender a pound of his flesh to Shylock, she offers unconventional value for what she seeks, and also like that merchant, she seeks to bargain for the sake of her affections, and not just out of mercantile self-interest.[1] The single "hour" she seeks to spend in the presence of the beloved may even have been designed to echo the single pound of flesh Shylock requires from Antonio, should he default on his contractual obligations.

The speaker's faux-childish, hyperbolic language affirms the primacy of subjectively determined values over conventional systems of exchange. The speaker offers birds, flowers, and bees, natural phenomena with no intrinsic commercial worth, yet with tremendous figural value as exponents of the sexual self. Other assets the narrator professes herself willing to exchange have a nominal worth inversely proportionate to the grandiose language she uses to describe them, as if she were a seller anxious to make her own offerings appear more attractive. The poem's diction probably draws consciously from the terminology of financial reports and stockbrokers' prospectuses, yet Dickinson uses clever puns to undercut her words' quotidian commercial meanings. "Banks" refers both to financial institutions and to banks of flowers, and "stocks" signifies simultaneously shares in a company and horticultural stocks of shrubs from which scions may be propagated.

In mixing terms drawn from finance with those from home and garden, Dickinson's wordplay also conflates gender-defined spheres to affirm an essential equality between men's and women's determinations of worth, and of self-worth. That the narrator would surrender "Daffodil Dowries" signals she is even willing to give up what women would ordinarily regard as a material benefit conserved for a future husband, the yellow daffodil, glittering like the gold they might bring as their contribution to the joint enterprise of marriage in the form of dowries. Such willingness may have been intended to convey to contemporary readers—particularly women—the desperation of the speaker's bargaining position, in that she proposes to trade away for the evanescent pleasure of seeing her beloved's face what would normally be seen as an inducement to a man to marry her.

The words "spicy" and "Stocks" again suggest to mind "I gave myself to Him –," in which an investment in mercantile fleets' voyages to distant shores, like "Zinzebar" or the Indies, promises rich rewards. Here, in an inversion of sea and sky, the speaker proposes to offer, first, property, in units of tremendous acreage ("furlong[s]") and even maritime rights, "Straits of Blue" and "Navies of Butterflies." These "properties" may constitute other assets in the portfolio of her dowry. Continuing in her vein of tying distant, hazardous voyages to the possibility of realizing huge returns, Dickinson refers to the pollen sacs bees bear away as "Doubloons," her figure indirectly comparing the bees to conquistadors shipping New World gold back to Spain, a supposition reinforced by her next reference to "Purple – from Peru," that is, the export of luxurious dyes like Tyrian purple from the Mediterranean. Perhaps the poem's reference to mercantile fleets helped prompt Dickinson's mentioning of Shylock, who privately hopes Antonio's far-flung ships will wreck, propelling his rival and enemy into bankruptcy. If so, the narrator is implicitly associating herself with Antonio, who risked virtually all he possessed to realize an emotional profit.

The narrator would also seem to be offering a female proxy for herself, "June": "You know who "*June*" is –/ I'd give *her* –." June is the month when the speaker's garden would burst into full bloom, and thus, by the poem's logic, also reach its peak of material, aesthetic, and reproductive value. Her verb "give" signifies not just the surrender of an asset, but also sexual surrender, as in the phrase "I gave Myself to Him –." Although the narrator does not begin "What would I give to see his face?" by saying that she would give *herself* to her lover, her natural and calendrical symbols function as erotic surrogates. The poem's sexual and reproductive agendas remain tacit, visible only behind a screen of ostensible artlessness and naïveté; the speaker seems a victim who invites her auditor to take advantage of her by depriving her of the metonymic equivalents of sexuality, leaving her only the actual sexually and emotionally charged experience of interviewing her lover in the flesh. In an economy that continued to withhold effective economic power and most real property from women, this poem's language connoting nature and reproduction gestures toward the only inalienable sources of wealth women possessed, that is, their affective capability, their dowries, and their reproductive potential, which is itself a function governed by nature.

The poem's deployment of direct address simulates, as I said, real-time negotiations, and the narrator's implicit auditor and potential contractual partner, "Shylock," is easily conflated with the poem's auditors and readers. As readers, we are being invited both to participate in the bargaining process antecedent to drawing up and signing the contract, and then to suffer some guilt by association in assuming "Shylock's" role in taking advantage of what would appear to be an almost laughably inexperienced bargainer. In contrast to her unknowingness, our own presumed sophistication in adult economies of value inevitably aligns us uncomfortably with the all-too-knowing, market-wise, devious Shylock. The speaker, seemingly in over her head, exemplifies the sort of person who would benefit from the advice of informed legal counsel, which is notably missing in the poem. Like Antonio, she may be heedlessly subscribing herself to a legally binding contractual relationship while remaining too much under the influence of her emotions, opening herself up to possible financial and affective repercussions. The narrator's folly is integral to the poem's theme: as a Romantic writer, Dickinson affirms the emotional wisdom of giving all for love, even to the point of self-impoverishment.

Other poems focus on contracts that do go awry—that is, those negotiated in bad faith, or those whose conditions cannot be fulfilled.[2] When a contract is broken, it is said to be *breached,* like a wall, dike, or dam. Typically, a breach occurs when one of the parties stipulating to the contract fails to follow through with duties set forth within the contractual agreement. But sometimes breaches turn out to be necessary or inevitable, as in the quatrain F1465:

> How ruthless are the gentle –
> How cruel are the kind –
> God broke his contract to his Lamb
> To qualify the Wind –

In this short poem questioning the limits, even the utility, of kindness, Dickinson's inversions and paradoxes rationalize and justify the existence of cruelty in the world, implicitly through God's sufferance.[3] By permitting Jesus to sacrifice himself, God enters into a contractual relationship with humankind (and also perhaps with the entire universe) to allow kindness and gentleness to exist, as emblematized by the figure of God's son, Jesus, as Lamb. Yet those who are kind and gentle may, ironically, employ those very qualities in mistreating others—killing them with kindness, so to speak. Dickinson is questioning an oft-quoted pious observation made by Laurence Sterne in *A Sentimental Journey,* "God tempers the wind to the shorn lamb."[4] Not so, says the narrator. Rather, God, as a contractual partner who had cooperated in authorizing kindness's existence, having witnessed subsequently the limitations and weaknesses intrinsic within the psychological (as opposed to the theological) concept of kindness, breaches the original contract by seeking, again unilaterally, a modification adding a third party, the Wind, to the original contracting principals. In law, one of the few plausible defenses for breach of contract is an act of God, and the poem describes such an act in the truest sense.[5] In a somewhat Manichean frame of mind, Dickinson proposes that elemental cruelty (not quite the same thing as evil) must be permitted to exist as a kind of corrective or counterweight to kindness, which may seek, in its own way, to monopolize the moral landscape. God's implicit endorsement of the wind, in direct contrast to Sterne's platitude, would seem designed to reestablish a fundamental equilibrium in both nature and morality.

One type of lawsuit alleging breach of contract that gradually fell out of favor during Dickinson's young adulthood was breach of promise, brought usually by women against men who failed to marry them.[6] Breach of promise actions sometimes alleged that a man had seduced a woman by pledging to marry her, a promise he later denied or reneged upon. Even disregarding, for the moment, the emotive cost to jilted engaged women, material costs to them and their families could be considerable. Wedding preparations perhaps already contracted for would have to be canceled; then too, in the aftermath of a broken engagement, a rejected woman might receive fewer, or less desirable, marriage proposals.

Yet breach of promise suits grew increasingly rare during the poet's young womanhood and adulthood. The legal community came to see them as self-defeating, if only because public revelations of intimate behavior might damage a woman's future marital prospects even further. Moreover, producing a statement from a man that could be construed as an offer of marriage was notoriously difficult, and even should such a document be forthcoming, disclosure of its contents could prove humiliating and embarrassing for both parties. Courts were often left with few good options. Women could sue for monetary damages, but assessing the cost of their disappointed expectations remained problematic. Equity, within whose purview the interests of women and other largely disenfranchised parties (such as children) traditionally lay, could issue an injunction for a man to fulfill his promise, yet plainly, a compulsory marriage would have a poor chance of succeeding. The application of contractual responsibilities to purported fiancés also ran counter to a general belief that an engagement, as opposed to a marriage, enjoyed an only quasi-legal status. Lawyers and laypeople alike believed that unmarried women and men should, by logic and practice, enjoy a period of preliminary affective relations during which the more exacting contractual obligations of marriage did not yet apply. Then too, courts were understandably reluctant to intrude upon relationships entered into by consenting adults.

It was also widely believed that some women attempted to coerce men into marrying them by alleging breach of promise. In the Dickinson household, breach of promise actions provided fodder for legal ridicule. The poet begins a letter to Austin written in 1853 (L108) by reminding him of their sister Lavinia's tale of "a Breach of promise Case where the correspondence between the parties consisted of a reply from the girl to one she had never received, but was daily expecting." Evidently the young woman in question had been so confident she would receive a proposal in the mail that she accepted preemptively. For all three Dickinson siblings, this story would have provoked a hearty laugh about the young woman's emotional, sexual, and legal naïveté. For his own part, Edward Dickinson defended a young man accused in a breach of promise case brought before the Massachusetts Supreme Judicial Court, which did find in his client's favor (Habegger, *My Wars* 415). We can reasonably assume that the entire Dickinson family would have winked knowingly at breach of promise suits.[7] Yet the poet, as an unmarried woman, would inevitably also have identified with the predicament of the betrothed woman who assumes considerable risk in committing herself to a man, sometimes without knowing whether she is being deceived.

Emily Dickinson's familial and personal antipathy to breach of promise actions likely helped determine her treatment of an anthropomorphized suitor bee in a handful of bee/flower poems. In "What would I give to see his face?," we have already seen one example of her employment of the bee/flower metatrope, a poetic convention of long standing by the time Dickinson took it up.[8] Particularly as written by women, poems describing relations between bees and flowers were widely understood as providing an only slightly covert method of discussing such tabooed topics as courting protocols, sexual intercourse, seduction, and abandonment. But, as I have argued elsewhere, by the time Dickinson composed her own variations on the theme, the trope had become so familiar and popular that she could approach it subversively and ironically. Thus Dickinson may align herself, through the medium of her narrators, with the masculinized bee, whose "infidelity," in visiting flower after flower, she, as an avid gardener, knew was necessary for *pollination* (a figural substitute for sex, impregnation, and child-bearing) to take place. Accordingly, the tone of these poems, which are so numerous as to constitute virtually a Dickinsonian subgenre, is typically lighthearted—satirical, parodic, and mischievous. The poem "Of Silken Speech and Specious Shoe" (F1078 B) exemplifies her practice, while simultaneously suggesting that, at least parenthetically, the poet has breach of promise actions in mind:

> Of Silken Speech and Specious Shoe
> A Traitor is the Bee
> His service to the newest Grace
> Present continually
>
> His Suit a chance
> His Troth a Term
> Protracted as the Breeze
> Continual Ban propoundeth He
> Continual Divorce.

The sexual terms employed in this poem are fairly straightforward. No feminized flower could profess herself in doubt about the courting bee's essential character. His habitual infidelity is evident at every stage of the courtship process, and the bee enters into relationships so carelessly as to make them seem virtually a matter of chance. His offer of engagement shifts with every wind that blows; his offers of marriage—suggested with the word "Ban," as in marriage banns, that is, public announcements of an intention to marry—are made serially, as is also then inevitably true of his suits for divorce each time his eye wanders to some new

"Grace," or bloom. The bee's troth is a "Term," and Dickinson's play on words constructs an expression of temporal duration as meaningless, empty palaver. Moreover, Dickinson's diction emphasizes the legal status of these various phases of the bee's amorous adventures. The buzzing bee is implicitly presented as a smooth talker whose diction alternates between the language of seduction and the language of the court, as when he *propounds* divorce. The word "Suit" also does double duty, signifying both the bee's attentions and the likelihood that his activities will land him in court, where he might yet have a "chance" of prevailing in actions brought against him.

The suitor bee would certainly seem to qualify as a type of the thoughtless seducer, and yet the narrator of this poem, rather as if she were acting as the bee's advocate, introduces extenuating circumstances in his favor. For one thing, the capriciousness of his romantic and sexual favors is apparently well known, even flagrant. Secondly, the bee, though a "Traitor," has only partial control over which flower he visits, as he is propelled about by the wind. No wonder, then, that his betrothals are brief and "Protracted as the Breeze." The poem's alliteration and sibilance, especially prominent in the first line, simulate the bee's humming, persuasive mode of speaking, while simultaneously serving to mitigate his promiscuity by implying an identification with his point of view. The bee behaves the way he does, the poem suggest, because such is his nature—and, as an agent of fertilization and fecundity, also in the nature of Nature. Someone expecting anything otherwise would be, implicitly, both naive and out of synchrony or harmony with normal natural processes.

An engagement that does move successfully from the stage of talking to one of action has been signified traditionally by the offer of a ring, one of the various physical tokens employed in negotiating contracts. The act of offering the ring, and the object itself, may be regarded as a *consideration*—a concept in contract law that deserves some clarification. Two factors critical to determining the validity of a contract are mutuality and consideration. In "I gave Myself to Him –," "The solemn contract of a Life" is "ratified," from a legal standpoint, because both parties incur "Mutual – Risk" to achieve a potential "Mutual Gain." Consideration, in law, signifies what each party is willing to give up for the sake of reaping that benefit. Either might submit as consideration money, a service, or an object, but crucially, consideration is a sacrifice made voluntarily. The underlying assumption here is that each party must be willing to forgo an advantage, that is, he or she must demonstrate a willingness to surrender an object or service as an indication of a good-faith intention to cooperate.

But consideration, particularly when used as a noun, as in "*a consideration*," also embraces a preliminary exchange of objects or services anticipating or rehearsing the more substantive exchange made once a contract is formalized. Hence, in ancient practice, rings, gloves, or other tokens served virtually as contractual instruments in their own right; they also provided testamentary evidence that an individual had indeed entered into a contract. These tokens could have a modest material value of their own, and they were often associated with the giver's own person, particularly his hand, so that the consideration served as a synecdochical surrogate for a handshake, or for the hand that would eventually sign a formal, written contract. Thus in *The Merchant of Venice* the disguised Portia, after she has successfully defended Antonio, demands of Antonio his gloves, and of her husband, Bassanio, his ring, an act that acquires added ironic significance because he and she had recently exchanged rings at their wedding. Even the pound of flesh to be extracted from Antonio's body may be regarded, within the figural economy of law, as emblematic of the idea of consideration.

In British and American jurisprudence, the offering of a consideration became, over time, increasingly abstract, especially as contracting parties were separated by ever greater physical distances, so that the object being tendered as consideration came to lose its association both with the offeror's person and with the actual or potential value of the goods or services being bargained for. To this day, a contract struck in the United States is considered valid and enforceable when the offeree—that is, the person approached by the offeror in the first place—tenders a single dollar as consideration, whatever the intrinsic value of the goods or services involved in the contract. This is called a nominal consideration, in recognition of its chiefly symbolic value.

In law, the actual worth of a consideration itself is now generally disregarded, so long as the surrendering of the object, money, or service signifies a contractor's willingness to convey an innate benefit. Virtually anything may be submitted, giving rise to what is called the peppercorn rule: that is, even a peppercorn may, theoretically, serve as a consideration. From a legal standpoint, then, in "What would I give to see his face?" the narrator's offer to sacrifice daffodils and primroses may not seem quite so far-fetched. Such objects have a legal validity, despite their apparent worthlessness as assets in a capitalistic and entrepreneurial economy. What looks to be an almost cloying ingenuousness on the part of the narrator may instead reflect a consciousness of the concrete legal reality that an element from nature, such as a flower, a seed, or a pepper-corn, might be used as consideration.

For reasons I will shortly explain, contracts for sale of land do not ordinarily require a consideration. Yet "The Judge is like the Owl" (F728), a poem offering to negotiate a sale of real estate, would seem to conflate the issues of mutuality and consideration, perhaps for the sake of humor:

> The Judge is like the Owl –
> I've heard my Father tell –
> And Owls do build in Oaks –
> So here's an Amber Sill –
>
> That slanted in my Path –
> When going to the Barn –
> And if it serve You for a House –
> Itself is not in vain –
>
> About the price – 'tis small –
> I only ask a Tune
> At Midnight – Let the Owl select
> His favorite Refrain.

I have discussed elsewhere Dickinson's reference here to a "Judge," the poem's projected reader or auditor (*Emily Dickinson's Vision* 159–60). Emblematic of wisdom, owls have a long pictorial association with judges. For present purposes, however, I want to emphasize this poem's resemblance to a legal contract, specifically a deed, to confirm that Dickinson did occasionally write poems as direct, often parodical, imi-tations of contractual legal documents. Many of the required elements of an enforceable contract are in evidence. The narrator possesses real estate she believes might interest the "Judge," figured as an owl: an oak tree in which he may build his nest. In this fictional transaction the narrator is offeror, the party who initiates negotiations. As potential consideration, she suggests a branch from the tree, an act that indicates simultaneously that she is indeed the tree's owner. In turn, she suggests, the owl may sing at midnight, his song serving as his own form of consideration, a preliminary sample of the nocturnal serenades he could provide throughout his tenure in the tree, should he accept her offer. In depicting the owl as possibly singing, the poem provides a nearly literal illustration of the idea that one acceptable form of consideration may be *performance,* rather than a synecdochical object such as the tree branch.

The narrator's language also imitates the diction of legal instruments and court proceedings. "Let the Owl select / His favorite Refrain" she says, employing the volitional subjunctive of legal bargaining and judicial protocol—as in, for example, "Let the record show." Dickinson's language mimics the entire process of negotiations, offering tangible tokens of her good faith while demonstrating that her terms remain flexible and open to further negotiation, at the buyer's discretion.

A contract for land does not require consideration because ordinarily it is formalized in a deed, often signed in the presence of witnesses. Nevertheless, even deeds contained token symbolic references to their negotiators in the form of affixed seals. Anciently in British common law, an actual wax seal was attached to a deed to land or other contractual agreements to signify one party's agreement to the stated terms. Over time, wax seals evolved into pressed paper wafers, and eventually to embossments made upon the contract itself. The seal affixed to a deed or contract, because it was usually personalized to indicate the name and family affiliation of the contracting party, functioned as an alternative means of identification to consideration, which once had been affiliated with the actual person of the contractor by means of an intimately associated object, such as a ring or a glove. The employment of seals took the original synecdochical basis of consideration one step further, substituting for the body of the contractor a more abstract symbolic indication of his name, family, and credit-worthiness. By the time Edward Dickinson was practicing law in Amherst, courts were already beginning to accept a flourish of the pen, or *scroll* (*Black's:* "A written mark; esp., a character affixed to a signature in place of a seal") in lieu of the actual wafer, and eventually, nothing more than the initials "L.S.," standing for *locus sigilli,* "place of the seal." Thus, over time, a symbol for a symbol for a symbol came to be accepted.

Consideration and seal coexisted within contract law as alternate forms of guaranty. But as the arena of commerce expanded and distances

between contracting parties continued to increase, the feasibility of trans-
ferring tangible considerations declined, so that, in law, an exchange of
considerations between the parties began to be replaced by more easily transmitted two-dimensional means. Then too, because of its often
implicitly ceremonial function, consideration began to be recognized as
being disconnected from the actual terms, values, and conditions set forth
in a formal contract. The acceptance of seals as the preferred means of
finalizing contracts, especially those for land, arose out of a consensus that
such signs, despite their abstractness, could be relied on as substitutes for
the physical presence of contractors rather than objects personally associated with them.[9] The formality of the sealed document itself, or rather
of the process involved in generating it, came to signify the seriousness
and intentionality—and even the implied presence—of the contracting
parties. As one legal authority notes, "The only formal contract of English
law is the contract under seal, sometimes also called a deed. . . . It is the
only formal contract, because it derives its validity neither from the fact
of agreement, nor from the consideration which may exist for the promise
of either party, but from the form in which it is expressed."[10]

Although the term "seal" possesses several significations in law, as applied
to contracts, the provision of a seal affects, above all, a contract's enforceability.[11] A contract under seal could not be modified, unless those modifications were *also* set under seal; fraud could not be alleged as having taken
place during negotiations; and the physical document had to be destroyed
once all contractual obligations had been fulfilled. When Antonio and
Shylock first negotiate the terms of their contract in *The Merchant of Venice*,
Bassanio, alarmed at the thought of flesh being cut from his friend, begs
him, "You shall not seal to such a bond for me." Shylock, the offeror in the
proposed transaction, invites Antonio to draw up a contract with him and
have it witnessed before a notary, who would affix to the document his own
seal: "Go with me to a notary, seal me there / Your single bond." Eventually
Antonio agrees, and he verbally confirms that a contract has been struck:
"Yes, Shylock, I will seal onto this bond."

In many ways, Shakespeare's tragicomedy pivots on the very concepts
of enforceability and inviolability, sealed contracts providing a powerful
bulwark against legal attack. During Portia and Shylock's confrontation
in court, she, as Balthasar, finds the contract, however repugnant, to
be legally enforceable and Antonio to be in breach, so that the bond is

"forfeit." Barring the discovery of evidence showing that the bond had been drawn up improperly in any way, the only legal recourse left to Antonio is a hope that the other contracting party will accede to having the document annulled, and physically destroyed. Accordingly, Portia implores Shylock, "Bid me tear the bond!" But Shylock refuses, compelling her to adopt, as Antonio's unacknowledged, unadmitted legal advocate, alternative legal strategies.

Antonio's original near-default of a pound of flesh would have reminded legally inclined Elizabethan audiences of the sometimes capricious behavior of bargainers, who might introduce symbolic, even seemingly trivial, terms in contracts that were nevertheless legally enforceable. One lesson the play teaches is not to enter into legal agreements imprudently or facetiously. Contract law has traditionally granted contractors wide latitude in defining the terms of their agreement and, should they define unwisely, the liberty to put themselves in legal jeopardy. Yet Shakespeare's tragicomedy also investigates the role of symbolism in legal thinking and in the legal bonds people establish with each other. Shylock is implicitly criticized in the play for treating the symbolic and substantive functions of law literally and vindictively. Portia's famous courtroom speech about justice, in comparing God's grace to the mercy of earthly potentates, reaffirms a symbolic connection between heaven and earth, yet she also draws a line at reducing human life to a symbolic term. The laws of Venice—a commercial capital—protect the rights of business contractors, but they also guard the lives of citizens, so that Shylock's acts become prosecutable within the separate domain of criminal law. Signs may be enforceable, yet they do not constitute the sum of the law.

For a sealed contract to be made executable, it also had to be signed and delivered. The word "sign" has long been regarded as being synonymous with "signature"; this usage presupposes an equivalency between the physical presence of the contractor and a graphic representation of that person's identity, expressed as an autograph (sometimes as rudimentary as an "X") or some other not easily duplicated placeholder. Webster's 1828 dictionary defines the noun "sign" as "The subscription of one's name; signature; as a sign manual"—that is, as a mark inscribed manually. Perhaps because they all refer implicitly to hands, historically, a good deal of synonymy has existed between the words "sign," "seal," and "ring." Signet rings, for example, by incorporating a coat of arms or dynastic logo, came to be accepted as a surrogate for the presence of the authorizing party, whether used to impress that logo onto a wax seal, or simply by association with the hand that signs documents and bears the ring. Dickinson occasionally conflates the legally inflected terms sign, seal, and ring, perhaps because she possessed at least a rudimentary understanding of their legal significances and histories. Thus, for example, the words "this Ring" and "the Seal" appear as variants in "Given in Marriage unto Thee" (F818 B):

> Given in Marriage unto Thee
> Oh thou Celestial Host –
> Bride of the Father and the Son
> Bride of the Holy Ghost –
>
> Other Betrothal shall dissolve –
> Wedlock of Will, decay –
> Only the Keeper of this Ring | this Ring / the Seal
> Conquer Mortality –

Two types of marriage are described here, mortal and immortal. In the temporal world, the poem says, ordinary troth may be broken, and marriages may founder, but God, in being tripartite, offers a superior sort of matrimonial guarantee to the believing individual Christian, here gendered feminine. Dickinson's ambivalence about using "this Ring" and "the Seal" may arise from a desire to formulate language connoting *lastingness,* a contract under seal offering the highest degree of legal protection.[12] Such a marriage might even "Conquer Mortality," in the sense that a sealed contract withstood legal efforts made to invalidate it, so that the durability of law approximated the immortality guaranteed to faithful Christians.[13] Also, the threefold, virtually polygamous "marriage" offered to the Christian was demonstrably superior to the wedding of a conventional bride to a sole groom. Such a communal marriage offered a better chance of maintaining the original pitch of passion than did conventional betrothals and marriages, which might "decay" by falling victim to tedium or infidelity. "Host" may thus signify both the consecrated bread and wine offered to congregants and the groom's composite nature.

Although some of Dickinson's poetic treatments of women's status as fiancées are apt to sound a comic note ("Of Silken Speech and Specious Shoe," for example) the tone of other poems comparing betrothal to marriage may be emotionally roiled, the register of their narrating voices ranging from proud indifference to frustration, anger, or despair. One source of anguish was the simple fact that married women enjoyed a higher societal, legal, and economic status than did unmarried women. These privileges were conferred by the very act of marrying, an event that utterly transformed lives of women in ways both private and public. In that regard, the sequence of courtship, betrothal, and marriage represented for women, much more so than for men, a profound legal and existential shift. With that in mind, and in light of Dickinson's personal awareness of the basic legal criteria required for a contract to be made enforceable, we may approach one of her more famous, and more difficult, poems (F194 B) with an informed cultural sensibility:

> Title divine, is mine.
> The Wife without the Sign –
> Acute Degree conferred on me –
> Empress of Calvary –
> Royal, all but the Crown –
> Betrothed, without the Swoon
> God gives us Women –
> When You hold Garnet to Garnet –
> Gold – To Gold –
> Born – Bridalled – Shrouded –
> In a Day –
> Tri Victory –
> "My Husband" – Women say
> Stroking the Melody –
> Is this the way –[14]

The speaker in this poem would seem to be asserting that a virtual betrothal and marriage are nearly identical to the real thing, save for the absence of outward indicators of status, particularly engagement and wedding rings. Whether set with a gemstone, like garnet, or made of gold like a wedding band, rings serve simultaneously as external signs of a woman's marital state and legal standing. Dickinson's figures implicitly associate rings with crowns, both of them circular bands signifying transformational shifts in status. In the poem's first line, the narrator revels in her own brand of social promotion, declaring that she now enjoys the emotional benefits of being a fiancée or wife, albeit without possessing the confirming jewels of betrothal or wedlock.[15] She asserts that the gemstone of her own strictly imaginary engagement ring or gold wedding ring ("When You hold Garnet to Garnet –/ Gold – To Gold –") could stand up to a jeweler's assay as well as any conventional jewelry could.[16] Dickinson's line "Stroking the Melody" may refer to preening wives who draw out or *stroke* the phrase "My Husband" to emphasize their superiority to, we may presume, any unmarried woman within range of sight or hearing. Married women's display of their rings is mere flaunting, the poem's narrator might say, confident that her own undefined relationship endows with her with a status equal to theirs and with bragging rights that she, for her part, need not feel compelled to assert.

Yet how strong is the narrator's argument, really? A legal analysis suggests she discerns serious weaknesses undermining her position. The "signs" of betrothal and wifehood the narrator lacks are the physical tokens of existing contractual or quasi-contractual arrangements. The narrator is reduced to citing only metaphoric equivalents of them, and, lacking tangible, visible proof, her claims remain baseless; analogously, a queen who lacks a crown is not yet "Royal." The "Acute Degree" of status to which she aspires has not been "conferred" upon her by any identified figure of authority, and the "Sign" she lacks may even refer indirectly to the marriage license itself, required in Massachusetts since 1639, and invalid until signed. Without the *sign,* whether made in pen or denoted by the possession of a ring, the narrator lacks confirmation of her subjectively determined elevation in status, and, however much she may disparage outward show, communal and public acknowledgment is integral to the contractual definitions of betrothal and marriage. The narrator's final, possibly rhetorical, question, "Is this the way?" (with the pronoun underlined, in an earlier version of the poem) may connote either a criticism of conventionally engaged and married women's smugness, or an expression of self-doubt as the speaker wonders whether her "way" of ignoring the public and legal dimensions of marriage is justified, after all. The passionate tone of "Title divine, is mine" may finally be symptomatic of a tension generated by an incongruity between the speaker's Romantically inspired efforts to redefine affective relations with the law's inherent conservatism in defining and codifying them. Throughout her poetic career, Dickinson may have sought various means of reconciling the private realm of the emotions and the imagination with the public reality of law.

4

LANDS WITH LOCKS
Property

Perhaps influenced by her family's bruising experience with bankruptcy, Emily Dickinson remained alert throughout her poetic career to the precariousness of property ownership. Control over land could offer a lasting source of family prosperity and dynastic stability, yet it could also be threatened by a number of legal hazards aside from debt. For one thing, ownership of land was itself a sort of legal fiction; rather, an owner held *title* to a piece of land.[1] As we saw in "Alone and in a Circumstance," that title might be challenged by interlopers of all sorts—neighbors, other family members, trespassers, tenants, the government itself. Proprietors might also encounter nonlegal threats—fire, flood, frosts, or other acts of God. And yet the poet knew that in matters pertaining to property, as well as in those pertaining to the affections, realizing a reward entailed an acceptance of risk, and her sympathies generally lay with investors and other risk-takers. The Dickinson family, ardent Webster Whigs, generally upheld the rights of property owners, and Edward and Austin Dickinson became skilled advocates for their clients' landed interests and for their own. Dickinsons had owned properties in western Massachusetts since colonial times, and, ignoring the lesson provided by his own father's imprudence, Edward Dickinson speculated eagerly not just in business schemes, but also in real estate parcels of various kinds, including local farms and town lots, as well as properties in distant Michigan, which enjoyed a land boom at midcentury.[2] Land offered the Dickinsons safety, security, and perhaps even profit—but at a price.

The poet's ambivalence about owning property may also have been rooted in her cultural inheritance, for New Englanders had always tended to view property ownership somewhat paradoxically. As Perry Miller points out, an ingrained Calvinism required of both the Puritans and their descendants a willingness to see material wealth as double-edged, even a snare. Owners should enjoy property and other forms of wealth while they had them, but they should also be prepared to surrender their profits to chance or to providence, even gladly:

> A logical consequence of Puritan theology [is that] man is put into this world, not to spend his life in profitless singing of hymns or in unfruitful monastic contemplation, but to do what the world requires, according to its terms. He must raise children, he must work at his calling. . . . Yet the Christian works not for the gain that may (or may not) result from his labor, but for the glory of God. He remains an ascetic in the world, as much as any hermit outside it. He displays unprecedented energy in wresting the land from the Indians, trading in the seven seas, speculating in lands: "Yet," says Cotton, "his heart is not set upon these things, he can tell what to do with his estate when he hath got it." (*American Puritans* 171–72)

The Transcendentalists inherited the Puritans' conflicted feelings about property ownership. Emerson's poem "Hamatreya," for example, emphasized that the land owned the man, and not vice versa. Much as Dickinson admired the Transcendentalists, she did not share their view that materialism merited consideration within a comprehensive agenda of personal or social reform. Instead, the poet's ambivalence about land ownership tends to focus on religious, ontological, and aesthetic issues. Specific property law topics such as landlord–tenant law and patent law may also have provided Dickinson with useful analogies for describing her own activities as artist and thinker.

In law, property may assume several forms. The oldest of these, and the most problematic, is real property, that is, land. Historically, ownership of land has enjoyed powerful legal protections in Britain and in America. Yet virtually from the start, land held in the New World was regarded very differently from the way it was viewed in the mother country. The most obvious cause for this divergence was sheer availability. English property laws were devised to preserve owners' rights to a finite supply of arable land, and land ownership was generally restricted to the wealthy, the aristocracy, and the nobility. In America, on the other hand, legislation was passed to encourage the claiming, cultivation, expansion, and transferability of nearly infinite territorial resources. British laws sought to make the transfer of property outside of an owner's immediate family difficult, if not impossible, while in America an abundance of land and a rapid influx of immigrants rendered it more important to facilitate sale and transmittal. During the early federal period, the American legal system did away with two British concepts that seemed to inhibit the rapid conveyancing of property: primogeniture and the fee tail.

A second form of property is chattel, that is, owned physical objects that may be moved, as opposed to immobile holdings in land. Jewelry, heirlooms, and livestock have traditionally been associated with the legal concept of chattel. Because they usually have lower monetary value than holdings in land, chattels have been awarded a somewhat lesser status in law, and consequently case law is dominated by decisions pertaining to real properties. Nevertheless, chattels may possess a sentimental value out of all proportion to their value in the marketplace, and laws—particularly those in equity—have striven to recognize that fact. Other forms of personal property are neither so personal nor so concrete as chattels or real properties. Because of an increase in public ownership of stocks, bonds, and other paper investments, nineteenth-century law also came to recognize an owner's rights in what were called intangible properties.[3] One subcategory of such assets is intellectual property, including patent and copyright, which are closely allied under law.

I want to begin by considering Dickinson's legal and poetical treatment of real property, that is, land and its potential value, which may come under assault by either legal or extralegal forces. Within Dickinson's entire oeuvre, the poem "I had some things that I called mine –" (F101, written around 1859) is distinctive for the specificity of its legal terminology and for its topical references in describing the seizure of a coveted piece of land. Although I have discussed this poem elsewhere,[4] here I want to emphasize Dickinson's integration of legal issues with religious and philosophical themes.

> I had some things that I called mine –
> And God, that he called his,
> Till recently a rival claim
> Disturbed these amities.

The property, my garden,
Which having sown with care –
He claims the pretty acre –
And sends a Bailiff there.

The station of the parties
Forbids publicity,
But Justice is sublimer
Than Arms, or pedigree.

I'll institute an "Action" –
I'll vindicate the law –
Jove! Choose your counsel –
I retain "Shaw"!

Who is threatening to sue whom here, and why? And what will happen to the disputed property, a garden?[5] The "Bailiff" seizing the property would seem to be another of the poet's personifications of the first hard frost, the "blonde Assassin" who, as in the poem "Apparently with no surprise," destroyed flower gardens overnight, an annual event of some import to the poet. As mentioned in my earlier discussion of "A prompt – executive Bird is the Jay –," bailiffs tended to be burly types who could face down resistance from scofflaws while delivering a summons or executing the will of the court. The third stanza's punning reference to "arms" may then signify simultaneously the bailiff's baton and the heraldic coat of arms specific to the patrician counterclaimant, God, who asserts his own right to the garden by authorizing the death of the narrator's flowers. The poem thus presents the seizure of the speaker's property as an opportunistic land grab made by an arrogant, well-to-do neighbor with whom the narrator had previously enjoyed amicable relations, but who now employs the bailiff/frost as his legal surrogate or stooge. This mock portrayal of a conventional Victorian fictional narrative—the appropriation of a fertile plot of land by a greedy baronial landowner—is also latent in the deployment of the terms "arms" and "pedigree," terms with limited application in egalitarian America. Although a flower garden may seem an unlikely site for a cosmic tug of war, the poem's diction presents the stakes as being significantly higher, and the poem would appear to be aimed at an informed reader who could appreciate the situation's legal and religious ramifications simultaneously.[6]

A plot an acre in extent would be much larger than the typical domestic flower garden, so that some of the poem's humor derives from discussing flowers as if they were crops seized illegitimately from a farmer's field, a not infrequent accusation in trespassing cases. But the narrator's threatened legal action is evidently intended to be understood as being virtually hopeless from the start, which indeed it is, because under law the destruction of property by natural causes is counted an act of God, or *force majeure;* then too, her wilted flowers could hardly be revived. Her current "crop" forfeit, she clings to the land nonetheless, not just out of principle, but because of its potential future benefit.

The tone of the narrator emulates shock and outrage, and she threatens to retain "Shaw" in defense of her rights. Dickinson's, or the narrator's, quotation marks indicate she is being ironic and facetious, perhaps because the Dickinson family employed a laborer named Shaw, although contemporary readers would have recognized the poet's allusion to Lemuel Shaw, chief justice of the Massachusetts Supreme Judicial Court from 1830 to 1860.[7] Thus the narrator is proposing to bring in some heavy legal artillery indeed: Judge Shaw was venerated by Webster Whigs for championing in his decisions the interests of corporations and property owners.[8] With the exception of Daniel Webster himself, the narrator could hardly have chosen a more highly respected advocate for owners' rights. Evidently the poem is intended for the ears or eyes of someone familiar with Shaw's legal reputation, but it may be aimed as well at readers having some familiarity with basic property law. For example, the term "acre" would resonate with law students, who learn legal "hypos" involving fictional properties denominated as "Blackacre," "Redacre," or "Greenacre."[9] Despite the celebrity of her potential legal counsel, however, the narrator is likely to have difficulty prevailing in court. The fact that a bailiff has shown up to take possession of the garden suggests her title to the property may be in question, and tacitly she admits as much by saying "I had some things that I *called* mine," as opposed to *were mine.* Even though the narrator vows that she will "vindicate the law," no remedy may, realistically, be available to her. The tone of the poem emulates the initial outrage adopted by someone who thinks her rights have been violated, but the precariousness of her legal situation may render her threats finally hyperbolic and ludicrous.

Even if legal title to land should be found unimpeachable, the obligation of ownership carried burdens of its own. In "I am afraid to own a Body" (F1050), Dickinson uses a contrast between British and American legal traditions regarding the transmission of property to develop a metaphor for philosophic imperatives resulting from the raw fact of our existence:

> I am afraid to own a Body –
> I am afraid to own a Soul –
> Profound – precarious Property –
> Possession, not optional –
>
> Double Estate, entailed at pleasure
> Opon an unsuspecting Heir –
> Duke in a moment of Deathlessness
> And God, for a Frontier.

This poem derives considerable power from Dickinson's troping of body and soul as real, inheritable property. In a sense, this is always true, in that we inherit physical and psychological traits from consanguineous ancestors. Consequently, heredity could be considered analogous to the legal concept of fee tail, in which, so long as valid heirs continue to be produced, real properties may be left to descendants in perpetuity— the lawyer's version of eternity. But the suggestive presence of the poem's final word, "Frontier," indicates Dickinson has in mind distinctly *local* circumstances, namely, the Connecticut Valley frontier, bounded to the west by the Berkshires. A combination of implied specific geographical locales and a contrast of British and American legal treatments of inherited property suggest that the poet is embedding this ontological consideration in a cultural context that would have been, for her, intimate and familiar.

Initially, at least, the pairing of an allusion to the fee tail with a reference to frontier lands would seem incongruous. The British law of primogeniture discouraged the breaking up of estates by placing ownership of inherited properties exclusively within the hands of eldest male heirs. Thus younger heirs were compelled to enter alternate fields, such as the military, the clergy, or the law, or to seek their fortunes elsewhere— perhaps by hazarding their lives and fortunes in distant colonial possessions. Yet for legal heirs of British properties, the responsibilities of unique ownership could constitute a burden in their own right. Lacking immediate financial reinforcement from younger siblings, heirs could find themselves solely responsible for the upkeep of estates whose original extents had been augmented, over time, by successive purchases of neighboring properties, by engrossing inheritances, or by outright seizure. British heirs could be land rich and cash poor, possessed of vast holdings yet hobbled by debts incurred through their maintenance and by a restrictive legal system that left them few ways to extricate themselves. So heavily did the dead hand of the past weigh upon heirs that only by, to use Lawrence Friedman's phrase, "tricks of conveyancing" (175) could some owners, and their attorneys, escape the ironclad laws of inheritance. Partly as a consequence, British property law acquired a reputation for Byzantine complexity and the attendant expense, incurred sometimes by heirs controlling enormous estates who nevertheless had little cash in their pockets with which to pay even their solicitors' fees. In this sense, inheriting land in Britain could indeed be seen as both a blessing and a curse.

Within the American legal community, a concerted effort arose in the nineteenth century, while Edward Dickinson was in law school, to do away, state by state, with British legal procedures governing ownership of land that had come to seem antiquated, cumbersome, or antidemocratic.[10] Westward expansion, rapid social change, and the near-constant arrival of immigrants made it desirable to enact comparatively simple and straightforward laws governing the purchase and disposal of property. Although the narrator of "I am afraid to own a Body –" may be, if we assume an identity between writer and poetic persona, a woman, and thus prevented under both contemporary British and American law from inheriting land, she speaks as if she were a reluctant heir. As a semi-ironic indicator of the speaker's new class status, Dickinson employs a distinctly British noble title, "Duke." Yet Dickinson converts an Old World legal process concerning the disposition of inherited properties into a New World philosophical meditation on the obligations assumed by any individual through the very fact of his or her existence. The *precariousness* of the narrator's situation is not owing to any legal challenge to her right to property; instead, the phrase "Profound – precarious Property –" refers to religious and ontological challenges faced by everyone and anyone, rather than simply dukes or duchesses.

As a human being and a Christian, the narrator of "I am afraid to own a Body –" could hardly have avoided inheriting body and soul; neither could she escape her biological inheritance from her parents. The word "deathlessness" connotes both the descent of title in a noble British family from one generation to the next and the indestructibility and immortality of the individual Christian soul. The duality of the narrator's "Estate" originates simultaneously in the binary of body and soul, which are not only proverbially difficult to reconcile but, at least in the case of the domain of the soul, so illimitable that the narrator, American though she may be, might as well have inherited a vast British estate that could only be maintained precariously, if at all. Dickinson uses the legal history of inheritance laws in both England and America to construct a figure describing destiny itself, which we may neither direct nor dismiss. The narrator is receiving his or her bequest at her ancestral testator's "pleasure," a word that signals the benefactor's willful intention that the bequest be made, whether his heir knows about it or not, or approves the decision.

In the "moment" of the testator's death, the scion's life is changed irrevocably—a parallel, somewhat ominous vision of eternity that contrasts with reassurances offered by Christian orthodoxy. Yet the eternity of God remains valid in "I am afraid to own a Body –" as a vision of time and of an individual's significance within time, figured as an immense expanse of "Profound" territory. Considered epistemologically, God is indeed a "frontier," in the sense that the concept of deity sets an intellectual limit, a border, between mortal and eternal varieties of knowledge. But Dickinson's use of the word "frontier" also inevitably guides us back to the poem's initial emphasis on the concepts of property and inheritance. Only two generations earlier, the Connecticut Valley represented for the poet's Puritan ancestors the limit of civilization itself, the edge of knowledge beyond which maps themselves became untrustworthy, if not useless. As presumptive "resident" of the terra incognita beyond that frontier, God did not pose the same immediate threat to early settlers that Mohawks and Mohicans did, yet in this poem, the concept of God may be thought of as occupying the same conceptual space, that of the unknown.

Significantly too, land on the American frontier was, partly because of its geographical proximity to dangers and uncertainties, ordinarily either given away or sold cheaply to immigrants willing to settle there, and, to justify later claims of ownership to land, early occupiers of frontier property in America often invoked the legal principle of first occupancy, or first possession.[11] "Duke" and "Frontier" may thus be seen in the poem as a binary denoting antithetical historical, cultural, and even geographic views of land, property rights, and disposal of property. According to English law, heirs had little choice about accepting estates bequeathed to them; in America, those who accepted the hazards of living on the frontier were rewarded with land. Dickinson may be suggesting in this poem that some risks in life are unavoidable, while others are taken on voluntarily, even though we may be, as she says, "afraid."

The precariousness of property ownership in the poems may, however, derive from situations much less dire than keeping body and soul together. In a handful of poems involving landlord–tenant law, Dickinson investigates frictions generated by human beings living in close, sometimes too close, proximity to one another, rather than on any "frontier." Again, the subject may have been prompted by personal and family experience. While the poet was a child, the Dickinsons learned perforce the realities of living as tenants in a house they had once owned, when the Mack family bought the Homestead and lived side by side with them, the families separated only by a wall. Although the family's relations with the landlord Macks were said to have been amicable, the fact remained that as a consequence of Samuel F. Dickinson's financial imprudence, the family had lost control of a domestic space they had once occupied independently. The memory of having once been a tenant may have helped motivate Edward to repurchase the Homestead and emulate his own father's erstwhile status as landowner rather than remaining a dependent debtor/renter. Emily Dickinson's own interest in landlord–tenant law focuses on the transience of renters, difficulties raised by owners and renters living in close proximity to each other, and, for either party, the trauma of eviction.

Amherst, a college town with a substantial transient population turning over regularly with the departure of each graduating class, profited by offering short-term lodging to students, visitors, and professors. For property owners in Amherst, becoming a landlord offered a dependable means of earning a modest income—if, that is, tenants were solvent, well-behaved, and cooperative. Issues covered by landlord–tenant law would, it stands to reason, have gained the attention of Amherst property owners and attorneys. Frustrations associated with being a landlord may be reflected indirectly in one of Dickinson's wittier poems (F1369 B):

> The Rat is the concisest Tenant.
> He pays no Rent.
> Repudiates the Obligation –
> On Schemes intent
>
> Balking our Wit
> To sound or circumvent –
> Hate cannot harm
> A Foe so reticent –
> Neither Decree prohibit him –
> Lawful as Equilibrium.

This delightful poem has much in common with "Alone and in a Circumstance." Both are legal satires that discuss, possibly from the vantage of a landlord, the presence of noxious, irresponsible tenants whose eviction poses legal problems. Reflecting, indirectly, the reality that enmity may arise between landlord and renters, both poems describe creatures ordinarily considered repellent. Dickinson could write humorously and sympathetically about animals deemed conventionally to be vermin—bats, flies, beetles, and snakes—and often they are covert protagonists of the miniature narratives in which they appear. For example, in "The Bat is dun, with wrinkled Wings –," the bat's abrupt flitting motions are shown to be both logical and beautiful, in their own way, and in "These are the Nights that Beetles love –," the june bug's ponderous flights knocking against our ceilings on summer nights are described as being "an improving thing . . . that keeps the nerves progressive." Taken as a group and examined from a legal perspective, these creatures are often Dickinson's perennial, wrongly accused defendants.[12] Ugly, ungainly, nonhuman and alien, they evoke from her a witty defense. Sometimes she depicts them as harmless and unpredictable housemates, rather like rambunctious student tenants prone to go on sprees. Yet the poet also celebrates them for the very fact of their *difference* from human beings, a point that I think deserves to be looked at from a legal perspective. For many attorneys, the defense of the apparently indefensible and representation of the less-than-presentable remain important reasons why they entered the profession in the first place. "The Rat is the concisest Tenant" is a brief for the underdog.

The poem is narrated simultaneously from the point of view of a landlord frustrated by a tenant's behavior and, indirectly, from a much more objective view recognizing both the rat's rights and his virtues.[13] From the viewpoint of the landlord, his tenant is evasive and elusive: whenever he comes to collect the rent, his renter seems to have vanished into thin air. Yet the poem portrays this avoidance on the part of the renter as shyness, a *reticence* upon which the property owner might feel guilty for having intruded. Moreover, as was true in "Alone and in a Circumstance," the relative statuses of owner and trespasser, landlord and tenant, native and alien become intermingled, even interchangeable. The rat behaves, paradoxically, as if he owns the place, refusing to pay rent at all, meeting visitors or avoiding them as he pleases, and, implicitly, going to law to defend himself, the poem's final line handing down a verdict in the rat's favor.

Dickinson's intensively concise and alliterative style reinforces her only somewhat covert championing of the rat's rights. Reclusive, efficient, eccentric, and astute herself, the poet implicitly aligns herself with the poem's deadbeat rodent hero, serving even as his advocate. The poem's insistently Latinate diction prepares readers to think of the rat's challenge to authority in mock-professional terms, particularly those drawn from the arenas of science and law. The poem's last line, "Lawful as Equilibrium," makes a clever joke on the intersection of the laws of physics and the common law. The *real* joke, of course, is that the rat, in opportunistically consuming our foodstores and fleeing when we approach, is behaving according to the dictates of his nature. *Our* mistake, in trying to trap, or "evict" the rat, is to anthropomorphize an animal rather than approach him on his own terms. Seeing a rat in our premises, we tend to think of him either as an intruder or as an undesirable housemate, yet our insistently dialectical approach does not succeed in either getting rid of the rat or accommodating us to his presence. The otherness of the rat is what ultimately disturbs us, and Dickinson's highly literate vocabulary operates satirically to illustrate the vast gulf separating us from the rest of nature. In this sense, the nonhuman majority of nature is what is being put on trial in this poem, and which the conclusion finally exonerates. We recognize the laws of physics, Dickinson suggests, but not the laws of biology, even though those two bodies of knowledge are interwoven and continuous.[14]

If we look at the poem's argument more narrowly, Dickinson's philosophic intentions become clearer. First, as a tenant, the rat does not even try to pay the rent, a refusal consistent with his overall strategy of exploitative occupancy—he's an opportunist, and proud of it. To his human hosts, the rat constructs himself virtually as their guest. His presence on the premises is tacitly the result of an invitation extended by someone he implicitly treats as host, not landlord. Guests don't pay rent, while renters and boarders do. The rat eats our food as if he were a fellow human being entitled to our hospitality, and not to any legal obligation to pay for his upkeep, or for the space in which he sleeps. The rat-protagonist "Repudiates the Obligation"; indeed, he denies that a landlord–tenant legal relationship adequately describes the connection between homeowner and affiliated occupant. Moreover, the "landlord" indirectly alluded to in the poem is not an absentee landlord, but rather someone who himself or herself resides on the premises, taking in boarders. Tenant, boarder, or guest, the rat actively schemes to evade both his human interlocutors and his obligations. The poem says as much: the rat contrives "Schemes" to avoid his responsibilities, yet these plans are so labyrinthine that his human hosts cannot "sound" them, Dickinson's choice of words paying homage simultaneously to the rat's quiet, scurrying movements.

A landlord retaining legal counsel and appearing before a judge would declare that his patience has been exhausted in dealing with a troublesome tenant. Any lawyer advocating for the landlord might try to show that the irresponsible tenant *planned* not to pay rent rather than omitting payment by accident, and the poem's emphasis on scheming and planning would support such a claim. In an effort to demonstrate intent, a retained lawyer might also look to establish a pattern of increasing irresponsibility, but the rat in the poem "Repudiates the Obligation" to pay rent entirely, as if he never had intended to compensate his host. Absent a written lease, the poem's projected property owner, in seeking to evict the rat, would encounter rough sailing in court, not to mention the difficulties entailed in deposing a reticent (and illiterate) defendant.

Any landlord seeking a "Decree" prohibiting the rat from continuing to occupy the premises would require the cooperation of a court, and subsequently a sheriff or bailiff, to serve an order of eviction. Like a malefactor avoiding a summons or a writ, the rat might flee at the sound of footsteps, so that he could not be served. Lacking any viable legal response, a landlord could do virtually nothing to prevent an unwanted tenant from occupying the premises indefinitely. Like a guest who won't leave, the rat remains, his continuing presence enabled by his ambiguous legal status. The term "Equilibrium" in the poem finally describes not just the physical laws binding human conduct to the rest of nature, but also the offsetting rights of property owners and of tenants. The rat triumphs from a legal standpoint not least because his occupancy of the house is an admitted fact, and, once he has gained entrance to the property, the rights of the rat remain proof against both legal challenges and physical efforts to expel him. According to the poem, it is not the rat's tenancy in our homes that is precarious, but rather the efficacy of our motives, methods, and laws in a world not populated solely by human beings directed by enforceable laws.

Dickinson's poems concerning landlord–tenant law move easily back and forth between the perspectives of owners and renters, yet she returns repeatedly in either case to the issue of available physical space. In nineteenth-century New England, landlords and boardinghouse owners chiefly let rooms rather than apartments, so that space for renters and roomers may indeed be conceived as severely circumscribed, rather like the quarters jointly occupied by the Dickinsons and the Macks. One term Dickinson probably employed to describe such a limited rental space is "tenement," defined in *Bouvier's* as "Rooms let in houses" (2: 1107). Poem F1210 describes the loved dead as occupying "Tenements of Wonder" in the afterlife, the narrator conjecturing that heaven or eternity resembles not an apartment block, but rather an immense boardinghouse. Poem F1358 describes clover plants as "tenements" for the bee, a transient who finds in the small space of the clover flower a "fitting" residence. Perceptions of volume are, Dickinson suggests, all relative: the rat doesn't require much room, and the bee (like the bees in Wordsworth's sonnet "Nuns fret not") finds his temporary lodgings in the clover's bloom spacious enough. But if the space enclosing landlords together with their tenants became too intimate and confining, frictions could arise. Physical proximity as a consideration in landlord–tenant relations resurfaces in F902, which again seems to capture, indirectly, the Dickinson family's early relations with their friends and landlords, the Macks:

Too little way the House must lie
From every Human Heart
That holds in undisputed Lease
A white inhabitant –

Too narrow is the Right between –
Too imminent the chance –
Each Consciousness must emigrate
And lose it's neighbor once –

I speculate that the "white inhabitant" in this poem is the soul, which, like a tenant, lives within the rest of an encompassing individual identity, signified here synecdochically as the heart. Such proximity is risky, since encountering its soul reveals to a human host both its own mortality and the soul's equally searing immortality, as in "Dare you see a Soul *at the White Heat?*" But human beings can hardly *evict* souls, considered as tenants: their leases are "undisputed," insusceptible to being revoked. The heart fears to meet its tenant, the soul, within the restricted confines of their mutual conceptual living space. "Too little way" exists between the heart and the soul, as if the spatial offset between them were too narrow, and Dickinson's use of "way" has, I think, a peculiarly legal emphasis, particularly in association with "Right," in the paralleling fifth line. In law, "right-of-way" is, according to *Black's,* "The right to pass through property owned by another," or "The strip of land subject to a nonowner's right to pass through" (1351). A right of way may thus be a walkway between properties, such as an alleyway or path, even such a one as existed between the Homestead and the neighboring Evergreens.[15]

In this poem it is not the tenant who is reticent about coming into contact with its landlord, as was the case in "The Rat is the concisest Tenant," but rather the property owner, who fears encountering her own renter. In both cases, shyness, or perhaps discretion, remains paramount in order for the two to get along. Still, the poem approves the adage that landlords and tenants should not live too closely together. Their legal relationship is apt to disturb their relations as neighbors—the "amities" referred to by the narrator of "I had some things that I called mine –." And yet neither resident thrives while apart. Dickinson may be grouping heart and soul together under the rubric "consciousness," so that when one leaves, or "emigrate[s]," the other must "lose it's neighbor," perhaps in the moment of death, when the immortal soul departs the body. The relationship between the two, as is often the case in Dickinson's poems describing landlord–tenant relations, may be described more accurately as symbiotic rather than hierarchical.

In "'Twas awkward, but it fitted me –" (F900), written apparently at around the same time as "Too little way the House must lie," Dickinson characterizes the heart as tenant rather than landlord. Here the space separating owner and renter has once again become problematic, and separation of one from the other may lead to death. Moreover, while the lease in the previous poem was "undisputed," that is, insusceptible to legal challenges, the lease described here may yet be invalidated by a technicality:

'Twas awkward, but it fitted me –
An Ancient fashioned Heart –
It's only lore – it's Steadfastness –
In Change – unerudite –

It only moved as do the Suns –
For merit of Return –
Or Birds – confirmed perpetual
By Alternating Zone –

I only have it not Tonight
It it's established place –
For technicality of Death –
Omitted in the Lease –

The narrator speaks as a landlord who has had a most reliable tenant, her own heart, dwell within the larger figural property of her body. Despite their long-lasting amity, the heart, lodged within her ribcage, had eventually proved "awkward," in both a physiological and a social sense. Now the narrator has *lost* her heart, perhaps as the result of falling into depression or despair. The tone of the narrating landlord or landlady seems wistful, as if she regrets losing her neighbor. Dickinson's language implicitly personifies the heart as an elderly person who is "Ancient," old-fashioned, set in her ways. The heart-tenant resists innovation, and Dickinson's language, particularly her Latinate words "perpetual" and "Alternating," and her professionalized, nearly bureaucratic diction in "technicality" and "Omitted," gestures toward modernity and social change, the significance of the trope being that the speaker characterizes her own heart as conservative, faithful, and constant in its affections, as opposed to her own more knowing and contemporary, fashionable intellect. The narrator implicitly contrasts the heart-tenant's "lore" with her own erudition. Within the poem's larger figural economy, the speaker draws a fairly conventional distinction between the untutored emotions and the analytical and totalizing intellect. This attitudinal, even generational, gap between two types of knowledge provides yet another connotation for "awkward" in the poem's initial line.

From the point of view of the landlord-narrator, the heart would seem, ostensibly, to have been an ideal tenant. She was dependable, rooted in place, and, we may infer, unobtrusive. Leaving only briefly and at regular intervals, presumably during periods of melancholy, or while missing those she loved, the heart ordinarily acted according to habits as predictable as the apparent movement of the sun across the sky each day, or the departure and return of migrating birds. Mentioning these phenomena helps align the heart with nature and natural "lore." The refined, somewhat dry persona of the narrator stumbles in the final stanza when she admits that her best tenant is gone again, perhaps for good. But the gap separating levels of diction hints at the narrator's own complicity in achieving that separation. The "old tenant," the heart, is not herself dead; her absence is the result of her having been *evicted*. The landlord-narrator's statement in the final stanza is framed as if in response to a query concerning the whereabouts of her old, familiar renter. The poem's legal terminology would have us believe that the owner contrived to get her old tenant thrown out by citing a "technicality," conveniently omitted in the original lease. In other words, the persona in this poem speaks as an exploitative landlord or landlady who has tricked her aged tenant into leaving, and the explanation she offers for the heart's absence should be understood as being disingenuous, at best. The narrator's elaborate diction and passive verbs in the final stanza obscure her own agency in the heart-tenant's departure, and her treatment of her lodger, her own heart, has been shabby indeed.

The image of the heart lends itself to poetic discussions of dependability and durability. In some poems, Dickinson describes the heart explicitly as a machine, a *device*. In so doing, she touches on yet another legal consideration involving contested property, in this case intellectual property, including patentable inventions and copyrighted materials. Unlike *real* property, exemplified by bricks and mortar, soil and surveyors, intellectual property deals typically with ideas. Despite being more intangible than land, intellectual property could nevertheless make patentees or copyright holders rich, even richer than speculators in real estate. At midcentury, America was awash in applications for patents, whether submitted by thoroughly subsidized researchers employed in industry or government, or by tinkering farmers who thought they had invented the next revolutionary labor-saving device. Lawyers made a good living by representing both, either by assisting them in preparing applications to the U.S. Patent Office or by defending their patents against competitors and infringers, sometimes in court; Daniel Webster, for example, earned a considerable income from defending Charles Goodyear's patent for making rubber. The poem "Hope is a strange invention –" (F1424, written around 1877) strikes a delicate balance between a sober recognition of the ingenuity required of inventors and a subtle humor directed at crackpot thinking and the marketplace's avidity for commodifiable ideas:

> Hope is a strange invention –
> A Patent of the Heart –
> In unremitting action
> Yet never wearing out –
>
> Of this electric Adjunct
> Not anything is known
> But it's unique momentum
> Embellish all we own –

Here Dickinson compares hope, an "Adjunct" of the heart, to perpetual motion devices—the elusive grail of amateur inventors. Designs for perpetual motion machines have long been derided by physicists as practically impossible, since they violate the first and second laws of thermodynamics. Even during the Victorian era, patents submitted for such devices were viewed with a mixture of scorn and fascination. In the poem, the heart assumes the role of inventor whose invention is hope, which, like systole and diastole in the sponsoring heart, keeps up a regular, reciprocal "action" by waxing and waning, yet without ever vanishing completely. Dickinson would have known from receiving even basic instruction in human anatomy that the heart is an organ remarkable for its capacity to maintain a relatively stable rate of activity over the lengthy course of a human lifetime. Thus inventor and invention also resemble each other in that the diligence of the inventor is transferred to the regularity of his creation, and Dickinson's term "momentum" helps direct readers' attention to a physical process that is simultaneously psychological, mechanical, and physiological.

Dickinson's language, however, even while alluding to the scientific or faux-scientific representation of hope as a perpetual motion device, also focuses on the actual legal ramifications of applying for a patent. The U.S. Patent Office's criteria for establishing patent dictated that a qualifying invention or process had to demonstrate, as one writer on intellectual property says, its "utility; . . . novelty; and . . . nonobviousness" (Sprankling 62). In Dickinson's poem, all three of these conditions are met either by the invention itself of hope, or, by extension, its alliteratively linked inventor, the heart.

First, hope has intrinsic usefulness, because possessing it "Embellish[es] all we own," enriching our lives both aesthetically and materially in helping us to remain optimistic.[16] Hope is also "strange," "unique," or novel in that its operation cannot be fully explained. Finally, because hope is insubstantial, not subject to empirical analysis, it again resembles its creator, the heart hidden from view within the chest, where it is unavailable for inspection. The legal criterion of "nonobviousness" subsumes ideas, processes, or devices already so widely understood that a patent applicant might be denied credit for doing nothing more than describe something already well known and understood. But Dickinson appropriates the concept of "nonobviousness" more literally to mean hidden from sight, and she may also be gently mocking inventors who, when they presented prototypes of their devices to a curious public (and to potential investors), refused to divulge crucial details of their operation. Hope is finally "nonobvious" too in that, as Dickinson says in other poems, it persists even when, logically, it should not—that is, when all hope should be gone. Thus the action of hope is illogical, like the physical principles animating a perpetual motion machine.

Especially during the nineteenth century, applications for patent of supposed perpetual motion machines became so notorious within the U.S. Patent Office for their frequency and their impracticality that eventually, barring any special considerations, they were rejected out of hand. The modern Patent Office description of regulations governing "utility" may have arisen out of Victorian mistrust of designs submitted for purported perpetual motion devices: "A rejection on the ground of lack of utility includes the more specific grounds of inoperativeness, involving perpetual motion" (*Manual of Patent Examining Procedure* sec. 706.03(a) II). The taint of fraud continued to be associated with patents submitted for perpetual motion machines, and in Dickinson's poem, uncertainty arises from doubts about whether the heart may be acting fraudulently in offering hope as a legitimate device or process. The description of hope as "a patent of the heart" indicates that, at least from a legal standpoint, the statutory criteria for establishing patent have been met, so indeed, the heart is effectively inventor and patent holder of *hope*.[17]

Yet despite this legal success, the emotional mechanism of hope remains obscure. To identify hope as an "electric Adjunct" calls into question not only its operation but its authenticity, electricity remaining, at the time of this poem's composition around 1877, an incompletely understood (and widely feared) phenomenon.[18] Fraudulent inventors took advantage of the general public's interest in, and ignorance about, electricity to make extravagant claims about how their devices were powered, as inventors in the previous century had worked up claims about magnetism. Here hope is neither "the thing with feathers" nor "a subtle Glutton," as in other poems defining the term, but rather a machine with moving parts ("In unremitting action") that, mysteriously, never wear out—another physical impossibility, according to the principle of friction. Like a labor-saving device, hope is an "Adjunct" to our lives, yet its motions and "momentum" remain inexplicable, "unique." Thus in mode of operation, materials, and function, hope continues to mystify, impressing us or, alternatively, inviting suspicion. Lingering doubts about the mechanism of hope may be exacerbated by the poem's diction, which blends officialese and legalese with advertising jargon. Such phrases and words as "unremitting action," "never wearing out," "electric Adjunct," "unique momentum," and "embellish" suggest that someone, somewhere, is being sold a bill of goods. Dickinson's knowing, legally informed construction of hope in this poem as a perpetual motion machine finally interrogates the poem's ostensible presentation of hope as an admirable, even amazing display of emotional resilience.

Written considerably earlier than the previous poem, the aphoristic "'Faith' is a fine invention" (F202), nevertheless shares with it several structural, tonal, and thematic features. Dickinson imports the language

of patent and technical innovation in describing a religious and epistemological crisis:

> "Faith" is a fine invention
> When Gentlemen can *see* –
> But *Microscopes* are prudent
> In an Emergency.

Here Dickinson—speaking once again, I think, without employing the
mediating narrative stance of a persona—distances herself from one
component of her subject, religious faith, by means of punctuation and
diction. Her quotation marks ironize the term *faith,* showing that from
the outset her poem will treat religiosity unconventionally and idiosyn-
cratically, yet her punctuation also serves to objectify the term, presenting
it, almost literally, as a physical *object,* a device—and perhaps a potentially patentable one existing in direct technical and commercial competition with other instruments dedicated to empirical analysis, such as
the microscope, a recognized investigative tool. Hope, and here, faith,
have dubious value as recourses in an emergency. Faith may be a "fine"
invention, but Dickinson's evaluative adjective generates its own irony,
casting doubt on claims made about a seemingly miraculous device, and
her diction may also convey doubt by alluding once again to the language
of advertising, the term "Gentlemen" parodying the language of sales-
men's ingratiating address of potential buyers.[19]

Overall, the poem recommends empirical analysis over the inaccessi-
ble "machinery" of faith. Faith may help us see what cannot be seen, but
a microscope allows us to view what we *can* see more clearly and effectively, helping to dispel doubts and uncertainties. Dickinson's language
also imitates warnings found on emergency equipment, as in the case of
fire, and the word "prudent" may gesture toward insurance policies and
legal liabilities, thereby reinforcing the poem's emphasis on response to
risks and hazards. Dickinson's goal in writing this poem would seem to
be to deliver a wry commentary on the purported certainties offered by
religious faith, her doubts reflected by a rhetorical distinction between
the language of belief and that of law and commerce.

These poetic discussions of the value of originality and the importance
of inventiveness indirectly raise the question of whether Dickinson may
have considered her own literary productions as *inventions.* Her entire

life was spent in a nearly rural environment located far from such literary centers as Boston, New York, or Philadelphia, cities large enough to support literary circles committed to the idea that writing poetry could be a vocation. Reared instead in a legalistically minded household, could Dickinson have envisioned herself alternatively as an "inventor" possessing a "patent" on the products of her ingenuity? Some textual evidence would seem to indicate she did. In an early letter (L110, March 27, 1853) she arraigns Austin comically as an artistic competitor who has tried to violate her poetic patent:

> And Austin is a Poet, Austin writes a psalm. Out of the way, Pegasus, Olympus enough "to him," and just say to those "nine muses" that we have done with them!
>
> Raised a living muse ourselves, worth the whole nine of them. Up, off, tramp!
>
> Now Brother Pegasus, I'll tell you what it is – I've been in the habit myself of writing some few things, and it rather appears to me that you're getting away my patent, so you'd better be somewhat careful, or I'll call the police!

Here, at the age of twenty-two, Emily Dickinson threatens to have her brother arrested for infringing upon her "patent" as poet. Poetic inspiration, being neither a process nor a device, would of course be legally indefensible as a patentable invention, and Austin, who had entered Harvard Law School only two weeks earlier, would have twigged the joke. The poet may also be nodding toward the education he is about to receive: should Austin become an attorney, he would have to stay current with legal decisions concerning both real property and intellectual property. Dickinson's letter admonishes her older brother for poaching on her intellectual territory, and she may refer indirectly to trespass in alluding to him as a superfluous tenth muse who must be shooed away like an intrusive tramp.

Austin probably would have understood his sister's flight of oratory as a self-consciously ironic exhibition of sibling rivalry. But he also must have been aware that she was presenting her own budding literary talents to him both as intellectual property and as evidence that she had embarked on a career path that paralleled his. She frames her talents rhetorically in a manner suited to the comprehension of someone who himself had one foot in the law and the other, evidently, in letters. As mock patentee and plaintiff, Emily Dickinson ironizes the phrase *"Brother* Pegasus," acknowledging the familial bond, while simultaneously criticizing him for aspiring to join her in the fraternity of poets. She also turns the tables on him by writing as if she too were versed in matters of law.[20] "I'll tell you," she says, how she will respond to his infringement of her patent: Austin had better cease and desist, the letter's diction implies, or she will have the law on him.

Dickinson was well aware of her own creative powers. Raised, however, in a family dedicated to mercantile and professional interests, she quite naturally adopted the vocabularies of business, science, and law to describe the ceaselessly inquisitive nature of the imagination. Acquainted with the concept of risk, she interpreted her own productions as the result of having entertained uncertainty, in pursuing the forbidden or thinking the unthinkable. The poem "What we see we know somewhat" (F1272, written around 1872) may be read either as a generic observation on the psychological process of creativity or as a credo, of sorts, written by Dickinson in recognition of the way her mind worked:

> What we see we know somewhat
> Be it but a little –
> What we don't surmise we do
> Though it shows so fickle
>
> I shall vote for Lands with Locks
> Granted I can pick 'em –
> Transport's doubtful Dividend
> Patented by Adam.

In these lines Dickinson talks indirectly by way of her narrator about the financial reward attendant on having been granted patent. Dickinson uses the term "Dividend" here somewhat miscellaneously to connote any ongoing source of revenue, such as dividends distributed to company shareholders and royalties. Paying wry homage to human persistence and perspicuity, the narrator honors Adam for having originated not a device, but an idea—the pursuit of forbidden knowledge. Adam's fall was to his credit, the narrator implies, and she, like he, aspires to live in a universe with visible causes and discernible effects, even if eating from the tree of knowledge should result in exile from Eden. She asserts that human beings, the implicit antecedent of "we" in the poem's first line, are so constituted as to search for causes and solutions: it is in our nature to do so. Visible reality may be initially opaque, "fickle," but human nature persists in *unlocking* the truths underlying appearances. In the moment of realization we experience an emotional and intellectual "Transport" of satisfaction and gratification, as if we had solved a puzzle. Dickinson concedes that acquired knowledge may or may not make us happy, another reason why the "Dividend" accruing to us after Adam's death is "doubtful." Yet that adjective has a highly productive dual resonance in the poem, since doubt is a species of curiosity, and we realize an intellectual benefit from having had our curiosity stimulated in the first place.

The innovation "patented" by Adam in this poem is intellectual inquiry itself, which typically advances through a series of starts and stops, with obstacles we encounter only encouraging us to look a little further and to dig a bit more deeply. Yet Dickinson's trope for this process relies on what was probably a much more common association of patents being awarded for a *device,* that is, a lock.[21] Dickinson likely draws on a contemporary reader's familiarity with the fierce competition waged during the nineteenth century among American and British companies and inventors to conceive, patent, and sell better locks. Locks manufactured in New England were famous—as, for example, Yale locks, made at the Yale Lock Manufacturing Company in Stamford, Connecticut, founded in 1868 by Linus Yale. Operators of stagecoaches, trains, and other forms of transport, in seeking to protect their cargoes, sustained a demand for new designs. To be patentable, each key or combination lock had to demonstrate superiority to earlier models.[22] In a contest of wits anticipating modern competitions waged by computer programmers and hackers, Victorian-era inventors and manufacturers set out to demonstrate that their respective designs could defeat or at least retard the efforts of lockpickers, or, alternatively, that a safecracker could work around or through an existing lock. This strenuous industrial rivalry provided Dickinson with an apt figure for the operations of an intellect stimulated by challenge.

Dickinson's figure is probably rooted as well in the use of locks to secure lands against potential trespassers. In the rural environment in which Dickinson was raised, farmers and other landowners installed locks on gates to keep out hunters, thieves, and vagrants. Poetically, the original model for such interdicted properties is, of course, Eden, and although Adam was exiled after the Fall, his inquisitive, risk-taking nature impels him to test the limits of the forbidden, to pick the lock barring his reentry. Dickinson thoroughly grasped the attractions of the unknown. "Forbidden Fruit a flavor has" she wrote in F1482, a poem I will examine more closely in chapter 7. Gifted with an analytical, inquisitive, and transgressive mind, Dickinson savored intellectual challenges. The precariousness of property in her poems is finally double-edged: she may present herself in her poems as the owner of lands subject to legal assaults by powerful forces, or as an actor in the drama played out between landlords and tenants joined in a battle over available space. Similarly, she may identify with a property owner, or the inventor of a new process or device. But her legal background also permitted her to identify with the trespasser, the rat in the wainscoting, the lockpick testing a bank vault. For Dickinson, property is, finally, analogous to knowledge itself—something to discover, define, and defend.

5

'HAS ALL A CODICIL?
Estates and Trusts

ulfilling the dying wishes of a client is one of the more important services an attorney can render, and one of the more problematic. Continued fidelity to the dead may be required even after family members have themselves ceased to mourn, and navigating among the competing claims of heirs and would-be heirs requires tact and discretion. Such qualities may also be demanded of attorneys serving as trustees for estates, since courts oblige them to maintain a high level of fiduciary duty to beneficiaries. Within Amherst's tightly knit legal community, a reputation for probity and prudence won Edward Dickinson various trust positions. He served as treasurer and trustee at Amherst College, as did his father before him and Austin Dickinson after him. Edward also served as trustee within his own family for two orphaned nieces, the Newman girls, who came from the New York City area to live in Amherst with their Dickinson relatives. Perhaps as a consequence of the family's professional involvement in such matters, Emily Dickinson's poems and letters evince considerable interest in the subjects of wills and codicils, dower and dowry, trusts and trustworthiness.

Dickinson grasped the delicacy of the estate attorney's professional duties, as is demonstrated by letters she sent after Judge Lord died in 1884 to his cousin, executor, and fellow attorney, Benjamin Kimball. In February 1885 she wrote (in L967):

Your task must be a fervent one – often one of pain.
To fulfill the will of a powerless friend supersedes the Grave.
Oh Death, where is thy Chancellor?

In these lines recognizing the professional and emotional difficulties some-times encountered by administrators or executors of estates, Dickinson also literalizes the meaning of a will, employing it to signify both the legal instrument and the intentions of a "friend" who, once dead, becomes "powerless." In wondering where death's "Chancellor" is, her capitaliza-tion suggests she is using the term in a special sense, that is, in reference to a legal office, with which Kimball would have been familiar. Chancellors, whether functioning as the "conscience of the King" or more informally as quasi- or de facto presidents at institutions such as colleges or universi-ties, combined the moral with the managerial in their professional roles. Dickinson implicitly answers her own rhetorical question: Judge Lord, troped as sovereign, has a "Chancellor" still, in the person of his cousin, executor of his estate. She taunts death itself, "supersede[d]" by the execu-tion of the judge's last wishes, for having no such advocate.[1] It is a lawyerly and friendly observation, made to confirm a bond with Kimball, and to flatter him by recognizing the significance of his task. Later, in a letter that was almost certainly written to Kimball (L1003), perhaps to thank him for carrying out the judge's wishes, she said:[2]

Dear friend.
Your Note was unspeakable strength.
May I keep it's promise in solemn reserve? To know that there is shelter, sometimes dissuades it's necessity – In this instance defers it.
Even to ask a legal question might so startle me that my Voice would pass to another World before it could be uttered.
In tribute to your fidelity I send you the face of my Father.
Thank you for the *Seal* – it covers the whole area of sanctity.

Confidingly,
E. Dickinson

Dickinson's complimentary close, "Confidingly," supplies the emotive keynote of this letter, reemphasizing the words "promise," "solemn," "fidelity," "Seal," and "sanctity." The poet wishes both to thank Kimball for his previous confidentiality and to thank him preemptively for his continued discretion. She does not recur, here, to the particular "legal question" she apparently has in mind, speculating that she herself might die (as indeed she would, about a year later) before she could frame it, so that her own "Voice," like Judge Lord's, would then be all that was left behind of her. Significantly, in implicit exchange for his services, she encloses what must have been a daguerreotype of her father, as if providing Kimball with an iconic reminder of the rectitude and integrity required of attorneys—as well as, perhaps, a not-so-subtle reminder of her own family's professional clout in Amherst.

The submerged message is that Kimball should carry out his duties and keep his mouth shut. Perhaps the poet had been mentioned in Judge Lord's will; if so, perhaps she was worried that the fact might become known, were the will to be read. Kimball could have been reassuring Dickinson that while wills are indeed public documents, some testamentary arrangements, perhaps with the cooperation of a probate judge, may be kept privy, under "Seal." Judge Lord, a longtime member of the bar who had already suffered a stroke and knew that his days were numbered, could have taken pains to ensure his estate would be handled discreetly, professionally, and sympathetically by his cousin. Lord himself had considerable experience in the drafting of wills, and several years previously he had likely advised the poet, and her mother, in composing theirs.[3] Thus the very concept of composing and acting on testamentary wishes would have provided Emily Dickinson and Judge Lord with something in common.

In her poems, Dickinson shows herself to have been keenly aware of death's legal ramifications for testators and legatees alike. I want to begin by examining "I heard a Fly buzz – when I died –" (F591), a classic within the Dickinsonian corpus, for its legal content and for its splitting of the consciousness of a dying person into both subjective experience and a curiously postmortem awareness of what death may come to mean, in its aftermath:

> I heard a Fly buzz – when I died –
> The Stillness in the Room
> Was like the Stillness in the Air –
> Between the Heaves of Storm –

The Eyes around – had wrung them dry –
And Breaths were gathering firm
For that last Onset – when the King
Be witnessed – in the Room –

I willed my Keepsakes – Signed away
What portion of me be
Assignable – and then it was
There interposed a Fly –

With Blue – uncertain – stumbling Buzz –
Between the light – and me –
And then the Windows failed – and then
I could not see to see –

Many of Dickinson's poems acquire an eerie power by deploying proleptic speakers, and indeed, this narrative strategy constitutes one of
the hallmarks of her style, manifested in other famous works such as
"Because I could not stop for Death –" and "I felt a Funeral, in my
Brain." And yet such impossible narrative stances may owe their existence
at least in part to the Dickinson family's legal heritage. Attorneys were
often retained expressly to speak for the dead, to provide a voice for those
whom death had silenced. The narrative perspective of a proleptic speaker
reifies the disembodied presence of the dead that "supersedes the Grave,"
as Dickinson wrote to Kimball. In "I heard a Fly buzz – when I died –,"
the speaker's narration resembles legal testimony rendered objectively,
minutely, and impartially. Here death is a door into a postmortem mode
of existence, one that both confirms and contradicts the comforting
metaphysical certainties offered by Christian orthodoxy. As depicted in
this poem, the afterlife is a confused state of being (or nonbeing) that is
at once alien and familiar, momentous and banal. The effect on a reader is
simultaneously reassuring and disturbing. Logic tells us that any speaker,
to speak, must exist, and yet this one seemingly does not; further, the
presence of a responsive auditor is implied, locating us disquietingly, as
we read the poem, at a prospect not far removed from that of the posthumous speaker.

In dying, the dead narrator of "I heard a Fly buzz – when I died –,"
whom I am reading as being gendered female, attempts to achieve what
the Victorians considered a "good death" by remaining fastidious, pious,

and observant even in her final moments.[4] She speaks to those gathered around her deathbed, distributes her "Keepsakes" by "will[ing]" them away, and summons the strength to sign a testamentary document.[5] At least initially, the narrator behaves according to customs sanctioned by religion and law. She distributes some gifts on the spot; typically, these would have been chattels, as opposed to real property, which would have been addressed in the contents of a will.[6] "Signed away / What portion of me be / Assignable" the narrator says, in reference to the standard language of wills, "I assign and devise," yet with a clever play on words in her juxtaposing of "Signed" and "Assignable." If we assume that the narrator is in fact intended to be construed as a woman, the poem's description of personal property is consistent with the legal doctrine of the time, in that women generally were prevented by law from controlling real property in their own names, so that what they left behind after their deaths consisted primarily of objects and heirlooms with a clearly defined intergenerational significance. The narrator employs the word "portion," another term with specific testamentary significance: *Bouvier's* defines "portion" as "That part of a parent's estate . . . which is given to a child" (2: 701). The poem subtly ironizes the idea that a dying person's estate could be conflated with her physical body, so that chunks of her physical and financial existence may be doled out piecemeal to offspring and other survivors.

Dickinson's legal puns and wordplay work subtly to undermine the implicit seriousness of this somber scene, helping to generate a wry tone that interrogates both Christian pieties and the conventions of deathbed etiquette. Funerary clichés and religious platitudes are also jarringly intermixed with the hard-edged language of law. Phrases such as "gathering firm," "last Onset," and "King / Be witnessed" participate in the deathbed language popular at midcentury, as does the phrase "wrung them dry," which literalizes, somewhat satirically, mourners' sobbing. Figural language predominates in the first half of the poem, but in the final two stanzas a professional and Latinate diction prevails. The words "portion," Assignable," and "interposed" redirect the poem from the rhetorical realm of sentiment and sanctimoniousness to that of law. This shift tracks the movement in narrative perspective from the present life into the afterlife: existence in the former is dominated by catchphrases, while the latter adopts a ruthlessly precise outlook in terms both of language and of empirical experience. The poem's second half thereby ventriloquizes, through the agency of its proleptic narrator, an attorney's more matter-of-fact approach to both the circumstances of death and its aftermath. The intrusion of the fly within the dying narrator's vision subsequently echoes and emulates, in imagery, this intrusion of a secular, professional, and unsentimental approach to death. The final line, "I could not see to see –," would lose much of its poignancy if a reader had not already been conditioned by preceding lines to interpret language more literally and less figurally. The metaphysical shift experienced by the narrator is thus reproduced by a shift in the poem's rhetoric, and the poem ends by denying, in essence, the presence of any comforting or comfortable epistemologies (the speaker cannot *see* things in those ways any more) and so does the poem, which effects, ironically, a movement from eschatological concerns back to the quotidian.[7]

While Dickinson was alive, women could compose their wills and bequeath chattels, but they retained little control over what is often the greatest single source of wealth in an estate: land. When the poet and her mother made out their wills in 1875, both documents referred to property held personally, yet effective control of what by that time had become fairly extensive family holdings in real estate would have remained firmly in the hands of Austin Dickinson, who became administrator of his father's estate after Edward died in 1874.[8] Although property rights for women slowly began to change after the middle of the century, during the greater part of the poet's life women continued to depend for their material well-being chiefly on the generosity of their husbands, and then, once widowed, on that of their sons, brothers, and brothers-in-law. Excluded from the direct line of succession, women often had to hope they were cared for virtually as an afterthought in the distribution of property specified in male relatives' wills. The theme of such patriarchal dispositions of property may be raised in the short poem F1296 B:

> Not One by Heaven defrauded stay –
> Although he seem to steal
> He restitutes in some sweet way
> Secreted in his will –

God's will, indicated by the metonymic "Heaven," is here conflated with ordinary testamentary wishes, Dickinson's legal emphasis being signaled by the word "defrauded." The trope implicitly compares God, or perhaps Jesus, to a dying patriarch who, to his heirs, may have appeared to cheat them of their patrimony while still alive. Yet Dickinson acknowledges the ways in which those about to die might seek to remedy such apparent financial injuries.

"Restitutes," a word that in its nominal form, "restitution," possesses wide application in law, seems here to signify the return of property unjustly seized by someone else. The speaker tempers the patriarch's ostensible theft, indicated by the verb "steal," with the word "seem," generating a nearly novelistic plot. A deliberate plan will be shown to have underlain what had looked, initially, to have been an act of spite or parsimony on the part of the testator. Afterward, in retrospect, the testator will seem "sweet" in the affections and memories of his heirs and heiresses. The long *e* assonance of the poem's terms surreptitiously invites a comparison of retrospective views. The phonetic similarity of "Steal," "sweet," and "Secreted" suggests an initially impenetrable design ultimately made clear. "Secreted" is, I think, an especially serendipitous word choice. It combines the *secretive* dimension of some testamentary documents (such as, for example, wills containing provisions put under seal) with the verb "secrete," which also signifies a sort of an organic distillation, a *secretion*. In that sense, the patriarch's will, by concentrating the essence of his character, is a more reliable indicator of his underlying personality than even his physical presence while still alive.

Dickinson's trope addresses, we may assume, the metaphysical mystery of God's will, not in a testamentary way but rather in the sense of providence, which, seen from a vaster temporal perspective, rewards as often as it robs (one is inevitably reminded of Dickinson's poem "I never lost as much but twice"). Yet I suggest that Dickinson's metaphor acquires added forcefulness from the reality that women were, at least for the first half of the nineteenth century, dependent on men's wishes for the distribution to them of an estate. For the most part, they could only hope and trust that testamentary arrangements had addressed their needs.

For an estate attorney, one source of professional concern was the sudden appearance of a previously unknown claimant to an estate. In "The Mushroom is the Elf of Plants" (F1350), written again on the subject of summer's annual "death" in autumn, Dickinson recurs to nature to find a figural vehicle appropriate for discussing legal quandaries presented by the perhaps unheralded arrival of a charming, transient, and only somewhat plausible heir:[9]

> The Mushroom is the Elf of Plants.
> At Evening, it is not –
> At Morning in a Truffled Hut
> It stop opon a Spot
>
> As if it tarried always
> And yet it's whole Career
> Is shorter than a Snake's Delay
> And fleeter than a Tare –
>
> 'Tis Vegetation's Juggler –
> The Germ of Alibi –
> Doth like a Bubble antedate
> And like a Bubble, hie –
>
> I feel as if the Grass was pleased
> To have it intermit –
> This surreptitious scion
> Of summer's circumspect.
>
> Had Nature any Plated Face | Plated / supple
> Or could she one contemn –
> Had Nature an Apostate – | Apostate / "Iscariot" / Iscariot
> That Mushroom it is Him.

This exuberantly playful poem recounts the brief, almost novelistic "Career" of the mushroom, its rascal hero, which springs up overnight from the cool turf of late summer and early autumn. The mushroom's dramatic efflorescence is likened to the tardy appearance of an irresponsible, and possibly fraudulent, heir, or "scion," who unexpectedly claims his "Spot," that is, possession of a miniscule site within the larger domain of the grass, which, like the rest of the vegetal world, faces extinction with the coming of the first frost.[10] In considering the dubiousness of the mushroom's claim, it is worth keeping in mind that Dickinson knew enough about botany to be well aware that despite her poem's initial line, mushrooms are not plants, although they may resemble them. The patriarch "Grass" is "pleased" rather than chagrined by this interposition of his prodigal, self-described heir. Dickinson employs the word "intermit," signifying both the mushroom's opportunistic occupation of its small space and its forceful intrusion into legal considerations of the grass's estate of real property, here literalized as the ground itself, thrust aside by the burgeoning fungus.

Strangely, Dickinson herself appears to have warmed, over time, to her own mushroom protagonist. She worked through several drafts of this poem, adding the final stanza and exchanging for her original choice of "Iscariot" in the penultimate line the less pejorative "Apostate." Moreover, the entire fourth stanza, in which the legator "Grass" is depicted as being not displeased to recognize, even embrace, his heir, was added as an afterthought.[11] Dickinson mitigates the moral culpability of the mushroom's intervention, adding more comic elements to her poem while deemphasizing its original judgmental tenor. Evidently Dickinson also took some pride in having composed this poem, enclosing it in a letter written to Thomas Wentworth Higginson in late May 1874 (L413). Prefatory to quoting her own lines to him, Dickinson says that she "slew a Mushroom –," implicating herself, we may suppose, in the capital punishment condign for such a rapscallion, either by serving it for dinner or by presenting her poetic treatment of the mushroom as a symbolic means of "slaying" it—that is, reducing the actual fungus to the status of literary subject. That Dickinson herself intermitted a stanza in this poem, in the process of composition, is mildly suggestive: she may be considered, deconstructively, as "slaying" her protagonist mushroom as an overreaching rival by modifying the moral tenor of her poem. Also, the scoundrel mushroom's methods are not that dissimilar from hers, in the seeming generation of something from nothing, perhaps in a very short time.

The tone of the poem overall is playful, as is indicated by the poet's anagrammatic combination of "stop" and "Spot," "tarried" and "Tare." Dickinson's reprobate hero is also a "Juggler," in the old sense of being an amusing *fraud*. Punning on the meaning of "germ" to signify seed or, in this case, spore, Dickinson associates the mushroom's seeming and duplicitous long-standing presence with "The Germ of Alibi," that is, a plausible excuse for his abrupt appearance on the scene. At the heart of the mushroom's deception is his nearly magical growth and substantial outward display; like any fraudulent person, he is adept at deceiving observers with a facade. His unforeseen appearance is also comparable to the inflated growth of a "Bubble," and here, in concert with the legally inflected term "antedate," Dickinson's employment of that term suggests that the mushroom is being analogized to out-of-town swindlers who promise vast returns to rural investors, although their schemes later prove to be no more than speculative bubbles.

In representing itself as a candidate heir for the patriarch grass's estate, the mushroom, like the King and the Duke passing themselves off as Peter Wilks's heirs in *Huckleberry Finn,* claims a family relation to a deceased testator. In the first stanza the mushroom erects its "Truffled Hut" hastily, a sham contrived to present the fungus "As if it tarried always," an oxymoron that helps point a reader toward the method of the fraud's deception, the mushroom's hastily constructed residence endowing its inhabitant with a fictitious air of permanence, stability, and the possession of local connections. The quick departure of frauds after their accomplishment of their aims (again, one can hardly avoid thinking of Twain's comic villains, leaving town as fast as their feet can carry them) is connoted by the bursting of a bubble, as the mushroom "hie[s]," disappearing from the forest floor as suddenly as it had appeared (or perhaps because it has been harvested by a hungry poet). A joke on "tarrying"—which is the last thing a fraud would wish to do at the scene of his imposture—is embedded in Dickinson's reference to a "Tare," or weed, which also springs up opportunistically, in a Darwinian sense, among crop plants, such as wheat. Although Dickinson does make hay, poetically, from the phonetic similarity of "tare" and "tarry," her underlying emphasis on the prodigious rate at which mushrooms and weeds grow ties them, through her figure, to the opportunism and facile creativity of frauds.

Aside from the potential appearance of unsuspected heirs, another potential headache for estate attorneys is the discovery of alternative versions of wills, often with attached codicils. Dickinson, habituated to using legal terminology as a sort of conceptual shorthand for more generic topics, employed "codicil" informally to signify addenda, postscripts, afterthoughts, or editorial emendations. The three known recipients of letters in which the poet employed that term were either near neighbors or themselves associated, directly or indirectly, with the practice of law, and thus perhaps accustomed to seeing the poet interpolate legal terminology in her casual writing. Because *codicil* is a comparatively specialized term used almost exclusively by attorneys, Dickinson is unlikely to have picked it up from readings in literature. Adding a codicil to a will was not, as Dickinson well knew, a trivial matter, and certainly not the same thing as simply rewording a document. In law, the presence of a codicil in a testamentary document may have far-reaching implications. Ordinarily, the discovery of a will containing a codicil would cause it to be received in court as the most recent version of a testator's last wishes. As such it could be used to cast doubts on other extant wills, affecting, to a greater or lesser degree, the final distribution of a decedent's estate.

In 1871 Dickinson asked her dear friend and sister-in-law, Susan Gilbert Dickinson, "Has All – a codicil?" (L366). Sue, married to an attorney, would have understood the logic, or rather the illogic, of the poet's legalistic question. Could a final, magisterial document be amended? And can a will that entails *all* of an estate on an heir contain qualifications or exceptions? Around 1878 Dickinson suggests to a traveling Mrs. J. Howard Sweetser, a lifelong neighbor, that if "Nellie" were to stay in one place for a while, the continuity of a still-fragile spring would be guaranteed: "Would she remain with the Robins April would need no Codicil, but Mrs Nellie has Wings –" (L550). Most poignantly, perhaps, in 1882 Dickinson composed a draft of a letter to Judge Lord, sympathizing with him while he suffered from a cold and expressing satisfaction that he was recovering "at Home" in Salem, with the added "codicil" that "My own were homeless if you were" (L750). That is, her own peace of mind would be as disrupted or dispossessed by worries about his well-being as his own health would be if he were convalescing somewhere away from the comfort of home. Dickinson's use of the word "codicil" in all of these letters would have gratified, rather than surprised, her several correspondents. In this way, the language of law functions as a means of intra-group communication among the poet and her friends, reflecting a shared awareness of the Dickinson family's legal heritage, as well as of their familiarity with professional and technical vocabularies.

These letters, and an awareness of the poet's familiarity with the way codicils could alter the expression of a testator's last wishes, may shed some light on the meaning of "Which is best? Heaven –" (F1021):

> Which is best? Heaven –
> Or only Heaven to come
> With that old Codicil of Doubt?
> I cannot help esteem

The "Bird within the Hand"
Superior to the one
The "Bush" may yield me
Or may not –
Too late to choose again.

That the promise of heaven to a Christian should include an "old" codicil of "Doubt" threatens to invalidate received religious precepts. Here the speaker deliberates before choosing between two "Heaven[s]," the conventional Christian afterlife and the sensually appealing "Heaven" of an earthly paradise, which is constantly accessible to those sufficiently appreciative of the present world's significance and beauty. The narrator speaks with a self-conscious logic: if we fail to understand that this temporal and sensual life is indeed the real paradise, we cannot recover from our mistake, once dead. The idea of the finality of testamentary documents is latent in this poem and connected as well to the ineluctability of empirical proof. Skepticism about religion is a "Codicil" that qualifies our belief in the existence of a postmortem paradise, yet we, as rational beings, must behave in ways consistent with self-preservation, and even self-gratification. If we wait until after we are dead to receive confirmation that an earthly paradise is inferior to an immaterial one, it will then be too late for us to write another "codicil" into our final opinions and wishes. Here, Dickinson's formal or informal training in logic, whether as an embellishment of a liberal education or as the ancillary effect of growing up amid a concentration of lawyers, is especially prominent.

That logic and belief could, and did, contradict each other the poet well knew. " 'Faith' is a fine invention," she wrote, but in an "Emergency" empirical evidence and reason usually provide better, or at least more "prudent," remedies. Religion resembled an estate in that it was inherited through one's family and culture; it descended from an ancient time; it was codified, in the written word; and, for the faithful, irrevocable—for the baptized, there was no turning back. Without mentioning either wills or codicils, the poem "To lose One's faith – surpass" (F623) exemplifies, I think, the poet's lay knowledge of the absolute quality of testamentary documents, and her sense of language in general as a precise instrument, whether deployed in contexts legal, poetic, or religious:

To lose One's faith – surpass
The loss of an Estate –
Because Estates can be
Replenished – faith cannot –

Inherited with Life –
Belief – but once – can be –
Annihilate a single clause –
And Being's – Beggary –

This version of Dickinson's figural equation of religious faith with an inheritance is especially trenchant. Faith is treated explicitly as a category of property, like real property or chattels, which may be preserved, or lost. As spendthrift scions may waste an estate, progeny of the faithful may disavow and discard belief. Unlike capital, religious faith diminished by apostasy, skepticism, or unbelief is difficult to replenish, so that, within the space of a single generation, an inherited condition of spiritual wealth may be reduced to spiritual penury. Yet the poem does not adopt a moralizing position on this intergenerational question. Rather, Dickinson investigates the grounds of religious belief on their own terms, which she borrows here from legal terminology, specifically estate law. Testamentary documents have to be drafted precisely and revised carefully, because usually they are followed literally to the letter, and, of course, the deceased cannot amend or clarify what had been said. If imprecise language is included, or if one codicil is superseded by another, an heir who had expected to be made wealthy might instead find himself destitute.

In the poet's figure comparing the high stakes involved in writing testamentary documents to an individual's subscription to religious faith, "Annihilate" has an especially potent meaning. For an attorney or for other writers, the verb refers simply to the editorial process, including either erasure or the rendering of a previous version obsolescent, as when codicils modify previous wills. On a metaphysical level, however, the word's significance is devastating. Financial pauperism is being likened to spiritual emptiness, yet the term also suggests utter erasure of a soul from existence, in direct opposition to the Christian's promise of eternal life. Being itself may then be *beggared,* that is, reduced to nonentity or nonbeing, and Dickinson leaves open the question of whether a nonbeliever in the temporal world may be made spiritually poor by skepticism and doubt, or whether a faith in the afterlife may even be entirely destroyed.

During Dickinson's lifetime, narratives describing legacies being handed down to unsuspecting heirs and trust funds being distributed to young survivors would generally have excluded women. Virtually the only exception to this exclusion from sources of economic security was the legal right of *dower,* a subject Dickinson recurs to in several poems. The word possessed dual significances that Dickinson, perhaps mindful of the concept's rich legal history, exploited. Cynthia Griffin Wolff cites the term's twofold, paradoxical meanings, both of them grounded in a woman's marital status: "A 'dower' is 'the property which a woman brings to her husband in marriage'; however, it is also 'the gift of a husband for a wife'" (172). That is, the first meaning coincides with what we might ordinarily call a "dowry," conveyed by a woman to her husband at the beginning of a marriage, and the second with what is known colloquially as the "widow's third," the one-third interest in his estate that came to her automatically, by law, after her husband had died. The latter may be understood as being a corollary or consequence of the former.

In common parlance, "dower" and "dowry" have been employed somewhat promiscuously, which is perhaps to be expected, since both terms have common roots in the Latin *dos,* or gift, and both have traditionally described a woman's contribution to a marital estate when she married, as well as her rightful share in the accumulation of real property realized during the marriage. In the latter case, "dower" particularly signified a provision for a widow's old age; by statutory law, it devolved to her even if she had not been named in her husband's will. The legal concept of dower was one of several issues pertaining to women undergoing substantial judicial and legislative review during Dickinson's lifetime, providing perhaps one more reason why she refers to it comparatively often in her poems. Indeed, Robert Lambert, who quotes Wolff in excavating the term's problematic legal definition, says "It is not surprising that the dually defined DOWER is one of the most widely used [legal] technical terms," with nineteen citations in Stanford Rosenbaum's concordance to the poems (72). The poet appears to have used the term generally as a means of describing women's ownership of property in the context of the marital relation.

Since it expired at the end of her own lifetime, dower gave a widow only a temporary interest in her husband's estate. Ordinarily she could not sell her third, bequeath it, or alienate it in any other way. Rather, the estate passed *through* her, and, after her death, continued on to her husband's named or unnamed beneficiaries.[12] A widow's existence could thus be considered, from a legal point of view, as a fragmentary and remnant extension of her husband's status as property owner while he was still alive, and after his death a wife's control of any portion of the estate was limited to her own upkeep and maintenance. In Massachusetts, until the state's adoption of the Married Women's Property Act in 1855, dower had been codified originally by a colony act passed in 1641:

> It is ordered by this court, and the authority thereof, that every married woman, (living with her husband in this jurisdiction, or other where absent from him with his consent, or through his mere default, or inevitable providence, or in case of divorce where she is the innocent party,) that shall not, before marriage, be estated by way of jointure, in some houses, lands, tenements, or other hereditaments for term of life, shall, immediately after the death of her husband, have right and interest, by way of dowry, in and to one third part of all such houses, lands, tenements, and hereditaments, as her husband was seized of to his own use, either in possession, reversion or remainder, in any estate of inheritance . . . at any time during the marriage, to have and enjoy for the term of her natural life.[13]

The terminological confusion between "dowry" and "dower" also points to a woman's volition in assigning property *to,* or receiving property *from,* a man. A bride gave her dowry to her husband freely, in a sense analogous to the way she also gave herself to him emotionally and sexually. A widow, on the other hand, passively and rightfully received her dower in consequence of having been married as a symbolic continuation of her deceased husband's solicitude for her material well-being. During an age when women were still largely excluded from the professions, a widow's third was virtually the only barrier against want wives possessed in old age. Ideally, the legal right of dower also provided a remedy for surviving wives against the potential postmortem spite of stingy husbands and the ingratitude of grasping children, while also helping reduce the number of women compelled to rely on the charity of town officials and church aid societies.[14]

Dickinson appears to have used the word "dower" in many of its multiple legal meanings.[15] Remaining unmarried throughout her life, the poet used the term to identify that portion of an estate reserved for women, married or single, to distribute as they pleased. She also used the word, or variants of it, simply to connote a *gift*. In either case, an explicitly distaff connotation usually attaches to her use of the word. For her, "dower," accepted in its traditional and historic senses, does not prompt meditations on legal inequities in the distribution of real properties among women and men. Instead, Dickinson uses the word to signify women's generosity to those whom they love, and to the world at large. It's a mark of honor, a woman's gift, and a substantial one at that, since "dower" sometimes referred to real property, that is, land. Dickinson's emphasis on the female gender of the dower donor is exemplified by "Precious to Me – She still shall be –" (F751), in which one of the poet's typically male-gendered bee figures reappears:

> Precious to Me – She still shall be –
> Though She forget the name I bear –
> The fashion of the Gown I wear –
> The very Color of My Hair –
>
> So like the Meadows – now –
> I dared to show a Tress of Their's
> If haply – She might not despise
> A Buttercup's Array –
>
> I know the Whole – obscures the Part –
> The fraction – that appeased the Heart
> Till Number's Empery –
> Remembered – as the Milliner's flower
> When Summer's Everlasting Dower –
> Confronts the dazzled Bee –

Here the speaker constructs herself as a flower designed to attract ("Confront") a suitor bee, who, in this case, is paradoxically identified in the first line as a woman, "She." The final stanza's emphasis on a "fraction" that "appeased the Heart" gestures, I think, to the poet's awareness that dower is legally defined as a fraction, usually one third of a decedent's estate, Dickinson's figure integrating the very concept of fractionality with an implied contrast to whole numbers, "Number's empery."

The speaker frames her own offering of herself as being a symbolic imitation of nature, betokened by the spray of buttercups she wears as an ornament during summer, or the milliner's artificial flowers adorning a woman's hat. The speaker's *gift* to the woman she admires is given as freely as the dowry is extended to the suitor bee, yet also fractional, in the sense that a recipient must content herself with the symbolic or synecdochical equivalent of a larger estate, until such time as fulfillment arrives. The phrase "Everlasting dower" is itself oxymoronic, since the legal concept of dower was circumscribed by the life of the surviving widow. In that sense, Dickinson may be referring here to the conditional nature of dower for widows, if they cannot, in the temporal world, re-create a marital unity in a sense pertaining both to the affections and to legal considerations of estate, until husband and wife *both* have died. Then, "Number's Empery" is indeed reestablished in the afterlife, as the deceased spouses once again share equally and posthumously in the joint enterprise of a marriage sustained beyond the grave.[16] Alternatively, "empery" may refer indirectly to women's fertility, multiplied across the generations by the generative power of their offspring. In either case, Dickinson's poems mentioning dower are apt to contrast fractions to wholes, perhaps reflecting a legally inflected consciousness of women's partial contributions to the marital relation conflated with a nearly Malthusian sense of how populations grow.

As opposed to wills, trusts are estate instruments generally intended to confer continuing benefits to survivors, rather than dividing up a decedent's holdings among heirs. The complex denotative context of the word "trust" may have drawn the attention of lawyer Dickinson's poetical daughter. More generally, the word "trust" is, of course, likely to appear in discussions of religion, love, and friendship, and these more general applications overlap with the term's specific legal meanings. Along with a letter (L637) sent to a neighbor, Mrs. Edward Tuckerman, around 1880, Dickinson placed a daphne flower in the envelope, expressing a hope that Mrs. Tuckerman would enjoy taking up the flower in her own hands:

> Almost I trust that they [i.e., Mrs. Tuckerman's hands] will, yet trust is such a shelving word – Part of our treasures are denied us – part of them provisoed, like Bequests available far hence – part of them we partake?
>
> Which, dear, are the divinest?

Dickinson draws a lawyerly distinction here between pleasures to be enjoyed today and those to be enjoyed tomorrow. Benefits to be realized in the future are "shelv[ed]," or put aside like portions of an estate withheld from a beneficiary's control. In saying "provisoed," Dickinson links trusts with wills, whose codicils or provisos sometimes withhold part of an inheritance until an heir reaches his majority. Her closing rhetorical question obviates the question of which are to preferred, present or contingent pleasures, counterbalancing the immediate sensory pleasure to be derived from looking at, handling, and smelling the daphne, with the pleasure of seeing Mrs. Tuckerman once again after she has returned.[17]

In law, the role of *trustee* implies absolute financial integrity, indifference to personal enrichment, dogged loyalty to the wishes of the deceased, and, not unusually, a nearly parental concern for the trust beneficiaries, who may be minors. These are all qualities Dickinson admired, both as the product of a zealously moral late-Puritan culture and as the daughter of a solicitous lawyer-father who could, at times, wax both overprotective and overbearing. For attorneys, the office of trustee epitomized their professional role as vigorous guardians of civic order, family privacy, and the responsibilities entailed on them by the voiceless dead. As attorneys, Samuel Fowler Dickinson, Edward Dickinson, and Austin Dickinson derived a measure of professional satisfaction in their appointments to positions with trust responsibilities. And yet such duties could conflict with family loyalties: for example, in 1842 Edward Dickinson served as court-appointed trustee to prevent his own father, Samuel, from disposing of property belonging to his wife in order to pay off Squire Dickinson's burgeoning debts. Thus, for the Dickinsons, being put into a position of trust was sometimes necessitated, ironically, by a lack of basic trust in the discretion of other family members.

The issue of possibly misplaced fiduciary trust shows up occasionally as a theme in Emily Dickinson's writing. I have written elsewhere about the poem " 'Remember me' implored the Thief!" (F1208), in which Jesus assures the thief crucified alongside him that they will be reunited in the estate of paradise.[18] The poem's speaker, like an attorney quoting precedent, says that to retell that story is to "cite this mightiest case / Of compensated Trust." "Compensation," in the context of chancery practice, is defined in *Bouvier's* as "Something to be done for or paid to a person of equal value with something of which he has been deprived by the acts or negligence of the party so doing or paying" (1: 375).[19] In that sense, Jesus's guarantee ("guaranty," in " 'Remember me' implored the Thief!") to the thief that he would be compensated for his death frames Jesus as the promissory in a trust relationship. Jesus performs his initial fiduciary duty as trustee for the thief not only by taking on himself the material burden of "rewarding" the thief for his fidelity but also by offering an equal posthumous share in the kingdom of heaven. Yet we, the living, cannot know whether Jesus was ever able to make good on these promises, and the only evidence we possess of whether the thief's trust in Jesus was indeed compensated is the "Affidavit" provided by the New Testament.

Dickinson also represented the connection between body and soul as a trust relationship. We have already seen the poet acknowledge "inheriting" the binary of body and soul as a condition of existence in "I am afraid to own a Body –," in which the speaker tropes both halves of her corporate—not *corporeal*—identity as parcels of property for which possession is both "precarious" and "not optional"; that is, however difficult it may be to reconcile the two, existence itself is an obligation that may not be shirked. Dialogues between body and spirit constitute a literary convention that has existed at least since the Renaissance (as, for example, in Marvell's "A Dialogue Between the Soul and Body") and yet in "Death is a Dialogue between" (F973), Dickinson situates their competing imperatives in the distinctly legal context of a trust:

> Death is a Dialogue between
> The Spirit and the Dust.
> "Dissolve" says Death, The Spirit "Sir
> I have another Trust" –
> Death doubts it –
> Argues from the ground –
> The Spirit turns away
> Just laying off for evidence
> An Overcoat of Clay.

I think the setting of this poem may be imagined productively as a courtroom, so that the two speakers could be thought of as competing attorneys, or, perhaps even more likely, judge and advocate. Thus the

"Dialogue" resembles a courtroom debate, in which Death, as judge, asserts the preeminence of the corruptible body, and the Spirit speaks on behalf of the immortal and enduring soul or spirit. Despite the seriousness of the topic, the poem's tone is once again playful, nearly comic. Dickinson's language is full of legal puns, as when Death, as presiding judge, orders attorney "Spirit" to dissolve a "Trust." Legally, trusts may indeed be dissolved, although rarely, by order of a court, that is, through a judge. Yet Dickinson's witticism refers rather to decomposition, the decay of a body as it dissolves into "Dust" and the enveloping "ground," a pun for "grounds of argument." Spirit, on the other hand, argues for the sake of his client, an individual identity that, even should one particular "Trust" be dissolved, he, as both advocate and trustee for the plaintiff, will remain faithful to by upholding another trust, the promise of resurrection. Dickinson's depiction of a courtroom scene is both inherently dramatic and acutely observed. The imperiousness of the judge's order suggests that Dickinson has in mind courts of equity, in which judges, rather than juries, handed down decisions unilaterally. One of the maxims of equity is "Equity will not allow a trust to fail for want of a trustee," and here, perhaps, death's "chancellor" finally cannot prevent the spirit's advocate from fulfilling his office as trustee for the trust's settlor, an individual identity.

Thinking legalistically, we might ask why Dickinson should have chosen, in "Death is a Dialogue between," to characterize the dichotomy of matter and spirit, death and immortality, as an attorney arguing the merits of a trust before a judge, rather than as an arraignment, or a criminal trial, or a sentencing. First, the poet may wish for a reader with a sophisticated lay familiarity with the law to have in mind, while reading the poem, the idea of *living* trusts. Although not so widely popular as they have been in the post–World War II era, even in the nineteenth century attorneys employed living trusts as an estate planning tool to protect clients' assets from being subjected to probate after death.[20] And, of course, Dickinson would achieve a submerged pun in emphasizing "living," in contradistinction to death and extinction. Then too, at a crucial moment in the proceedings described in this poem, Attorney Spirit introduces in court the paradoxically material evidence of the body, which may be shed like an outworn overcoat. True to the genre of dramatic courtroom narrative, this empirical evidence becomes dispositive: it's a display of courtroom showmanship, and subsequently, Judge Death could hardly deny the soul's independence from fleshly limitations.

Yet Attorney Spirit's shrugging off of the coat is not evidence of his client's innocence, as could be true during a criminal trial, when a defense attorney might, by demonstrating that a garment introduced as evidence did not fit his accused client. Rather, the body, or the coat itself, is a sort of document in its own right, specifically a trust document, indicative of the alternative "trust" the Spirit claims to be still in effect for his client, and therefore immune to court-ordered dissolution. Despite the production in court of evidence, the procedure described in the poem would seem to be a civil suit, not a criminal one, so that what is at stake is the client's material, and eternal, circumstances, and not his (or her) guilt or innocence. In law, trusts may be financial, custodial, or both, and conceivably Spirit, figured here as attorney, assumes a court-appointed, or *ad litem,* role as guardian of the individual identity. In a proud gesture of forensic and legal supremacy, Spirit finally "turns away" from the bench, dismissing it symbolically as a valid arbiter while simultaneously illustrating his point by disappearing into thin air, an act constituting proof of the soul's immunity to limitations imposed by material existence, and a trust's immunity to judicial interference.

"Death is a Dialogue between" may also contain topical allusions to a case that became a cause célèbre in 1844, when Dickinson was fourteen years old: *Vidal v. Philadelphia.* In that case, tried before the Supreme Court, Daniel Webster, the most famous forensic attorney of his generation, argued against the notable Philadelphia lawyer Horace Binney. At the center of the dispute was a will left by Stephen Girard, a native of France and a naturalized citizen of Philadelphia. One of the wealthiest men in the nation, known for his benevolence and for his generosity to his adopted city, Girard died a childless widower. He bequeathed the bulk of his immense estate to found a school for fatherless boys, but he also set up a trust to finance, after his death, canal and street improvements in Philadelphia. The dollar amounts involved were prodigious, and Girard's relatives in France sought to have these testamentary bequests set aside. At the heart of the heirs' attack on the will was a provision Girard had made that the school he was endowing was to be operated on entirely secular principles—for example, no teacher who identified with any sectarian view was to be hired, and the campus was to bar speakers espousing religious views of any sort. Webster, representing Girard's heirs, argued that such restrictions flouted the common law of the United States, which, Webster asserted, was inherently predicated on Christian principles. Despite Webster's customary eloquence, the court ruled unanimously against the heirs, upholding the testator's stated wishes. Perry Miller, in his recounting of the trial, suggests that this defeat may have resulted soon after in a failure of the Whig party to nominate Webster as their presidential candidate (*Life of the Mind* 201). Instead, the Whigs chose Webster's perennial intraparty rival and fellow attorney, Henry Clay.

Dickinson wrote "Death is a Dialogue between" about twenty years after Story handed down the verdict in *Vidal*. Still, if we look at some of the legal details involved in the *Vidal* decision, we may discern at least an echo of that case's ancillary impact on Webster's fellow attorneys and Whigs. As Dickinson alluded to in her letter to Benjamin Kimball, wills and trust agreements serve to prolong the presence of the deceased, and, in law, respecting decedents' wishes enjoys substantial legal protections, as is demonstrated by the outcome in *Vidal*. That case involved two testamentary documents, a will with attached codicils and the trust instrument itself. Even if the Girard heirs had succeeded in breaking the will (which they did not), dissolution of the trust represented a separate legal matter. Thus it is suggestive that counselor "Spirit" in Dickinson's poem, despite having suffered, apparently, an initial legal defeat, says to the court, "Sir / I have another Trust," that is, an auxiliary shield against attacks on a client's estate. Moreover, when counsel introduces "An Overcoat of Clay" in court as evidence, Dickinson's capitalization of *clay* may be an indirect, punning reference to Webster's political rival, in the same way the name "Shaw" in "I had some things that I called mine –" may possess more than one meaning.

It is difficult to say whether the presence of a topical pun would signal that the poet, speaking indirectly through the agency of her narrator, is expressing partisan support for the man her father admired, or for Clay, the man who supplanted him. But clearly Dickinson's major emphasis is religious, rather than legal or political. The poem evidently reaffirms Christian pieties about *trust* in the existence of an afterlife, and spirit's superiority to the flesh. If the poem does indeed refer indirectly to *Vidal*, a piquant irony would seem to be present in that Dickinson's religious theme asserting the superiority of the immaterial to the material contradicts the *Vidal* decision's reaffirming the wisdom of separating church and state.

As *Vidal* showed, honoring the wishes of the dying and the dead, as expressed in testamentary documents, is a bedrock principle in law. Wills, of course, express the *will,* or the wishes, of the testator, while trusts emphasize the *trust* the dying place in the hands of the living. While wills are a matter of public record, trusts may be entirely private. Trustees are required to notify beneficiaries if they are named in a trust document, but otherwise, only the trustee and the court overseeing it need be privy to its contents, whether the instrument is *inter vivos,* that is, a living trust, or testamentary, as in *Vidal.* One of the more famous literary treatments of a living trust appears in *Great Expectations,* in which Pip is made beneficiary to a secret living trust.[21] Pip learns he will receive a generous allowance to finance his raising as a gentleman, but his benefactor's identity remains a mystery until Magwitch chooses to make himself known to him. Dickens's dramatic handling of Magwitch's trust emphasizes the surreptitious nature of such arrangements, which could be as secretive as the settlor wished them to be. In *Great Expectations,* Mr. Jaggers, trustee for Magwitch, fulfills his legal duty to communicate with Pip, while telling him nothing about Magwitch.[22] Without mentioning Dickens's fortunate young heir, the poem "Nature and God – I neither knew" (F803 B, written around 1864) seems to reinterpret Pip's legal situation as a philosophic, almost existential, statement about the obligations of existence:

> Nature and God – I neither knew
> Yet Both, so well knew Me
> They startled, like Executors
> Of My identity— | My / an
>
> Yet Neither told – that I could learn –
> My Secret as secure
> As Herschel's private interest
> Or Mercury's Affair –

In Dickinson's opening simile, the narrator compares herself to someone "startled" to learn she has been named beneficiary of an estate, as Pip was surprised to discover that he was the recipient of some unidentified person's generosity. The speaker's mixed legacy resembles both an inheritance and a trust property. The benefit itself is mere existence; as ordained by both nature and God, the speaker possesses body and soul, a binary already encountered in "I am afraid to own a Body –." The word "Executors" points to a testamentary bequest, that is, nature and God promote whatever primal cause brought the speaker into being in the first place. Legally, an executor has been defined as "One to whom another man commits by his last will the execution of that will and testament" (*Bouvier's* 1: 727).

Like partners in a supposititious law firm, "Nature & God," the speaker's two benefactors are entrusted with the fact of her existence, God and nature behaving toward her as if she were a minor not yet fully capable of comprehending the duties requisite to Being. Dickinson's emphasis in this poem on surprise and secrecy, however, gestures toward the distinct legal formulation of a trust. In *Great Expectations,* Pip is surprised to receive news of his fortune from Jaggers, who, although a stranger to Pip, possesses a mysteriously profound personal knowledge of a boy heretofore considered to be thoroughly insignificant, and similarly, the speaker in this poem is astonished by Nature's and God's intimacy with her. As the daughter of an attorney, Dickinson would undoubtedly have been acquainted with situations in which unsuspecting young adults found themselves named in estate documents they did not know existed, predicated on legal and familial relationships that they, while still young, understood imperfectly, if at all. The death of a distant, perhaps childless relative could result in completely unforeseen, life-altering bequests being made to a named heir or beneficiary. Such information might arrive like a bolt from the blue, and the poem replicates the shock attendant on receiving this news, as well as a dawning comprehension of the responsibilities entailed in assuming so radically redefined a role. Dickinson's variant for "My," "an," suggests that she remained undecided whether to emphasize the particular identity of the poem's narrator, reinforced later in the poem by "My Secret," or an executor's duty to retain in confidence any heir's or trustee's identity, should a will or a trust so specify.

Dickinson's topical reference to "Herschel" and to Mercury is also significant. Sir William Herschel and his son John were notable astronomers during the eighteenth century and the early decades of the nineteenth. The mention of Herschel, a name synonymous with scientific achievement, helps reinforce the narrator's inclusion of Nature as one of the mysterious agents entrusted with her welfare. In 1802 the elder Herschel's observations of the transit of Mercury permitted a more accurate calculation of solar and interplanetary distances. Dickinson's reference, then, is probably to Sir William, in that she is comparing the very great distances between the sun and the planets existing on a scale heretofore unknown, and thus "secret," to the shroud of secrecy enveloping some trust arrangements. Determining the distance between Mercury and the sun is "Herschel's private interest," a matter of professional ambition for the astronomer, yet the poem's diction also introduces legal themes and words by using language generally reserved for the drafting of trust documents, which may be sealed by the court.[23] Dickinson's theme here would seem to be the opacity of the unknown, whether embodied in undisclosed legal facts or in undiscovered scientific facts.

Dickinson once stated to Susan Dickinson, in a note written around 1871, "Trust is better than Contract, for one is still, but the other moves" (L365). As a legal instrument, a trust agreement is superior to a contract, Dickinson seems to be implying, because it cannot be easily amended and because it requires such a high degree of fidelity from a trustee. Contracts operate within the realm of business, while trusts, although they too usually involve fiduciary duties, carry an additional moral burden. As characterized by Roger Andersen, trustees approved by a court must be "squeaky clean," above reproach, and they must "place the beneficiaries' interests above their own" (296). The constancy and durability of a legal trust in regulating the dispersal of testamentary assets may be referred to in "She laid her docile Crescent down" (F1453 B), written around 1877:[24]

She laid her docile Crescent down	| She / He her / his
And this mechanic Stone	| mechanic / confiding
Still states to Dates that have forgot	
The News that she is gone –	
So constant to it's stolid trust,	
The Shaft that never knew –	
It shames the Constancy that fled	
Before it's emblem flew –	

Here, in recording the birth and death dates of the deceased, whether female or male, the headstone of a grave is "constant to its stolid trust," with a superhuman devotion. The insentient stone cannot know what it records, its ignorance serving to insulate it, as if it were an automaton, from the emotional significance of the life it memorializes. Even the deceased woman, who may have faced her own death with resignation and equanimity ("She laid her docile Crescent down"), and who is remembered by the living as an exemplar of loyalty and "constancy," cannot rival the unconscious fidelity of her own memorial. In carrying out their duties either as guardians of the living or emissaries of the dead, trustees, like memorial stones, seemed to be held by the rigor of the law to an almost impossibly exacting standard of personal conduct, fiduciary rectitude, and enduring remembrance.

The necessity of maintaining so high a standard for legal and moral rectitude came home quite literally for the Dickinsons in Edward Dickinson's trusteeship and guardianship of his two nieces, Clara and Anna Newman. Mark Newman, Edward's brother-in-law, had been a well-to-do Brooklyn publisher. He died of tuberculosis when his five children were still quite young; Mary Newman, Edward Dickinson's sister, had already died of the same disease earlier that same year. Although possessed of a considerable estate, Mr. Newman prepared what Alfred Habegger describes as an "ill-advised will" bequeathing a good deal of his wealth to religious charities and benevolent societies. "Newman left only $25,000, a third of his net worth, to his five orphaned children," Habegger says (*My Wars* 283), requiring them to depend for a large measure of their material support on the benevolence of relatives, including the Dickinsons, who took in the youngest girls. Edward Dickinson pledged, as legal trustee of Mark Newman's estate and his nieces' guardian, to raise the girls in a Christian setting and to educate them until they became independent. Edward sought to place the Newman girls with various relatives in Amherst until he hit upon the solution of moving them into a new residence he would cause to be built for the newlyweds Austin and Sue, the house that would come to be known as the Evergreens.[25] After the birth of Austin's and Sue's children—Ned, Mattie, and Gilbert ("Gib")—Clara and Anna functioned informally as nannies or babysitters for their young second cousins.

At the heart of the controversy over Edward Dickinson's conduct as trustee for the Newman girls is his taking some of the money left in trust for their upkeep and education to build the Evergreens. It is unclear how Edward rationalized the transfer of funds; perhaps he could have justified it legally, if pressed to do so, by describing it as a measure taken to help ensure the girls' future security and educational advantages. In any event, after the house was built, Clara and Anna moved in with Austin and Sue in October 1858, with Clara remaining there until she married in 1869, and Anna for fourteen years until she herself married. Relations between the Newman girls and their hosts did not always run smooth. The sisters evidently resented being treated implicitly like servants, and Austin and Sue may have been only too keenly aware that the girls' trust funds had helped finance the roof under which they all resided. The degree of Edward's culpability in managing the Newman sisters' money is debatable. Nevertheless, no evidence has been forthcoming to indicate that the girls themselves resented the original trust arrangement bringing them to live in Amherst. In a memoir written after Emily Dickinson's poems were published posthumously, Clara Newman Turner remembered her poetical cousin fondly, while refraining from criticizing her uncle. According to Clara's own niece, Clara Newman Pearl, "His two nieces never wavered in their love and loyalty to their Uncle Edward" (Sewall 265).

Yet Edward Dickinson's borrowing from the Newmans' trust threatened to become a source of future legal headaches. Within the Dickinsons' extended family, Edward had already witnessed at first hand the legal difficulties that could arise from the misuse of trust funds. Loring and Albert Norcross, Emily Norcross Dickinson's brothers, were trustees to the estate of their brother William for the care of his children. Loring and Albert requested permission of the court of probate to invest trust funds in land in New Jersey, outside of their home state of Massachusetts. Attorney Edward Dickinson himself composed the brothers' petition to the court, where it was rejected; the Norcross brothers invested anyway, and managed to turn a considerable profit on resale of the land. The brothers claimed the profit, but the court subsequently decided they had enriched themselves at the expense of William's children, found them in breach of their fiduciary duty, and ordered them to pay the profit back into the trust. Once again, Edward Dickinson represented the brothers and, once again, lost. Thus lawyer Dickinson proved unable to defend his own wife's brothers successfully against allegations that they had, in effect, stolen from their nieces and nephews.

Habegger suggests that this consciousness of intrafamily feuds over trust fund monies and of defeats in court may have preyed on Edward

Dickinson's mind when he himself was entrusted with the Newman girls' care. Certainly Edward borrowed freely from the trust to build the Evergreens in 1857, so much so, according to Barton St. Armand, that when Clara wed in 1869, Edward had become indebted to the trust to the tune of $13,600, a huge amount (308). Edward finally compelled his son to begin paying for the house in which he and his wife had been living, yet Austin did not receive a deed to the house until his father died and he inherited ownership of the Evergreens as an asset in Edward Dickinson's estate.[26] Thus up until the very end of his life Edward Dickinson was saddled with complex familial, legal, and financial responsibilities as trustee for the Newman girls.[27]

Edward was present at Anna's wedding on June 3, 1874, which Jay Leyda has identified as the final social event he attended before succumbing two weeks later to complications brought on by a stroke (1: lxiv). For Anna's wedding, as well as for her older sister's some years earlier, Edward Dickinson would have been expected to distribute to the brides and their husbands a considerable portion of the trust estate as informal dowries, but it is unclear if he had the wherewithal to do so at that point. Penalties for mismanaging trust funds, or diverting them to one's own use (called "self-dealing"), were, and are, severe. Courts may compel trustees to repay such funds with interest, or they may order a transfer of custodial control to an alternative trustee. The question of whether financial embarrassments contributed to the mental and physical pressures working on Edward Dickinson at the time of his death cannot be answered definitively, and neither can the question of whether he really did breach his fiduciary duty in his handling of his nieces' estate.[28]

A few of Dickinson's poems may obliquely reflect her family's complicated legal and financial status at about the time of her father's death. Around 1874 she composed "The things we thought that we should do" (mentioning procrastination and speculative investments), "The Mushroom is the Elf of Plants –" (mentioning heirs' competition to be named in an estate), "Not One by Heaven defrauded stay –" (mentioning wills and fraud), and "Elizabeth told Essex" (employing the words "suing," "clemency," and "reprieving"). All of these legally inflected poems discuss futurity, in one way or another, sometimes explicitly in connection to the settling of estates. Yet at the time of her father's death, when she herself was forty-four years old, Dickinson may have been looking at law both retrospectively and prospectively. Convinced that her father represented a type of his generation which had adhered to high legal and moral standards exceeding those attained by her own contemporaries, Dickinson could nevertheless hardly avoid absorbing the example her father had also provided of human fallibility. For lawyers and for laypersons, the lesson was clear: the wishes of the dead are not always easily fulfilled, and not all trusts may indeed be compensated.

6

FELONIES, TRIALS, AND TRANSCENDENTAL PRISONS

Crime and Punishment

In the spring of 1850, John Webster, professor of chemistry at Harvard Medical School, was tried in Boston for killing his colleague Dr. George Parkman. From its opening day, March 19, the Parkman–Webster murder trial caused a sensation throughout New England, with sixty thousand people witnessing at least some part of the courtroom drama. Newspaper reporters commented on the stellar reputations of the attorneys who declined to represent Webster, including Daniel Webster (no relation) and Rufus Choate; on the Brahmin status of both victim and accused; and on the crime's grislier details, including the murderer's dismemberment of his victim before burning pieces of the body in a laboratory furnace and throwing the rest down a privy. Webster owed Parkman a considerable sum, and, when Parkman visited a lab at Harvard demanding payment, Webster impulsively killed him on the spot.

After deliberating for less than three hours the jury found Webster guilty, and on April 1 Judge Lemuel Shaw condemned him to be hanged, which sentence was duly carried out at the Leverett Street Jail on August 30.[1] One year later, in June 1851, Emily Dickinson wrote to Austin, who was teaching in Boston before he entered law school, many of his pupils drawn from recently arrived Irish immigrant families: "We are quite alarmed for the boys, hope you wont kill, or pack away any of em, so near Dr. Webster's bones t'ant strange you have had temptations!" (L43). Later in the same month she asked Austin, "have you whipped any more bad boys [?]" (L44). Humorously and grotesquely, the poet encourages her brother to emulate Webster by killing his troublesome pupils, and she also suggests that he has been using a whip to keep them in line.

A decade later, once Emily Dickinson had matured as a poet, her mind continued to revert often to the subjects of crime and punishment. She concerned herself with all stages of the legal system's treatment of arrested felons: trial, conviction, sentencing, punishment. Trials particularly attracted her attention, perhaps because, as public events, they manifested a wide range of human behaviors and emotions, providing a literarily minded observer with a nearly novelistic panorama of human types. Inside the courtroom, the voices of attorneys blended with those of witnesses, judge, and jury, and some of Dickinson's poems appear to emulate this legal heteroglossia through the deployment of a dialogic narrative voice. The treatment of convicted felons elicited her particular attention, and she vacillated between approving of corporal punishment, as she suggests in her letter to Austin, or empathizing intensely with the accused and the convicted.[2] She also recognized that new penal systems implemented during her young adulthood promised to make imprisoned life either more tolerable or more horrific than in times past. Unexpectedly, she herself also received a taste of what it was like to be jailed, blindfolded, and kept in solitary confinement.

Crime and punishment appear to have been much on Dickinson's mind during the winter of 1850, when she had turned twenty years old and a few months before she wrote her letter to Austin. At least, so we might assume after examining three other letters she wrote at that time which continue to treat the subject of criminality humorously and facetiously. At that early point in her adulthood Dickinson was in high spirits, having returned from her brief sojourn at Mount Holyoke Female Seminary to her cherished home and friends in Amherst. She had not yet established herself as a poet, yet all three of these passages adumbrate leitmotifs concerning crime and punishment that would resurface once she became a consciously literary artist. All contain topical references to issues absorbing the legal fraternity in the decades preceding the Civil War, including the insanity defense, corporal punishment, and penal reform.

Early on, Dickinson's assumption of the felon's role in her writing was apt to be both facetious and only mildly transgressive. On January 11, 1850, she composed a letter (L29) to a favorite uncle, Joel Norcross (her mother's brother), in which her exuberant wit is especially prominent:

> Harm is one of those things that I always mean to keep clear of – but somehow my intentions and me don't chime as they ought – and people will get hit with stones that I throw at my neighbor's dogs – not only hit – that is the least of the whole – but they insist upon blaming me instead of the stones – and tell me their heads ache – why it is the greatest piece of folly on record. It would do to go with a story I read – one man pointed a loaded gun at a man – and it shot him so that he died – and the people threw the owner of the gun into prison – and afterwards hung him for murder. Only another victim to the misunderstanding of society – such things should not be permitted – it certainly is as much as one's neck is worth to live in so stupid a world – and it makes one grow weary. Life is'nt what it purports to be. Now when I walk into your room and pluck your heart out that you die – I kill you – hang me if you like – but if I stab you while sleeping the dagger's to blame – it's no business of mine – you have no more right to accuse me of injuring you than anything else I can think of. That we understand capital punishment, and one another too I verily believe – and sincerely hope – for it's so trying to be read out of the wrong book when the right one is out of sight.

Dickinson's fondness for adopting personae is already on display here, long before she became a practicing poet. She presents herself to her uncle as a criminal, yet one who has been "a victim to the misunderstanding of society." She also hints broadly that she is insane, in that her justification for her criminality is legally preposterous. Her assignment of blame for her crimes to the weapon she wields is a parody of legal logic. But her implication that she is mentally ill refers indirectly to an absence of *mens rea,* that is, criminal intent, a subject much debated in antebellum America, partly as a result of some states' adoptions of Britain's M'Naghten rules. These were set forth in 1843 after Daniel

M'Naghten shot and killed Edward Drummond, Sir Robert Peel's secretary, thinking Drummond was the prime minister himself, and subsequently they became the basis for defenses made on the ground of insanity.[3] The M'Naghten rules or variations of them "won rapid acceptance in the United States," according to Lawrence Friedman (450–51). In Massachusetts, as early as 1844, Lemuel Shaw invoked a similar standard in *Commonwealth v. Rogers,* in which an inmate of the Massachusetts state prison alleged that disembodied voices had told him the prison warden wished to kill him. Dickinson poses as a homicidal maniac who is willing to risk being hanged for ridding the world of troublesome people: "it certainly is as much as one's neck is worth to live in so stupid a world – and it makes one grow weary." Elsewhere in the letter she threatens Joel directly: "I shall kill you."[4]

Joel Norcross almost certainly would have appreciated his talented young niece's extravagant impersonation of a deranged potential murderess.[5] But Dickinson's comical threats were not limited to members of her family. Only two weeks later, Dickinson wrote to her friend and former preceptress at Amherst Academy, Jane Humphrey, who had recently moved away. The future poet ventriloquizes various legal authorities who might inflict punishments on Jane for having deserted her: "The immortal Pickwick himself could'nt have been more amazed when he found himself soul – body and – spirit incarcerated in the pound than was I myself when they said she had gone – gone! Gone *how* – or *where* – or *why* – who saw her go – help – hold – bind – and keep her – put her into States-prison – into the House of Correction – bring out the long lashed whip – and put her feet in the stocks – and give her a number of stripes and make her repent her going!" (L30).

Although Samuel Pickwick is incarcerated for breach of promise (see chapter 3), not murder, Dickinson's comparison of herself to Dickens's bumbling hero was surely intended to be understood as being ridiculous on its face. Then, however, she veers toward the point of view of the accusers, rather than the accused. As Dickinson had reversed the roles of victim and assailant in the previous letter, here Jane is cast as the miscreant. For the crime of abandoning her friend, Jane is to be confined in "States-prison" and punished cruelly with a whip until she is made to "repent" her crime.

About one month later, Dickinson wrote, in a humorous valentine likely composed for George Gould, one of Austin Dickinson's classmates at Amherst: "But the world is sleeping in ignorance and error, sir, and we must be crowing cocks, and singing larks, and a rising sun to awake her; or else we'll pull society up to the roots, and plant it in a different place. We'll build Alms-houses, and transcendental State prisons, and scaffolds – we will blow out the sun, and the moon, and encourage invention. Alpha shall kiss Omega – we will ride up the hill of glory – Hallelujah, all hail!" (L34). Here Dickinson mocks the language of both revivalists and social engineers by importing stock phrases drawn from religious tracts and reform pamphlets. She facetiously invites Gould to join her in her ameliorating campaign, proposing that together they will save not only the country but the entire universe, as is signaled by her apocalyptic phrase "Alpha shall kiss Omega." But her references to "Alms-houses, and transcendental State prisons, and scaffolds" are, in their yoking of religion and reform, kindness and correction, internally contradictory, and thus examples of the same sort of rhetorical inversions made for the sake of satire she employed in the two previously quoted letters. The erecting of almshouses falls within the precincts of religious charity, but her adjective "transcendental" gestures instead toward antebellum penal reform, a cause taken up by Transcendentalists, including Emerson and Thoreau, as well as by Unitarians such as Emerson's fellow Bostonian Dorothea Dix. Penal reformers sought to emphasize penitence (as indicated by the newly minted noun "penitentiary") over punishment in the treatment of convicts, represented here metonymically by the word "scaffolds." Dickinson's helter-skelter coupling of these various, sometimes contradictory, clichés borrowed from social improvers of all sorts is a clear indication that Gould should not take her seriously, and that she does not yet take such ideas or people very seriously either.

Once Dickinson began actively pursuing her avocation as poet, these various references to crime, trial, and punishment found their way into her poetic metaphors and her formulation of narrating personae, although with several important modifications, including a tonal shift from satire to sympathy. The psychological effects of guilt and the obloquy connected with being identified as a convicted criminal are topics raised in two versions of a poem written when she was about twenty-seven years old (F57 A and B). According to Thomas Johnson, Dickinson penned these lines around 1858; Franklin dates the draft's composition to 1859:

I robbed the Woods –
The trusting Woods –
The unsuspecting Trees
Brought out their Burs and mosses
My fantasy to please –
I scanned their trinkets curious –
I grasped – I bore away –
What will the solemn Hemlock –
What will the Oak tree say?

Two or three years later the poet produced another version with radically altered pronouns, as well as few other more subtle changes:

Who robbed the Woods –
The trusting Woods?
The unsuspecting Trees
Brought out their Burs and Mosses –
His fantasy to please –
He scanned their trinkets – curious –
He grasped – he bore away –
What will the solemn Hemlock –
What will the Fir tree – say?

Major differences distinguishing these versions include who the criminal is and whether the mystery of the crime has been resolved. Dickinson moves from a personal statement of guilt made by a presumably female persona to a more objective, and possibly public, accusation of an identifiably *male* thief who has yet to be apprehended. In the first version, the narrator dreads that her crime will be discovered; in the second, although the crime is known the criminal is not, and the narrator speaks from the perspective of a shocked, but uninvolved, onlooker. The crime itself remains the same in both versions: shoplifting. In search of fragrant boughs (from the hemlock or the fir tree) and attractive curiosities of nature (burs, mosses, acorns), the female perpetrator in the poem's first version pilfers from the woods, taking whatever "trinkets" attract her eye without paying for them.[6] The underlying comparison is to jewelry put out on display by merchants in shop cases or on tables. Shoplifting is often a crime of opportunity, and it also tends to be a young person's crime, committed on impulse. The thief takes merchandise not for profit, but to "please" a "fantasy"; after all, these items are mere "trinkets." The perpetrator's youth is implicitly contrasted to the age and propriety of the venerable merchants, figured in the earlier version as the "solemn Hemlock" and the oak, a species celebrated for its sturdiness and longevity.[7] Punishment for having committed this petty theft is subordinated to the shame attached to being identified as the thief and to what people will say about her once her crime has been discovered.

Dickinson's shift in pronouns between versions produces a tangible difference in tone. The first is a confession, while the second generates an ongoing mystery. The initial version concentrates, from a subjective point of view, on the psychological effects of guilt, while the second takes a more objective, investigative, and even prosecutorial tone, as the narrator wonders aloud who could be so debased as to filch a nearly worthless item from an old and trusting shopkeeper. In both versions, an underlying irony obtains in that taking souvenirs from nature results in no monetary loss, so no actual crime has been committed. The projected juvenile speaker of the first draft is just beginning to comprehend how merchandise might be appraised according to capitalistic systems of exchange, as opposed to the gratification of her own desires or "fantasy." In the second draft, the transferal of responsibility for the "crime" to a male suggests that during the process of revision Dickinson decided that doing so might make the unknown perpetrator seem more menacing and mysterious. Readers may judge for themselves whether the second version's narrative suspense represents an aesthetic improvement over the first draft's psychological impact as a first-person expression of a young person's guilt, remorse, and shame.

Aside from the first version of "I robbed the Woods –," a handful of other poems refer to the commission of crimes from a first-person point of view. Of these, one of the more notable examples is "I know some Lonely houses off the Road" (F311), in which the poem's speaker would appear to be identifying with someone intending to commit a burglary.[8] From an early age, Emily and Lavinia had been warned by their parents to watch out for "prowling 'booger[s]'" (L281), and the poet's instilled fear of burglars and second-story men may be reflected by the scene the poem describes:

I know some lonely Houses off the Road
A Robber'd like the look of –

Wooden barred,
And Windows hanging low,
Inviting to –
A Portico,
Where two could creep –
One – hand the Tools –
The other peep –
To make sure all's asleep –
Old fashioned eyes –
Not easy to surprise!

How orderly the Kitchen'd look, by night –
With just a Clock –
But they could gag the Tick –
And Mice wont bark –
And so the Walls – dont tell –
None – will –

A pair of Spectacles ajar just stir –
An Almanac's aware –
Was it the Mat – winked,
Or a nervous Star?
The Moon – slides down the stair,
To see who's there!

There's plunder – where –
Tankard, or Spoon –
Earring – or Stone –
A Watch – Some Ancient Brooch
To match the Grandmama –
Staid sleeping – there –

Day – rattles – too –
Stealth's – slow –
The Sun has got as far
As the third Sycamore –
Screams Chanticleer
"Who's there"?

And Echoes – Trains away,
Sneer – "Where"!
While the old Couple, just astir,
Fancy the Sunrise – left the door ajar!

Here, the narrator adopts the perspectives of both victim *and* perpetrator. Although the speaker begins, almost conspiratorially, by declaring she (or he) knows of a house ripe for burgling, Dickinson's narration derives a good deal of suspense by identifying not just with the human actors in this crime drama, but also with various nonhuman mute witnesses. For example, the rooster, although he "speaks" by crowing, cannot make himself understood to the farmer and his wife. The "I" in the poem's initial line exists in tension with the elided—virtually *gagged*—voices of the household's nonhuman inhabitants: clock, mice, walls, spectacles, almanac, mat, star, moon, "Chanticleer," and echoes. All are potential reporters of the robbery, yet, being inarticulate or inanimate, they literally cannot alert the old couple to what is happening. Their muteness also emphasizes the robbers' stealth, while simultaneously generating an atmosphere hinting at the supernatural, as if the house were already haunted by silent specters. Finally, by allying shifts in point of view with the activity of *witnessing*, Dickinson reinforces a nearly complicitous stance the poem takes toward the crime: the narrator won't tell what happened, and neither will various household objects. It's important to note that the burglary detailed in this miniature crime narrative was successful, the old couple left gaping, at the poem's end, to discover their door has been left open by the criminals, yet unconscious even of the fact that they have been robbed.

Dickinson's phrase "Trains away" may also indirectly reflect early civic misgivings about bringing the railroad to Amherst, in that although it did promise to spur commerce, the railroad also threatened to give undesirable outsiders easy access to the town and a quick means of escaping the forces of the law. The "old fashioned" nature of the crime victims, partially emphasized by the inclusion of virtual farmhouse clichés such as the almanac, mice, and "Chanticleer," is set in implicit opposition to the sophisticated technology of rail travel. Dickinson's elided first-person narration in the poem, which hovers, in the initial stanzas, between objective narration and subjective identification with the robbers, helps situate her own sympathies between an enthusiasm for innovation (such as her father may have had, in bringing rail travel to Amherst) and traditional rural or small-town values, emblematized by the "Ancient Brooch."[9]

Jury trials may have provided Dickinson with an especially rich example of perspectival multiplicity. They were the great public spectacles of the

Victorian age, and newspapers competed to report not only what was said in court but also the public's reaction to courtroom events, providing yet another layer of narratological complexity. The Parkman–Webster murder trial, the Beecher–Tilton adultery trial in 1875, the trial of Lizzie Borden in 1892—all of these elevated trial participants, whether defendants, attorneys, or judges, virtually to celebrity status. Lawrence Friedman has written of major Victorian trials in America, "Cases of this sort were, in essence, great theater. . . . Everybody loves a mystery; everybody loves a courtroom drama. The great cases were also the ones in which all the stops were pulled out; juries were carefully and laboriously chosen; trials were long and crammed with detail; both sides marshaled evidence, introduced experts, battled and sparred on cross-examination, and due process was meticulously observed. These trials were replete with sensational events, witnesses who wept or fainted, grisly evidence and exhibits, and vast flights of purple oratory" (436–37). For famous trials, such as the Webster murder case, courts had to issue tickets to cope with the crush of spectators vying for good seats. Textual evidence suggests that Dickinson was particularly drawn by the inherent theatricality of jury trials, and that she enjoyed replicating their polyvocalism in her poems. Dickinson was already adept at delineating personae of all sorts from a comparatively early point in her artistic maturation, and the poems she wrote about legally inflected situations provide especially trenchant examples of what Paul Crumbley and others have identified as her distinctively dialogic voice, that is, her facility for identifying with, and speaking through, the narratival perspectives of several speakers within a single work.[10]

Criminal trials involve several features allying them to novelistic and dramatic productions—dialogue, character development, a narrative (the crime itself), plotlike turns in the discovery of facts, suspense, and perhaps a denouement, in the delivery of a verdict and the pronouncing of sentence. But trials are not intended, of course, to serve as public entertainments; instead, they resolve disputes. Dickinson, as the daughter of an attorney, would have understood that many legal actions involve competing *legitimate* claims, and accordingly some of her poems demonstrate a relativistic, and ultimately realistic, attitude toward complex interpersonal relations existing in a society operating under the rule of law. Courts, in their hearings, labor to find equitable solutions and resolutions amid what may seem at first a cacophony of voices, and

Dickinson's dialogic voice, exercised through the medium of her various narrating personae, provides a powerful tool for representing that effort.[11]

We have already seen Dickinson conveying the varied voices of law through the speech of her poetic speakers, such as the outraged, litigious property owner in "I had some things that I called mine –," the diffident, prudish deponent in "Alone and in a Circumstance," and the panicky bargainer negotiating a contract in "What would I give to see his face?" She may have understood her own dialogic process as being both internal, in the generation of a poem, and external, in her representation of the contesting voices of the law. "Shall I take thee, the Poet said" (F1243) depicts a poet listening to various inner promptings before settling on a means of expressing her thought—or, alternatively, rejecting the need to express herself altogether:

> Shall I take thee, the Poet said
> To the propounded word?
> Be stationed with the Candidates
> Till I have finer tried – | finer / vainer / further
>
> The Poet searched Philology | searched / probed
> And was about to ring | was / just / when
> For the suspended Candidate
> There came unsummoned in – | There came / Advanced
> That portion of the Vision
> The Word applied to fill
> Not unto nomination
> The Cherubim reveal –

Despite the poem's objectification of "the Poet," its presiding consciousness may also be imagined simultaneously or alternatively as that of an attorney or a judge, perhaps as they participate in a preliminary stage of trial, a voir dire, the selection of jurors. Legally freighted words are given prominence throughout. The adjective "unsummoned" calls to mind summonses issued to potential jurors, or veniremen, and "finer tried," in its echoing of *trial,* suggests that the speaker is sifting the qualifications of the various "Candidates." "Propounded" is a term applicable in several legal contexts, here, evidently, as a synonym for "suggested" or "eligible"—although it remains to be seen for what office, exactly, these personified words are submitting themselves.[12] In a variant, Dickinson considered replacing "searched" in the third stanza's first line with "probed," a word suggestive both of an attorney's investigations into a potential juror's background, and of the *probative* habit of mind common to attorneys and magistrates. "Came unsummoned" may echo the archaic phrase used to begin a pleading, "Comes now," as in the phrase, "Comes now the plaintiff, John Doe. . . ." That Dickinson may have meditated using a variant for line 8, "Advanced" for "There came," again suggests that what had been a deliberative process is interrupted peremptorily by a "portion of the Vision," which seizes a position antithetical and oppositional to the applicant "Word."

One of the more important aspects of jury empanelment is the selection of a foreman, a procedure that may also be reflected in "Shall I take thee, the Poet said." Before a trial begins, a foreman (or, today, foreperson) is elected by the seated jury members or appointed by the court. Judges have often looked among members of a jury for an individual demonstrating particular acuity, maturity, or educational attainment. If the rest of the jury elected this individual, well and good; yet courts also reserved the right to accept or refuse the jury's selection of a foreman. As *Bouvier's* describes the process: "Being called into the jury-box, they [i.e., members of the jury] are usually permitted to select a foreman, whom the court appoints; but the court may exercise the right to nominate one for them" (1: 898). Selecting an appropriate foreman could be crucial to the conduct of the trial in several ways: he might speed proceedings along by interpreting them for the benefit of fellow jurors, he might maintain order and discipline among their ranks, and, when the time arrived for reaching a verdict, he might urge them toward unanimity. Although judges did have the discretion to nominate a foreman, the spontaneous, voluntary appearance of such an individual from among the jurors would have lifted a burden from a judge's shoulders. One of the speakers, or actors, in "Shall I take thee, the Poet said" may be such a judge. Dissatisfied, initially, with various candidates for the position of foreman, the judge is pleasantly surprised when a jury member comes forward "unsummoned" and plainly demonstrates that he is suited for the task. The court is gratified to have found its wish fulfilled, despite the absence of a "nomination."

But "nomination" has, of course, a twofold sense. Dickinson may be anthropomorphizing her own creative process in the poem or, alternatively, an occasion on which her muse had failed or even *transcended* her. A comparison of words to persons pervades the poem. While a trial attorney interviewing prospective jurors might search the range of humanity, the Poet searches "Philology." That Dickinson could conceive of the poetic process as resembling jury selection has several potentially far-reaching implications. First, she may equate the professionalism displayed by poets engaged in the act of writing with that of legal practitioners. Second, she may have envisioned the process of drafting and selecting words as not just being judicial, but also egalitarian and democratic, with the words themselves given some voice in how or whether they are to be used. Third, she may suggest that the entire poetic process itself could be invalidated by chance: a rogue thought or insight might render her search for *le mot juste* superfluous.

There are other poems in which Dickinson presents the process of writing as being only somewhat volitional—"Publication – is the Auction," "Myself was formed – a Carpenter –," or (most appropriately, perhaps) "I found the words to every thought." "Shall I take thee, the Poet said," in describing its protagonist poet cum attorney cum magistrate, evidently frames the creative process itself as objective, deliberative, and painstaking, yet also subject to forces beyond the poet's control. Early in the poem, the projected "Poet" of the first line appears confident of her abilities and her duties, and she is determined to see the business of the muse done. Dickinson's language aptly captures her own poetic method, as, in draft after draft, she composed arrays of variants in striving to articulate her meaning. The poet in the poem treats the various candidates for inclusion in her poem fairly and equitably, addressing them in a tone that is simultaneously respectful and imperative before seating them together in her figure ("Be stationed"), as if their ranks in the jury box resembled her assembly of words into lines and stanzas.[13]

When inspiration does finally arrive, unheralded, its very authoritativeness derives from a private conviction that although it may be courted, inspiration will not be commanded or cajoled. As Emerson wrote in "Merlin" (a poem included in his 1847 collection *Poems,* which Dickinson owned):

> Sudden, at unawares,
> Self-moved, fly-to the doors,
> Nor sword of angels could reveal
> What they conceal.

For Dickinson, poetic inspiration could have seemed inherently hazardous in that the arrival of the muse, however tardy, might obviate the need for language itself. Like a "candidate" whose qualifications far outdistance his competitors', the missing "portion of the Vision," once it appears, may transcend the need for poetic expression altogether.

Jury trials could encounter the unforeseen as well, and within the legal community the risks involved in going to trial have been proverbial.[14] However strenuously legal professionals might attempt to control events unfolding within the courtroom, surprises or new information could upset the applecart. For example, new evidence might utterly alter a case's complexion, exonerating the defendant or shifting responsibility to someone not yet indicted. On the eve of trial, a defendant might change his mind and confess or stipulate to a plea, eliminating the need for a jury altogether. Such unexpected developments could obviate hours of legal labor already invested in gearing up to go to trial. On a more positive note, courtroom surprises might save an attorney the effort of mounting his case before a jury, or relieve a judge of the moral responsibility of sending a potentially innocent man to jail or the gallows.

A comparatively early and playful poem by Dickinson (F371) depicts a courtroom situation in which the outcome is indeed a surprise, one not revealed until the poem's last line, which replicates the announcement of a verdict. The poem also imitates the sort of real-time reportage that riveted Victorian readers to accounts of events transpiring within the courtroom, although in this particular instance the decision may come down not from a jury but from the bench, and the matter at law is presented perhaps intentionally as being trivial in comparison to major jury trials. The projected dialogic narrator, while staking out a position as an interested, first-person participant, may also inhabit various voices involved in the conduct of a trial:

> Is Bliss then, such Abyss —
> I must not put my foot amiss
> For fear I spoil my shoe?
>
> I'd rather suit my foot
> Than save my Boot —
> For yet to buy another Pair

Is possible,
At any store –

But Bliss, is sold just once.
The Patent lost
None buy it any more –
Say, Foot, decide the point –
The Lady cross, or not?
Verdict for Boot!

That Dickinson wishes us to read the poem as a mock legal argument is indicated not just by the final line's reference to a verdict, but also by the presence of other legally inflected terms, including "suit," "Patent," "cross," and "point." Her intent is also signaled by the poem's construction, which follows the classic rhetorical form of a legal brief. The first stanza presents the "question in point," that is, whether to abandon oneself to bliss by walking through a puddle. The second stanza presents the argument mounted by the plaintiff, in this case the foot, and then the position of the defendant, the boot. The last three lines distill the underlying question—to splash through the puddle or go around it?—and deliver the court's opinion. Nevertheless, that opinion may not be the one we expected or even were hoping for, and to see what Dickinson might be trying to accomplish in this poem, we could begin by considering what "Bliss" in the poem's first line means. I offer two, perhaps not mutually exclusive, readings.

The first concentrates on moral dilemmas and choices. Although the obstacle confronting the narrator is only a puddle, Dickinson's selection of the word "Abyss" as the rhyme for "Bliss" inevitably brings to mind the figural void into which, during the Victorian era, fallen women were thought to have cast themselves. Read in this light, the poem becomes, especially in the first stanza, a protest against a puritanically rigid moral climate in which the slightest sexual indiscretion may be interpreted as the first step taken on the road to perdition, from which the body, represented synecdochically by the foot, cannot ever be returned to a state of unfallen virginity. After her fall, which may be a consequence of having pursued sexual "bliss," the sinning woman's body is equated with damaged goods that "None buy . . . any more," meaning that such a woman might as well give up all hope of finding a marriage partner. Indeed, the poem may be read as a satirical attack on narrow-minded priggishness, particularly if we concentrate on Dickinson's humorously ironic comparison of a moral abyss to a mud puddle.[15] Then, the subsequent "lawsuit" brought by a foot against the encasing boot becomes part of the poem's satirical apparatus as well, a sort of reductio ad absurdum that pokes fun at the way prudes think. However much we may applaud Dickinson's playful, perhaps pointed characterization of the "Abyss" into which a fallen woman may plunge as the merest shallow puddle (an *anti*-abyss) and her evident dismissal of the conventional notion that women should remain paragons of virtue who never permit themselves to stray, the poem's ending is not at all we might expect, or perhaps hope, to see. The jury, or the judge, or the foot itself comes down firmly in favor of playing it safe by going around the puddle, avoiding temptation altogether by skirting the abyss.

A second possible reading, concentrating instead on hedonic values and the law, might go as follows. A nineteenth-century New England woman shod in a pair of expensive patent leather boots encounters a puddle in her path. If the puddle is very shallow, she may be able to walk right through it without harm, since the water will reach up only to her boot soles. Moreover, she enjoys walking through puddles in this manner; it is a minor form of "Bliss" for her, reminiscent, perhaps, of childhood. If the puddle turns out to be deep, however, walking through it will damage her boots beyond repair. As can be the case with puddles, she may not be able to gauge precisely how deep this one is, so she is confronted momentarily with the dilemma of balancing the risk to her property against a potential hedonic reward, "Bliss." Then the poem becomes a straightforward economic analysis. First, the poem's nominal speaker reasons that even if the puddle is deep and she does ruin her shoes, she can always buy another pair, and easily, "at any store." Moreover, if she refrains from indulging her impulse, she might not enjoy another chance to splash through so inviting a puddle. Unlike her shoes, bliss—once lost—cannot be replaced or traded for. In other words, the "Patent" on bliss expires, the pun on *patent* serving as a figural pivot around which the poem turns, representing simultaneously the endangered shoe, made of patent leather, and the opportunity to experience bliss. Dickinson's conflation of economic and emotive incentives may be intentional. The "price" of bliss is loss of her shoes, but her footwear is, in the language of law and economics, a "fungible good," while this particular form of bliss will never be available for purchase again, at any price: "None buy it any more." Foregone bliss also resembles the shoe that is no longer fashionable, or the boot that laces up according to a proprietary design for which the patent has now expired, in that such bliss cannot be bought because it cannot be *found,* whether in the stores or within the adult self. The speaker (whoever that may be) finally resolves the problem by resubmitting the question to the plaintiff foot, which decides pragmatically to conserve shoe leather and save money.[16]

Both of these readings work, in that they provide contextual foundations for the poem's humor, as well as rationales for its having been structured as a legal argument. What we have not yet clarified, however, is why Dickinson employs so many different narrative points of view. After all, the poem begins by being narrated in the first person, but in the final stanza, the conflicted walker is objectified as "The Lady." And who delivers the verdict? A judge? A jury foreman? The defendant, her foot? A court reporter addressing a waiting public? Of course, all of the poem's personae are, to some extent, avatars or manifestations of the narrator's internal dialogue as she debates whether to wade through the puddle. But Dickinson's dialogic voice also serves to represent competing interests involved in a legal action, as well as to resituate a private dilemma within the larger forum of public opinion.

The primary speaker in the poem does not seem to know what she will do until the end of the poem, and neither do we. Dickinson lays the groundwork for her surprise ending carefully by leading us to believe the decision will be made for foot, not boot.[17] For one thing, we would probably expect a poet to be biased toward bliss, not to come down conservatively on the side of economic prudence and adult self-restraint. Secondly, the "legal brief" Dickinson supplies in this poem appears to be inclining, right before the poem concludes, toward the pro-bliss, pro-foot faction. A third, and more unconscious, reason we may be surprised is the rhyme between "foot" and "boot." Phonetic similarity helps imply an ostensible relative equivalency between the two positions for which they are metonymic exponents. The poem's ending may finally also surprise readers because it doesn't make legal sense, at least not from a procedural standpoint. If the plaintiff "foot" has decided to pass up the pleasure of walking through a puddle in order to preserve the shoe, then a settlement, of sorts, has been reached, negating the necessity of seeking a decision from the bench. But Dickinson's representation of this mundane fashion decision as a legal question for which there is no single, clear-cut answer points to the relativism of law, that is, its role in resolving disputes. Relativistic thinking is demanded particularly of trial judges in untangling plaintiffs' and defendants' contending claims and interests. Thus the judge in this poem says, as if to a plaintiff or a jury foreman, "Say, Foot, decide the point – / The Lady cross, or not?" Dickinson's assumption of competing, dialogic voices replicates the law's forensic methods.

Dickinson's use of polyvocalism to depict the various and complicated interrelationships of the principals in a lawsuit, of the individual's connection to the state, and of court functionaries' and employees' performance of their courtroom tasks is also evident in another comparatively early poem (F432), whose miniature trial narrative addresses the resolution of a matter much more serious than protecting one's shoes: capital punishment.

> I read my sentence – steadily –
> Reviewed it with my eyes,
> To see that I made no mistake
> In it's extremest clause –
> The Date, and manner, of the shame –
> And then the Pious Form
> That "God have mercy" on the Soul
> The Jury voted Him –
> I made my soul familiar – with her extremity –
> That at the last, it should not be a novel Agony –
> But she, and Death, acquainted –
> Meet tranquilly, as friends –
> Salute, and pass, without a Hint –
> And there, the Matter ends –

The narrator of this poem occupies, I suggest, five different roles, possibly six: the accused, a second accused, defense attorney, judge, prison chaplain, and the poet herself. The fact that two prisoners are involved is indicated by the narrator's inclusion of both "Him," in the eighth line, and "her," in the ninth. Although they may be a couple, possibly lovers, still we are presented with several choices for determining who the "him" and "her" in this poem might be—perhaps an external-ized, apostrophized body and soul, as in Whitman's "Song of Myself," or two different facets of the soul, perhaps a mortal and an immortal part. Whatever their identities, these twin prisoners have been convicted of a "shame," a sin or a crime, which, although unspecified, is apparently so egregious as to be considered a capital offense.[18] Although Dickinson inverts the order of handing down verdict and sentence, her deployment of such specific legal terms as "sentence," "Form," and "Matter" (*Bouvier's* defines "matter" as "a fact or facts constituting the whole or a part of a ground of action or defence"; 2: 342) and her emphatically dispassionate, almost bureaucratic, syntax emphasize the precision, correctness, and propriety of these proceedings, traumatic though they may be for the defendant(s).[19] The narrator of the poem's final line, in assuming a mag-isterial, almost imperious point of view, may represent simultaneously overbearing, nearly irresistible, authority, as well as the numb, submissive attitude of the condemned.[20]

At the same time, however, the poet permits other words to accumu-late extralegal meanings leading toward other interpretive possibilities, some of them deconstructive. The word "sentence" can also mean, of course, a sentence written by a poet, and "extremest," in conjunction with "extremity," conflates a clause's syntactical position with the severity of legally sanctioned punishment, as well as with the extremity of life, as in *extreme* unction. In distinguishing among, or rather in surrendering the necessity of distinguishing among, the various voices and actors in this courtroom drama, we should begin, I suggest, with the poem's initial pronoun. "I" may stand, concurrently, for the condemned prisoner who dreads reading the sentence he has received; the judge, who, like virtually all judges (and especially those adjudicating capital crimes) expends great care in crafting a deliberated final sentence so that it cannot be appealed or overturned; the defense attorney, who must be able to explain the legal language of the court's sentence to his guilty client; the chaplain, who comforts the condemned by making the "soul – familiar – with [its] extremity –," and the poet herself, who continuously checks her own *sentences* for flaws of wording or syntax.

Let us suppose, for a moment, that Dickinson is commenting on the precision of her own writing of *this* poem. Significantly, the "extremest clause" of the first sentence of this poem, following Dickinson's apparent syntax, is "The Jury voted *Him* –." We might also speculate that the poem's primary narrator intends to emphasize the dual gender(s) of the accused—it is no "mistake." Moreover, although the phrase "Reviewed it with my eyes" may initially strike us as redundant, Dickinson's intention may be to clarify the meaning of "read" in the first sentence; that is, the court's sentence is being read by the prisoner, after it has been pronounced out loud by the judge. Furthermore, the poem's entwining of exact writing and careful reading is also sustained by a recurrent emphasis on *form*. An official death sentence had to conform to strict formal criteria—first the date of the offense, the nature of the crime, and then the punishment to be meted out, followed by the ritualistic injunction, "May God have mercy on your soul."

The presence of an identified "Other" in Dickinson's writings would seem to be one more corollary of her dialogic practice. Many poems involve paralleling punitive experiences suffered by a primary narrator and an externalized Other; together, they constitute a nearly twinned corporate identity. Discerning these poems' narratological stances may be made problematic for readers by perhaps deliberately obscured pronominal references, and by the porosity of the margin separating a poem's speakers from its actors. Such is the case in " 'Twas Love – not me –" (F562), which describes a whipping or beating administered for some unspecified moral transgression, the speaker suggesting that she and the Other are victims of a case of mistaken identity:

> 'Twas Love – not me –
> Oh punish – pray –
> The Real One died for Thee –
> Just Him – not me –
>
> Such Guilt – to love Thee – most!
> Doom it beyond the Rest –
> Forgive it – last –
> 'Twas base as Jesus' – most!
>
> Let Justice not mistake –
> We Two – looked so alike –
> Which was the Guilty Sake –
> 'Twas Love's – Now Strike!

Like a convicted and sentenced defendant, the narrator of this poem protests she has been found guilty only of the crime of love, which, she quite logically points out, Jesus committed, too. The narrator may be addressing a lover, protesting that he or she has convicted her of loving him or her too much. In such a case, Dickinson suggests, the instrument and not the agent should be held accountable, as the "dagger" deserved to be convicted, in her letter to Joel Norcross, rather than whoever wielded it. The narrator's lover/persecutor/prosecutor has unwittingly confused two perpetrators, herself and Love; small wonder, she says, since they look so much alike. Despite the chance that she might be able to construct a defense based on an allegation of mistaken identity, she volunteers herself for punishment, inviting her shadowy inquisitor, named only as abstract "Justice," to carry out the sentence, her altruism serving as indirect proof that she is in love, and that therefore love itself is to blame, not she. Alternatively, her invitation to authority to punish her may serve as an admission of guilt—she is Love, and Love is she—so that her defense of her actions merges powerfully with an admission of culpability. The emotional reality of losing oneself in love is exemplified by the speaker's own confusion over whether she is responsible or not. In this poem, Dickinson's polyvocalism serves to complicate the issue of guilt and responsibility, the mistaking of identities and personae, and the question of agency.

The Other, in Dickinson's descriptions of punishment and imprisonment, may be a complementary component of the Self, an absent lover, a missing twin, or an accomplice in crime. Often the narrators of such poems state that they must find, or at least attempt to find, the subtracted halves of themselves, who are, like them, locked away in a prison cell or dungeon. I have commented elsewhere on Dickinson's fondness for Byron's poem "The Prisoner of Chillon."[21] Drawing on the isolate heroism of Byron's imprisoned narrator, Bonnivard, who must witness his brothers dying beside him in the cell they all occupy, Dickinson constructed her own metanarrative integrating the themes of solitary confinement, a missing other, and the threat of corporal punishment. "I had not minded – Walls –" (F554), written around 1862, is representative of the subgenre:

> I had not minded – Walls –
> Were Universe – one Rock –
> And far I heard his silver Call
> The other side the Block –

I'd tunnel – till my Groove
Pushed sudden thro' to his –
Then my face take her Recompense –
The looking in his Eyes –

But 'tis a single Hair –
A filament – a law –
A Cobweb – wove in Adamant –
A Battlement – of Straw –

A limit like the Vail
Unto the Lady's face –
But every Mesh – a Citadel –
And Dragons – in the Crease –

Without revisiting comments I have made about this poem elsewhere
(*Emily Dickinson's Vision* 72–73), I want for the moment to concentrate
on details characterizing the speaker's carcerative experience. As readers,
evidently we are being invited to enjoy vicariously the potential reunion
of imprisoned halves, one male, one female. Reunion is each prisoner's goal, and an essential equality between the two is established by
their mutual determination to tunnel from their respective cells to meet
again, almost as if each prisoner were reduced to a geometric abstraction,
and the distance between them to the shortest distance between two
points.[22] Note that these separated prisoners don't tunnel to escape, but
rather to be reunited, so that the image of reunion may suggest sexual
union, fraternal (or sororal) sympathy, or the reconjoining of separated
twins.[23] The narrator, despite her avowed willingness to exert herself in
achieving the desired rendezvous, confesses that she has been defeated
from doing so by abstractions, societal interdictions, and moral prohibi-
tions. She and the Other are isolated from each other by rules, not walls.
The insubstantiality of the narrator's situation is reinforced by a corresponding consciously Romantic, even Gothic, diction gesturing toward
fictions—"Battlement," "Citadel," "Dragons." This last term serves to
indicate not only the moral obloquy the lovers would face should they
be reunited, but also their physical punishment: it would be comparable
to being incinerated by a dragon's breath.[24]

Whipping, isolation, a missing Other—all of these Dickinsonian topoi
may be rooted, to some degree, in nineteenth-century debates about

penal reform. Dating from Dickinson's 1850 references to "transcendental" prisons and to whipping in her letters to Jane Humphrey and to George Gould, the poet's references to methods of incarceration and to corporal punishment participate in the larger cultural context of America's antebellum reconsideration of how prisons should be designed, and how prisoners should be managed and treated. This debate took place as part of wider campaign waged largely by Transcendentalists, Unitarians, and other reform-minded groups seeking to reassess how marginalized populations—prisoners, the mentally ill, and, ultimately, slaves—should be restrained.

American reform movements at midcentury coincided with the poet's transition from girlhood to adulthood. The Dickinsons, staunch law-and-order Whigs, may be presumed to have been more receptive to schemes concerning penal reform and the treatment of the insane than they would have been to the outright abolition of slavery. In the decade preceding the Civil War, proposals for reforming prisons appeared regularly in liberal New England periodicals such as the *Christian Examiner* and the *North American Review.* An avid reader of contemporary journals, Dickinson would have been acutely aware, especially while a young woman, of various penological theories being advanced by antebellum reformers. Chief among these was Dorothea Dix, who discovered sympathetic audiences in the clergy, in government, and in fellow reformers such as Ralph Waldo Emerson. Herself the product of a Boston Brahmin upbringing, Dix lobbied indefatigably for the rights of various disadvantaged groups. Her work on behalf of the insane, for example, in agitating for better conditions in state asylums and the establishment of a federal system to fund mental hospitals, won her plaudits in the press and from legislators.[25] Before turning her attention to the insane, however, Dix had already established a reputation as a champion of prison reform, her 1845 survey of American penal institutions, *Remarks on Prisons and Prison Discipline,* having been reviewed warmly on both sides of the Atlantic (Brown 134–35).

Dix's intercession in the cause of prison reform was timely. In the three decades preceding the Civil War, Americans were engaged in a sometimes heated debate over the treatment of prisoners. Emphasis was shifting overall from the punishment of convicts to their rehabilitation; as Lawrence Friedman observes, "The modern prison—the penitentiary—is a product of the nineteenth century" (219). Pennsylvania and New York took the lead in experimenting with prisons constructed and administered on revolutionary principles of incarceration and correction. Generally penal reformers split into two factions: those favoring the "congregate" approach and those favoring the "separate" approach, also known as the Philadelphia system, or, more often, the Auburn system, after Auburn Prison in New York State, an early adopter of the plan (Brown 129; see also Friedman, 220–21). The congregate system, true to its name, permitted prisoners to work together in prison factories; nevertheless, as Thomas J. Brown writes, "while these activities went on, prison guards sought to enforce absolute silence, often with a whip" (130). Prisons run on the Auburn system, on the other hand, rather than depending on physical intimidation to maintain order, isolated inmates from each other both day and night, while simultaneously enforcing the same rule of silence observed by the congregate system. At Cherry Hill, a model prison in Philadelphia conceived according to the "separate" doctrine, the architecture itself replicated the omnipotence and omniscience of penal authorities: "Great stone arms radiated out of a central core. Each arm contained a number of individual cells connected to tiny walled courtyards, one to a cell. The prisoners spent their lives in their cell and courtyard, utterly alone, night and day. Sometimes they wore masks. Through peepholes, the prisoners could listen to religious services. In both Auburn and Cherry Hill, absolute silence was imposed on the prisoners—a punishment crueler perhaps than the flogging and branding that were, in theory, done away with" (Friedman 220).[26]

Charles Dickens visited Cherry Hill and came away appalled. Interested in prison reform himself—one has only to remember such characters as Pickwick, William Dorrit, and Micawber—Dickens concluded that the Auburn system was a dreadful mistake. In *American Notes* he wrote, "Those who devised this system of Prison Discipline, and those benevolent gentlemen who carry it into execution, do not know what it is that they are doing. . . . Over the head and face of every prisoner who comes into this melancholy house, a black hood is drawn; and in this dark shroud . . . he is led to the cell from which he never again comes forth, until his whole term of imprisonment has expired" (131, 133). Massachusetts adopted the Auburn system at the state prison at Charlestown in 1828, not abandoning it until the 1840s (Friedman 220–21).

Dorothea Dix, however, after visiting various prisons and jails in several states, generally favored the separate scheme over the congregate, if only because the latter emphasized beatings and whippings, which she deplored (Brown 130).[27] During her investigations she corresponded intermittently with Emerson, who sympathized with her interest in prisons and encouraged her to publish her findings. Dix, while admiring Emerson's efforts on behalf of reforms in institutions, never warmed to the version of personal reform endorsed by Transcendentalism or the Transcendentalists; rather, to the end of her life she subscribed to a Calvinistically rooted Unitarian orthodoxy emphasizing not just reason, but also self-discipline and an acceptance of moral responsibility.[28]

In the public mind, at least, all such efforts at prison reform may have come to be lumped together, an attitude perhaps responsible for Dickinson's joking reference to "transcendental State prisons" in her valentine. Five years before Dickinson wrote those words, Dix's pamphlet *Remarks on Prisons and Prison Discipline* was published, its expenses underwritten in part by Emerson. No direct evidence exists to show that Dickinson ever saw the pamphlet, although it was reviewed positively in the *Christian Examiner* and endorsed by James Kent, eminent jurist and chancellor of the New York Court of Chancery (Brown 134–35). Edward Dickinson probably read about Dix's study with professional interest, but his daughter belonged to a younger generation for whom once-revolutionary ideas concerning prison reform had become outdated and perhaps tiresome—thus the facetious tone of the poet's reference. Moreover, by 1850 the issue had lost much of its currency, Massachusetts having abandoned the Auburn system a decade earlier as a failed experiment.

Later in life, however, Dickinson may have renounced her youthful insouciance on the issue of prison reform. In a letter sent to Thomas Wentworth Higginson in 1860, she wrote "I am sorry I smiled at women. Indeed, I revere holy ones, like Mrs Fry and Miss Nightingale" (L223).[29] Following her service as a nurse in the Crimea, Florence Nightingale became a heroine to women on both sides of the Atlantic, and the English Quaker Elizabeth Fry had won renown for her championing of prison reform; indeed, Dorothea Dix was called "an American Mrs. Fry" (qtd. in Brown 135). But another possibly transformative personal experience may have been Dickinson's treatment for an optical ailment requiring her to endure long periods with her eyes bandaged, often in isolation, during the mid-1860s and perhaps earlier than that.[30] In light of some of the cultural influences I have been discussing and of the poet's figural treatments of prison narratives and punishments, including solitary confinement and whippings, I will conclude by looking more closely at her own experience with physical pain and confinement.

Whipping was certainly not uncommon in New England domestic life: employers whipped servants, teachers whipped pupils, riders whipped horses. As we have seen, while young, Dickinson liked to joke about the rod of correction with Austin, as she also did with her future sister-in-law, Susan Gilbert. While Sue was employed in Baltimore herself as a teacher, Dickinson joked in 1851 about her best friend's enforcement of classroom discipline: "I hope you whip them Susie – for *my* sake – whip them *hard* whenever they don't behave just as you want to have them!" (L56). Yet twenty years later, after the poet had undergone treatment for her eye problems, she sent a letter to her friend Elizabeth Holland (L369), sympathizing with Holland over her own treatment by an eye specialist:

> "Whom he loveth, he punisheth," is a doubtful solace finding tart response in the lower Mind.
> I shall cherish the Stripes though I regret that your latest Act must have been a Judicial one. It comforts the Criminal little to know that the Law expires with him.
> Beg the Oculist to commute your Sentence that you may also commute mine. Doubtless he has no friend and to curtail Communication is all that remains to him.

About three years after writing to Mrs. Holland, Dickinson was capable of empathizing poetically with the victim of a beating (F1349 B):

> Not with a Club, the Heart is broken
> Nor with a Stone –
> A Whip so small you could not see it
> I've known
>
> To lash the Magic Creature
> Till it fell,
> Yet that Whip's Name
> Too noble then to tell.

Magnanimous as Bird
By Boy descried –
Singing unto the Stone
Of which it died –

Shame need not crouch
In such an Earth as Our's –
Shame – stand erect –
The Universe is your's.

"Now, strike!" the narrator of " 'Twas love – not me –" exhorts her unknown auditor, inviting punishment for the crime of having fallen in love, and in this poem, the heart, lashed by the whip of love, also endures punishment in the service of passion.[31] Like a prisoner abused by an ironically "noble" superior, or by a prison guard, the heart should be able to find a kind of solace in its punishment. For shame is, after all, the ordinary condition of the world and the universe, Dickinson writes in the final stanza. Whether nobly or masochistically, a personified Shame should "stand erect" to take the blows, not cringe.

Dickinson's emphasis in her poems on attempts made by shackled, imprisoned personae to find the Other, a twin, or a similarly restrained lover, helps capture the psychological effects of isolation. Speakers are willing to tunnel through walls to find companions, and in Byron's "The Prisoner of Chillon," Bonnivard is heroic largely for enduring much of his long imprisonment in solitude, following the deaths of his brothers. Like prisoners sequestered under the Auburn system, many of Dickinson's poetic personae do not experience isolation as an opportunity for self-evaluation and spiritual renewal, but rather as an exquisite form of torture. Solitude and silence are closely allied themes in many of Dickinson's more celebrated poems, including "I felt a Funeral, in my Brain," in which the speaker proleptically interprets a vision of her own death and burial as exile to a kind of void, saying "I and Silence, some strange Race / [are] Wrecked, solitary here –," the adverb "here" serving to indicate an imprisoning, isolate space in which her only companion, Silence, intrinsically cannot speak or respond to her.

In "I tried to think a lonelier Thing," Dickinson envisions another landscape of loneliness, the Ultima Thule of a virtually existential isolation from all other human contact, "Some Polar Expiation – An Omen in the Bone." That the speaker should feel the need to expiate her crimes by dwelling in such solitude suggests that Dickinson had penal methodologies in mind, and in "I tried to think a lonelier Thing," the fellow prisoner, the Other, might validate her own experience by suffering comparably, within his own intolerable isolation:

I plucked at our Partition
As One should pry the Walls –
Between Himself – and Horror's Twin –
Within Opposing Cells –

As I have said, scenes of liberation from incarceration in Dickinson's poetry tend to emphasize not escape from oppressive authority, but rather reunion with the sympathetic and complementary Other. Speakers don't seek to escape imprisonment so much as they strive to find someone in circumstances identical to theirs. In the Auburn system, prisoners were discouraged from talking to one another as part of a deliberate effort to prevent them from building up a shared sense of human suffering. In a cruel, and perhaps peculiarly Calvinistic, way, inmates held under the Auburn system were compelled instead to turn in upon themselves: everyone his own prison.[32]

Dickinson's isolation throughout her treatments in a Cambridgeport boardinghouse taught the poet perforce quite a bit about what it felt like to be a prisoner. She was then in her thirties, and this health crisis followed hard upon her surge of poetic creativity in the early 1860s. References to having her eyes covered by bandages, probably in obedience to doctor's orders, indicate that Dickinson may have lived virtually blindfolded for extended periods during consecutive summers in 1864 and 1865. While in Boston, she was under the care of Dr. Henry W. Williams, a prominent ophthalmologist. As patient and convalescent, the poet was compelled to live apart from her immediate family, estranged from voices that would ordinarily have lent her support and encouraged her in enduring a regimen of self-deprivation. In June 1864 she wrote to Higginson, "I was ill since September, and since April, in Boston, for a Physician's care – He does not let me go, yet I work in my Prison, and make Guests for myself" (L290), a phrase that may refer to her dialogic poetic methodology. The next month she wrote to Lavinia, "You remember the Prisoner of Chillon did not know Liberty when it came, and asked to go back to Jail" (L293). In November, she wrote again to her sister, "I have been sick so long I do not know the Sun" (L296).

Like a prisoner confined to the nearby Charlestown prison, located only blocks away from her own rented room, Dickinson was compelled to embark on a program of self-renewal, although her ultimate goal was not parole, but rather the freedom to *see* again. "Renunciation – is a piercing Virtue –," Dickinson wrote, "The putting out of Eyes –/ Just Sunrise –." Even in the years preceding her treatment in Boston, Dickinson may have been constrained by other doctors to submit herself to similar therapeutic regimens involving self-deprivation of light and sight. "The Soul has Bandaged moments –" (F360) appears to have been written perhaps in the summer of 1862, during the very peak of her artistic productivity:

> The Soul has Bandaged moments –
> When too appalled to stir –
> She feels some ghastly Fright come up
> And stop to look at her –
>
> Salute her, with long fingers –
> Caress her freezing hair –
> Sip, Goblin, from the very lips
> The Lover – hovered – o'er –
> Unworthy, that a thought so mean
> Accost a Theme – so – fair –
>
> The soul has moments of escape –
> When bursting all the doors –
> She dances like a Bomb, abroad,
> And swings upon the Hours,
>
> As do the Bee – delirious borne –
> Long Dungeoned from his Rose –
> Touch Liberty – then know no more –
> But Noon, and Paradise –
>
> The Soul's retaken moments –
> When, Felon led along,
> With shackles on the plumed feet,
> And staples, in the song,
>
> The Horror welcomes her, again,
> These, are not brayed of Tongue –

I surmise the poet came to expect such temporary confinements as a matter of course during the years in which her eyes were afflicted, yet without ever being able to accommodate herself to them emotionally, especially during her cherished, all-too-brief New England summers. Without rehearsing what I have already said about this poem elsewhere (*Emily Dickinson's Vision* 23–24), I want to close by emphasizing the poem's penal imagery, which may draw on Dickinson's likely familiarity with the Auburn system.

The speaker in "The Soul has Bandaged moments –," who I will assume in this particular instance is rooted in the poet's own subjective experience, has her eyes covered or "Bandaged" during daylight hours, that adjective conflating both the palliative effect of a doctor's recommended method of treatment and a prison's suppression of inmates' vision achieved through the forced donning of masks under the Auburn system. Blind or semi-blind, the speaker cannot see people approaching her and consequently feels vulnerable, especially in a sexual sense: the first two stanzas describe a scene of potential sexual assault, made all the more horrifying by an intrinsic comparison with the welcome intimacy and physical proximity of the "Lover['s]" lips in former times. The speaker's suffering may be interrupted occasionally by real or imagined excursions outdoors, when, no longer "Dungeoned," she may briefly experience "Liberty" before being led inside again, her incarceration having been made all the more painful by such intervals of sensory freedom. Returned inside, and with her blindfold reapplied, she may feel hindered once more in moving about, or even in talking about her experience, her "shackle[d]" feet and "staple[d]" lips preventing her from "bray[ing]" about her sufferings to others. In the absence of the freedom to see, speak to, or hear others, Dickinson may have found solace in populating her poems with the presences denied her.

The poem's deliberate deployment of the literarily associated term "theme" and its implicit contrast of topics and images commonly found in Romantic literature—gothic "Goblin[s]," the Byronic trope of imprisonment and liberation, the erotic dyad of bee and blossom—with confinement and sensory deprivation suggest that Dickinson understood her illness may have imperiled her creativity. Indeed, in the years succeeding 1864 and 1865 her poetic output underwent a sharp decline. In that sense, Dickinson may have, at some level, perceived her extravagant outpouring of poems in the early 1860s as a sort of imaginative profligacy, a spree, so that, after her treatment in Cambridgeport, she could divide her years between the carefree half-decade she had enjoyed "Before I got my eye put out," and those years in which she occasionally had to endure a blind, mute solitude. In her youth she had jokingly advocated whipping and prison for wrongdoers, but by the time she began to approach middle age, she may have begun wondering sometimes what she herself had done to deserve so harsh a fate.

7

A KISS FROM
THERMOPYLAE
The Rule of Law

Throughout her adult life, Emily Dickinson ordinarily appreciated and endorsed law's role in preserving civic order. Yet her final decades spanned an era during which public anxiety over whether the rule of law was being obeyed steadily increased. Although the rate of serious crime actually fell in the nation (including Massachusetts) after 1860, Reconstruction-era Americans, already left grief-stricken by the war, expressed further uneasiness in enduring the successive shocks of Lincoln's and Garfield's assassinations, sporadic urban rioting, lurid accounts of crimes and trials, and news of political unrest in Europe.[1] The citizenry grew increasingly anxious about its personal safety, its property, and the durability of its institutions. As Lawrence Friedman writes of the postwar decades, "Crime did not go down fast enough for some people; the public demand for law and order, perhaps, more than kept pace with supply" (450). By the time the poet reached her final years, the lofty bar for civic integrity she thought had been set by the previous generation, including her father and his friend Judge Otis Phillips Lord, had begun to seem antiquated, even scorned and discarded. One of Dickinson's last letters, written to an aunt in the year she died, bemoaned what seemed to her a local lapse in morality: "Don't you think Fumigation ceased when Father died?" (L1041).[2]

And yet a fin-de-siècle spirit felt nationally during the poet's last few years may also have inspired in her a late optimism about her own personal liberty that itself seemed to border, at times, on a kind of lawlessness. Her love affair with Lord, one of the more powerful judicial figures in the Commonwealth, helped bring into sharp relief an apparent paradox generated by her faith in the stabilizing influence of law and new imaginative possibilities unleashed by a self-identification with transgressive forces, including art, eroticism, intellectual skepticism, and even crime. Such destabilizing influences, she may have come to believe, might be either destructive when manifested in the form of groups, such as mobs, or tonic at the individual and personal level, as exemplified by legally liminal figures appearing in Dickinson's late writings—wayfarers, rascals, and rogues.

This peculiarly bifurcated attitude may also be attributable to the poet's understanding of law's importance to society overall, and for this reason I will begin with a brief cultural and historical overview of the rule of law. Then I will turn to Dickinson's repeated references to an event resonating with several Victorians: the battle of Thermopylae, which provided the poet with a metatrope that evolved over the course of her adulthood from a conventional recognition of a military sacrifice made for the sake of the state to an intensely personal symbol of selflessness and emotional steadfastness.

What does the term "rule of law" signify? The concept is more slippery than one might imagine. For some, the phrase signifies a society's willingness to abide by rules applicable to all, rather than permitting the rich or the powerful to dominate the poor, the weak, or the disenfranchised. For others, it characterizes an orderly society in which disputants resolve arguments in court rather than trying to settle them privately, perhaps vindictively. For still others, it refers simply to the observance of legal precedent, or *stare decisis*. "Rule of law" is defined by *Bouvier's* as "A general principle of law, recognized as such by authorities. It is called a rule because in new cases it is a rule for their decision; it embraces particular cases within general principles" (2: 938).[3] But the word "rule" in "rule of law" is itself ambiguous. Does it refer to statutes or other written codifications of the law subsequent legal opinions should follow, or to governance, law holding sway over society in a manner analogous to the power a king, a president, or a prime minister wields in ruling executively?[4] Thus the phrase may be seen as possessing connotations ranging from the most local and immediate, in a reliance on statutory law and precedent, to broad political and philosophical meditations on how societies should conduct themselves.

In that latter, wider sense, the phrase "rule of law" has been employed to describe a legal philosophy upheld continuously within a Western tradition extending back to Charlemagne and the Salic Franks, to the Romans, and ultimately to the Greeks. Thus the rule of law may be construed as being nearly synonymous with "civilization," particularly in the sense that people collected in a polity agree to submit to a set of rules that maintains an existence independent from the rise and fall of rulers and regimes. Law itself becomes king, *rex lex* superseding the concept that a ruler was a law unto himself; as Aristotle said, "law should rule." We have already seen Dickinson refer to the principle that no one is above the law. In "I had some things that I called mine –," the narrator, in defending her claim against the interests of an implicitly wealthier and more prestigious neighboring property owner, God, declares, "Justice is sublimer / Than arms, or pedigree." The aggrieved speaker resolves to "institute an 'Action,'" that is, go to law rather than try to settle scores. "I'll vindicate the law" she promises, and in defending her own interests, she will uphold simultaneously the validity of law itself.

Despite a domestic existence spent largely in the company of small-town attorneys attending to everyday concerns such as contracts, deeds, and trusts, Dickinson did demonstrate she was capable of stepping back and considering the law more abstractly as a social, historical, and philosophic construct. Consider, for example, the late poem "The way Hope builds his House" (F1512):

> The way Hope builds his House
> It is not with a sill –
> Nor Rafter – has that Edifice
> But only Pinnacle –
>
> Abode in as supreme
> This superficies
> As if it were of Ledges smit
> Or mortised with the Laws –

Always interested in the psychological phenomenon of hope, Dickinson describes it here not as a device, as in "Hope is a strange invention –," but rather as a house. Hope is a structure built solidly on architectural principles that are, nonetheless, manifestly counterintuitive, rather like the mythical perpetual motion machine that earlier poem describes. The house of hope has no sill—that is, no preface—nor rational support, consisting almost entirely of facade, or "superficies." Hope's orientation is consistently upward, an expression of the intrinsic optimism of that state of mind, even in defiance of the law of gravity. Through the words "Ledges smit" and "mortised," Dickinson implies that hope is nevertheless built enduringly, as if of stone, so that despite its violation of essential logical and structural principles, hope's house is virtually indestructible. As law serves to bind bricks—representing, perhaps, an aggregate of individual citizens' interests—into a coherent whole, hope, at a personal level, finds its own reasons to persist, despite disappointments and internal contradictions.

Particularly in the years succeeding the War of 1812, the law acquired an intellectual glamour that came to be shed indirectly on its practitioners.[5] Seen previously chiefly as a handmaiden to trade, and even accused invidiously by some as being too closely identified with the interests of property owners and the patrician class, law came to be seen instead as equalizer, civilizer, and a medium for transmitting the fruits of Western thought to the hinterlands, even to foreign lands. This evolution took place against the wider background of the previous century's neoclassical appropriation of Greek and Roman historical events and cultural artifacts to justify contemporary opinions, beliefs, and policies.

One incident that appealed particularly to the Victorian imagination was the battle of Thermopylae, fought in 480 B.C. At Thermopylae, a small squad of Greeks, chiefly Spartans led by one of their kings, Leonidas, withstood repeated assaults by a horde of invading Persians before being finally overwhelmed. For Victorian writers, the famous story served various moral and political purposes. Above all, it provided an example of patriotic altruism and of personal courage in the face of certain defeat. Thermopylae was also used to extol the superiority of a democratic Western form of government, the Greek confederation, over a slave-owning Eastern tyranny, that is, Xerxes' vast Persian empire.[6] The battle also came to signify dedication of oneself to the principle of law, for which the Greek defenders were said to have been willing to lay down their lives. In this latter sense, the battle of Thermopylae came to represent love of the law for its own sake, even to the point of death.

In *Modern Painters,* Ruskin, whose writings Dickinson followed,[7] linked the battle to foundational concepts about the relation of the individual to the polis, while simultaneously imposing a Christian and revisionistic interpretation of what Leonidas and the brave Spartans he commanded had died for:

> Obedience in its highest form is not obedience to a constant and compulsory law, but a persuaded or voluntary yielded obedience to an issued command. . . . Thus far then of practical persons, once called believers, as set forth in the last word of the noblest group of words ever, so far as I know, uttered by simple man concerning his practice, being the final testimony of the leaders of a great practical nation, whose deed thenceforward became an example of deed to mankind:
>
> *Ō xein', angellein Lakedaimoniois hoti tēide*
> *keimetha, tois keinōn rhēmasi peithomenoi.* (481)

The epitaph Ruskin quotes, written by Simonides and as reported by Herodotus, has often been translated as:

> Stranger, announce to the Spartans that here
> We lie, having fulfilled their orders.

One assumption underlying the existence of the epitaph is that because the Spartan defenders were nearly annihilated, few or none were left to report what had happened to their friends and families. The inscription thus functioned as a voice for the voiceless dead, informing passersby what had happened on the site, who had died, and why.

Dickinson mentions Thermopylae in her writings directly three times, and indirectly at least once.[8] This latter instance occurs in poem F524, written probably during the early years of the Civil War, and with a martial theme appropriate to the times. The poem refers to a "Spartan" who must be "put away," or buried, after mounting a heroic defense of the liberties survivors continued to enjoy. The narrator wonders if the sacrifice was worth a valiant soldier's death:

> It feels a shame to be Alive –
> When Men so brave – are dead –
> One envies the Distinguished Dust –
> Permitted – such a Head –

The Stone – that tells defending Whom
This Spartan put away
What little of Him we – possessed
In Pawn for Liberty –

The price is great – Sublimely paid –
Do we deserve – a Thing –
That lives – like Dollars – must be piled
Before we may obtain?

Are we that wait – sufficient worth –
That such Enormous Pearl
As life – dissolved be – for Us –
In Battle's – horrid Bowl?

It may be – a Renown to live –
I think the Men who die –
Those unsustained – Saviors –
Present Divinity –

In this encomium to the noble dead, the speaker refers to the "Stone" erected over the grave of an individualized, representative Spartan, quite probably an allusion to the monument at Thermopylae. Dickinson's trope caustically compares systems of monetary value to a more intangible system of moral worth emblematized by the soldier's willingness to die for his country. Thus the "pile" of dollars wryly parodies the Greeks' burial mound, on which the famous monument was erected, and where the bodies of the Spartan defenders lay heaped. Dickinson's allusion strongly suggests she has the story of Thermopylae specifically in mind, yet it is also important to consider the battle's significance for her when she composed this poem.[9] "Liberty" is the political abstraction for which the Greeks are portrayed by the poem as having been willing to lay down their lives. As a concept integral to American thought, liberty has a political valence closely allied with the national definition of freedom, particularly in the sense of living free from tyranny. The American Civil War provides Dickinson here with a means of associating a single Union soldier's death with classical virtues and fairly conventional Christian pieties.

Another reference to Thermopylae appears in Dickinson's correspondence long after the Civil War had ended. In a letter to Thomas Wentworth Higginson (L519), himself a war veteran, Dickinson reverted to the ancient battle to praise private struggles waged by individuals against ill fortune, whether male or female. She wrote of a friend of Higginson's who had evidently succumbed recently to illness:

> She reminded me of Thermopylae – Did she suffer – except to leave you? That was perhaps the sum of Death – For the Hand I was never permitted to take, I enclose my own, and am tenderly
>
> Her's –

As Thomas Johnson says in a note on this letter, sent in September 1877, Dickinson "associated *Thermopylae* with uncomplaining bravery in the face of certain death" (*Letters* 592). In that sense, at least during the early years of her own middle age, Dickinson did not deviate from the practice observed by contemporaries who appropriated the classical episode as a validation of personal sacrifice. While patriotic imperatives receded in importance during the years following the Civil War, Dickinson's emphasis in deploying the trope evolved into praise for individual courage, now demonstrated in a more intimate and personal context.

A third reference to Thermopylae appears much later, in poem F1584, written around 1882, late in the poet's life, while she was engaged in her affair with Judge Lord. Her reference to the historical event has undergone another subtle shift:

> "Go tell it" – What a Message –
> To whom – is specified –
> Not murmur – or endearment –
> But simply – we obeyed –
> Obeyed – a Lure – a Longing?
> Oh Nature – none of this –
> To Law – said Sweet Thermopylae
> I give my dying Kiss – | give / Convey

Here Dickinson, through her speaker, converts the epitaph affirming the heroism of the Spartan defenders into a message both passionate and erotic, rather than pat and patriotic. The concept of heroism is transferred from a wider political and national cultural milieu, and from the acknowledgment of courage in the face of physical pain and suffering to the more private, and perhaps implicitly female, realm of emotional courage and fidelity. The erotic content of Dickinson's version of the defenders' message is signaled by her intimate diction: "murmur," "endearment," "sweet," "kiss." Plainly, obedience in military matters is being equated with obedience to the wishes of the beloved, and the laws of the land are subtly conflated with the laws of love. Now Dickinson's reference to the heroic Spartans' posthumous message would seem to draw on William Lisle Bowles's translation of the couplet (1833):

> Go tell the Spartans, thou who passest by,
> That here, obedient to their laws, we lie. (North 970)

In Bowles's version, "orders" has been transmuted subtly into "laws."[10] The fundamental source of her allusion would seem to be classical, rooted in Simonides' entreaty to passersby, "report this word," that is, tell surviving Spartans that the rule of law had been upheld by Leonidas and his demolished phalanxes, Dickinson's pronoun "it" in "'Go tell it' – What a Message –," referring to the message itself.

Considering its proposed date of composition, 1882, an assumption that the poem is to be read autobiographically and that it refers to Judge Lord is not unreasonable. In that year he became so ill that his family feared for his life and he was compelled to step down from his judicial duties.[11] While on the bench, Lord enjoyed a reputation for moral conservatism, forensic relentlessness, and eloquence. Like a Union soldier killed in battle or a Spartan hoplite, Lord had shown himself willing to make the ultimate sacrifice for his ideals. In that sense, the poem may also be regarded as a provisional epitaph or poetic obituary for Lord penned in advance. Like Simonides, Dickinson may have been fulfilling, informally, a state function by erecting a sort of verse cenotaph for a fallen warrior. Judge Lord's imminent death would represent a loss not just for her, but also for the Commonwealth of Massachusetts. In "'Go tell it' – What a Message –," Dickinson's stilted, somewhat oratorical syntax and peremptory tone of voice exist in a productive tension with the poem's recurrent romantic, intimate terms. The social pronoun "we" in the fourth line operates ambiguously to suggest that the narrator is speaking simultaneously for the state, for herself, and for them as a couple.

Over the years, Dickinson's presentation of the Spartans' message from Thermopylae shifted in tone from the martial to the nearly *marital,* as is indicated by the introduction of romantically laden terms emphasizing obligation and unquestioning loyalty at the personal, rather than national, level. The phrase "sweet Thermopylae" may be the poet's euphemism for Judge Lord, who could be seen as having given his all for law, and thus a figure deserving affection and respect at both the national and personal levels. Although Leonidas, king of Sparta and commander of his troops, could only with difficulty be described as "sweet," Dickinson's trope may be understood as equating military courage now with emotional bravery and fidelity. The "Kiss" conveyed back to the Spartans at home could then be construed more narrowly and intimately as a gesture of devotion and possible farewell to one's beloved. Although Dickinson characterizes her attraction to Lord erotically by way of the terms "Lure" and "Longing," she asserts (somewhat unconvincingly, I think) that their relationship exceeds the promptings of "Nature" and ascends instead to a higher level of commitment reflecting or emulating Lord's devotion to law. Yet despite the poet's emphasis here on Lord's public reputation, the affective dimension of their affair may have been intensified, for her at least, by his state-sanctioned power.

A fourth reference to Thermopylae appears in a short letter with an appended poem (L906, F1661) sent to Mabel Loomis Todd on July 19, 1884, four months after Judge Lord had died and only two years before the poet's own death. Dickinson may, in writing this note, have assumed some knowledge on Todd's part of her involvement with the judge:

How martial the Apology of Nature! We die, said the Deathless of Thermopylae, in obedience to Law.

Not Sickness stains the Brave,
Nor any Dart,
Nor Doubt of Scene to come,
But an adjourning Heart –

Strangely, Thomas Johnson cites this letter as a reference to "dying nature" (*Letters* 906), although, in mid-July and even in a harsh New England climate, the descent of vegetal nature into autumn's frosty death would not yet have begun. Rather, the poem likely refers to the death of Judge Lord, and to the forces of nature and age which had combined to kill him; alternatively, "Nature" may signify here, as it likely did in "'Go tell it' – What a Message –," a susceptibility to natural impulses.

Dickinson's emphasis in discussing the import of the doomed Spartans' message remains a dedication to law rather than obedience to orders. The legally inflected term "adjourning" strongly suggests that the poet had Judge Lord in mind in writing this note and poem, whether her reference was understood by Mrs. Todd or not (or by Austin, for that matter). Dickinson may again be representing Lord as one of the Spartan dead, having given his life nobly for the sake of his fellow citizens, an act of self-sacrifice performed in preserving the rule of law, indicated here by the phrase "obedience to Law." That virtual epitaph may signal simultaneously the Judge's willingness to enter into a career of public service and his adherence to the laws of love.

Although the judge did ultimately succumb to long-standing medical problems, Dickinson dismisses in her poem the idea that her lover had been felled by illness, or the "Dart" of enemies, a direct reference, I suggest, to historical accounts of the Spartans being destroyed finally by Persian spears and arrows, or, in light of contemporary accounts of Judge Lord's customary combativeness in politics and law, the antagonism of his enemies. Moreover, she asserts her departed lover's moral fearlessness, in that Lord, who combined personal playfulness with a reactionary Calvinist's temperament, would have died, she infers, without any "Doubt of Scene to come." As his lover, Dickinson is assuming as her prerogative the right to pronounce upon the judge's posthumous moral deserts. His reputation with her, at least, remains "Deathless" as that of the Spartans.

Despite Dickinson's apparent praise of her lover's professional dedication, her writings from 1882 to 1886 would also seem to indicate she believed that work responsibilities had hastened Lord's death. Up until his final years Otis Lord maintained a strenuous judicial pace, and the poet chided him for not allowing himself sufficient time for pleasure or rest. After he died, Dickinson wrote to Benjamin Kimball, "Abstinence from Melody was what made him die. Calvary and May wrestled in his Nature" (L968); evidently she thought a predisposition toward self-sacrifice, or "Calvary," ultimately prevailed.[12] After his death, Dickinson believed that Lord had "obeyed" the law, sacrificing himself for it as the Spartans had at Thermopylae. Subsequently, she too "obeyed" the law in continuing to love and remember him. Even while he still lived, her writings probably directed to him emphasize the theme of compelled obedience, portraying her relation to him as that of subject to sovereign, trespasser to landholder, criminal to judge.

If the rule of law also involves being *ruled* by law, Dickinson occasionally encouraged Judge *Lord*, a name that would have invited wordplay focusing on noble status and obedience, to see her as being *un*ruly even while professing herself subordinate to him, both in prestige and in age.[13] Especially to older male figures of authority, Dickinson was prone to portray herself somewhat flirtatiously and opportunistically as a lawless child. To Higginson, for example, she wrote, "You think me 'uncontrolled' – I have no Tribunal" (L265). In the same letter, one written early in their lengthy correspondence, she characterized herself to Higginson as well as being a victim of unruliness, in describing the death of an early mentor (probably Benjamin Newton): "My dying Tutor told me that he would like to live till I had been a poet, but Death was much of Mob as I could master – then –." While Judge Lord lived, the poet flattered him by contrasting her own self-avowedly unsophisticated, even wayward, life with his distinguished career: "Our Life together was long forgiveness on your part toward me. The trespass of my rustic Love upon your Realms of Ermine, only a Sovreign could forgive" (L750; May 1, 1882).[14] Dickinson's metonym ties the ermine-trimmed gown worn by British judges with an almost kingly power, for monarchs, too, donned such robes of office. Moreover, Lord presided, she implies, over a "Realm" of law comparable to domains ruled by a king, upon which she, like a "rustic" clown, was apt to trespass.[15]

What are these various forces of disorder with which the poet, in her writings, tended to associate, and disassociate, herself? They manifested themselves in ways both public and private. *Mobs* were on the minds of many following three days of rioting in New York, from July 13 to July 16, 1863, in protest of the nation's first draft law.[16] In response to these disturbances Melville wrote "From the House-Top," in which he praised the deployment of draconian federal force—in the form of companies of artillery—to put down the "roar of riot":[17]

> Wise Draco comes, deep in the midnight roll
> Of black artillery; he comes, though late;
> In code corroborating Calvin's creed
> And cynic tyrannies of honest kings;
> He comes, nor parlies; and the Town redeemed,
> Give thanks devout; nor, being thankful, heeds

The grimy slur on the Republic's faith implied,
Which holds that Man is naturally good,
And – more – is Nature's Roman, never to be scourged.

Melville's cynicism here about human nature and the inherent weakness of democracies reflects a conservative law-and-order philosophy that has much in common with Dickinson's own expressed attitude toward law-breakers. Yet Dickinson's response to the danger posed by mobs was more internalized and less political than Melville's. Around 1864, she wrote (F824):

A nearness to Tremendousness –
An Agony procures –
Affliction ranges Boundlessness –
Vicinity to Laws

Contentment's quiet Suburb –
Affliction cannot stay
In Acres – It's Location
Is Illocality – | Is Illocality / It rents Immensity –

In referring to urbanism and suburbanism, this poem may be commenting topically on New York's riots. The speaker contrasts the illusory safety of the "quiet Suburb," where residents believe themselves to be comfortably distant from "Affliction," to the center, from which chaos spirals outward. Dickinson appropriates the landscape of urban unrest to describe the psychological phenomenon of anxiety itself. The individual who believes herself to be removed and therefore comfortably immune to pain and loss resembles the suburbanite who thinks himself isolated from the virulently contagious "Affliction" of urban rioting. Contentment itself is thus a "Suburb," and, like a citizen living in lower Manhattan, or even the outer boroughs, the isolate self complacently ignores his or her own proximity to internal anarchic forces. In a fashion analogous to the way churchgoers in Melville's poem give thanks for their physical and conceptual distance from urban rioting, yet refuse to consider what those upheavals signify about the fragility of republics and the fallibility of human nature, the objectified consciousness, renamed "contentment" in Dickinson's poem, deludes itself in believing that it, too, is immune to the sorrow whose existence an "Agony" reveals.

Within Dickinson's internalized cityscape, the "Suburb" of "Contentment" derives its peaceful ambience from its location, which is in "Vicinity to Laws," as if the law itself were an edifice or wall separating suburban estates from a turbulent inner city. Alternatively, like the presence of a police station on the block, law provides citizens living close by to it a sense of security, yet one which, Dickinson suggests, may be illusory. The mind, she observes, derives an impression of stability by carefully compartmentalizing emotions and experiences as if they were contiguous yet separate neighborhoods whose integrity, in the presence of riot, has to be preserved in order for contentment, an internalized representation of law, to prevail. Yet Dickinson's final paradox points to the essential intractability of suffering, which vaults barriers erected by the mind between itself and chaos. Again, to superimpose the poet's schema of the mind onto a conceptual map of a major city, the tight pattern of blocks and neighborhoods is threatened by riot to be dissolved into a preexisting rural landscape consisting of implicitly unfenced, boundless "Acres," thus re-creating the primeval "Tremendousness" of the yet-unsettled American frontier from which cities first emerged. In that sense, between anarchy and civilization the law interposes a flimsy barrier, itself vulnerable to retrograde forces of political upheaval and emotional unraveling. In the midst of the Civil War, Melville and Dickinson were both concentrating their attentions on what the national struggle disclosed simultaneously about the fragility of political constructs and of purportedly "civilized" modes of human conduct considered collectively and individually.

Mobs, as a manifestation of democracy run amuck, menaced onlookers, and perhaps especially property owners, not just with the prospect of theft, vandalism, and arson, but also with a nearly explosive, ungoverned growth analogous to the exponential growth of a city over time from its core to its outermost suburbs. In that sense, Dickinson's trope may pertain as well to demographic changes in nineteenth-century urban America. In a representative democracy, and particularly in the northeastern sector of the country, burgeoning growth threatened to overwhelm the voices of the landed, invested, chiefly Protestant majority. During the 1850s such growth was attributed by many nativist groups, including the "Know Nothings," to what they regarded as the indiscriminate admission to American residency of European immigrants, particularly those coming from Ireland and Germany. In the previous poem, "Affliction" is figured as a pathology that threatens to metastasize beyond prescribed limits, "rang[ing] Boundless[ly]" until it infects an entire body politic. Another association of a nearly Malthusian growth with urban rioting appears in the undated poem F1763:

> The mob within the heart
> Police cannot suppress
> The riot given at the first
> Is authorized as peace
>
> Uncertified of scene
> Or signified of sound
> But growing like a hurricane
> In a congenial ground.

Here, as in the previous poem, mob action results indirectly from an inciting catalyst whose potential danger may not be evident initially. An unnamed generic "Agony" opens the door to a much larger, more ungovernable "Affliction." In this poem, the mob arises from a small, perhaps officially sanctioned (indicated by the adjective "authorized") demonstration that rapidly gets out of hand, becoming "Uncertified" presumably by the very same civic authorities who had originally given permission for a limited and voluntarily restrained demonstration to take place. In Dickinson's metatrope of consciousness considered as a city, we see once again the explosive growth of emotions imitating the unrestrained growth of "natural" agents—infection, or the exponential growth of a hurricane battening over warm waters (and an apt metaphor as well for a milling, circulating, swelling crowd). These metaphors stand for sociologic or demographic factors spiraling out of institutional control.[18] The paradox, once again, is that the "mob within the heart" is as quiet as an actual one is noisy, but the similarities private discord shares with public disorder include rapid, explosive growth and an immunity to the forces of reason and restraint.

In "The mob within the heart" the poet may be adopting a politically conservative position critical of civic authority, of which the police are but one extension, for being too "congenial" in their dealings, at first, with forces of anarchy and disorder.[19] Officials have "given at the first" permission for the demonstration to take place and have "authorized" the assembly of an initially manageable group of disaffected people; as protest turns to riot, however, the police, their ability to perform their duties perhaps compromised by other civic authorities not present on the scene, abruptly find themselves unable to "suppress" an increasingly unruly crowd. Dickinson's figure in the poem describes, as in "A nearness to Tremendousness –," the mind's inability to govern strong emotions. The internalized city, protected by a thin facade of law and order from powerful anarchic forces within its midst or from a "mob" of feelings that cannot be mastered, is threatened by a reversion to a natural, "rural" state of open spaces and uncivilized territories.[20]

During the poet's lifetime, such conceptualized raw spaces still existed within living memory of the oldest citizens of Amherst, a small town founded originally and somewhat precariously on the old Connecticut Valley frontier. In terms of a larger geographical metatrope, then, Emily Dickinson herself occupied a liminal position on the very borders of consciousness, a prospect from which she might observe the interplay of civilizing and decivilizing forces, as we saw in "I am afraid to own a Body –." She may have viewed her own proclivity for writing poems as a potentially destabilizing force that threatened to invalidate whatever civilizing influence the production and consumption of literature putatively offer, as benefits of civilization. When she began corresponding with Higginson in 1862, she characterized her own creative existence as a realm without a monarch, an anarchic state in which forces for maintaining law and order could not be organized. In L271, she may even have likened herself to an insurrectionist's bomb:[21]

> Are these more orderly? I thank you for the Truth –
>   I had no Monarch in my life, and cannot rule myself, and when I try to organize – my little Force explodes – and leaves me bare and charred –

The poet's language is reminiscent here of the closing of her letter to Susan Gilbert, in which she cautions, "open me carefully," as if the envelope itself might explode (L94). Although Dickinson's reference to explosions in her letter to Higginson may have been prompted by a proliferation of military terms—including those describing ordnance—in the national press during the war's opening months, her earlier reference to Sue would seem to indicate a preexisting pattern in which the poet presented herself to others as an explosive shell, which, although ordinarily placid in appearance, was capable of causing damage, disorder, and disruption.[22]

Her letter to Higginson also implies that her impulses toward personal anarchy and disorder are the result of having no "Monarch" or sovereign to impose order upon her. Bombs figure in several poems: "I tie my Hat – I crease my Shawl –"; "The Soul has Bandaged moments –"; "To interrupt His Yellow Plan"; "These are the Nights that Beetles love –." Like a bomb itself, Dickinson's creative work threatens the very forces of law and order she otherwise upholds, and, in the poems' creation, even herself, like a bomb maker left with skin burnt and clothes blasted off when her device detonates prematurely.

Although Dickinson thanks Higginson for helping her become a more orderly writer, other evidence would seem to suggest that she discerned in her own lawlessness the wellspring of her creativity and expressive power. Breaking the "laws" of regular rhyme and standard punctuation and capitalization, as well as gender-based conventions about which topics women should write about, Dickinson must have realized that her poetic style would always stand in the way of her potential attainment of poetic renown, even while it allowed her greater artistic, psychological, and emotional access to subjects that drew her irresistibly.[23] Many critics have pointed out the frequency with which disruptive and transgressive figures appear in her poems, exponents, perhaps, for the eccentricity and difference that the poet knew were keeping her literary productions out of the mainstream of conventional taste, even while they invested her work with its distinctiveness. These various destabilizing figures in her poems tend not to be outright criminals, but rather shady characters who contest authority, challenging the law to assimilate their divergent points of view, behavior, and beliefs. I wish to scrutinize three different such figures who appear with some regularity throughout Dickinson's poetic career, yet with increasing frequency during the final decade of her life: the *wayfarer,* the *rogue,* and the *rascal.*

Particularly in the wake of journalistic reportage of riot and crime in larger cities during the century's second half, smaller towns such as Amherst may have become infected with a mood of heightened alertness and some degree of xenophobia.[24] In such an atmosphere of unfocused distrust, if an unexplained event occurred or an item of property went missing, suspicions tended to fall initially on outsiders and transients, whether of the type who could afford to pay for a night's lodging or wandering poor vagabonds, such as gypsies, itinerant workers (chiefly

Irish), or the Native Americans who showed up from time to time on the Homestead's steps, begging for work or food. But the ethnic identity of the outsider was not necessarily overdetermined as being non-WASP or non-white. Sometimes Dickinson characterized the disruptive outsider in her poems as someone capable of blending in with the "indigenous" (in the sense of citizens of chiefly British ancestry who had settled the Connecticut Valley) local population. Thus the frost, in "Apparently with no surprise," may be figured as a "blond assassin" who prowls during the night, leaving slaughtered flowers in his wake like a charming serial killer, his hair color serving initially to divert suspicion from him.

In notes evidently written to Otis Lord, well-traveled judge and resident of Salem, a venerable Puritan town, the reclusive poet was prone to represent herself, too, as a rural wanderer, a "wayfaring woman" who might or might not be held accountable for her eccentric sojourning. Certainly a degree of irony attaches to such self-characterizing by a poet who left her home so rarely and reluctantly, but in letter draft L562 she says, "I am but a restive sleeper and often should journey from your Arms through the happy night, but you will lift me back, wont you, for only there I ask to be," and later in the same draft, "but then what I have not heard is the sweet majority – the Bible says very roguishly, that the 'wayfaring Man, though a Fool – need not err therein'; need the 'wayfaring' Woman? Ask your throbbing Scripture."[25] Dickinson's scriptural reference here is, as Thomas Johnson points out (*Letters* 618), to Isaiah 35:8, "And an highway shall be there, and a way, and it shall be called The way of holiness . . . ; the wayfaring men, though fools, shall not err therein."[26] Dickinson's message to her lover, conveyed through the mutually understood medium of the Old Testament, endorses the quality of serendipity. The process of trial and error may indeed lead to error, but it may also lead to the *right road* of happiness, even of holiness.

Dickinson's reference to "sweet majority" echoes her addressing of Lord as "My Sweet One," while also flattering him for being a judge, in that judicial panels issuing decisions may divide among themselves between majority and minority opinions. The emphasis on sweetness is also reminiscent of "sweet Thermopylae" in the poem " 'Go tell it' – What a Message –," written perhaps four years earlier. In L562, the poet implicitly asks the judge whether he agrees with her that a wanderer may have motives more lawful than unlawful. "Sweetness" may be allied to "roguishness," and in Dickinson's letter draft the adverb "roguishly" does double duty, directing the judge's attention to sexual connotations that may be read into the scriptural passage, in the sense that sexual dalliance may direct lovers to happiness rather than leading them astray, while suggesting simultaneously that "rogues" and "wayfarers" are natural confederates as mischievous outliers who may be viewed as potential agents of misrule and chaos—or, alternatively, explorers and innovators.[27]

In his 1828 dictionary, Noah Webster provides a specific legal definition for "rogue": "In law, a vagrant; a sturdy beggar; a vagabond. Persons of this character were, by the ancient laws of England, to be punished by whipping and having the ear bored with a hot iron." Implicitly, punishment is administered not just because the rogue is a wanderer or vagabond, but also because he is a liar, in that he is a "sturdy beggar" who remains intentionally idle, declaring himself unfit for work. The element of *lying* as part of the rogue's behavior and of a torturing punishment administered as a result appear in the a poem written to Susan Dickinson around 1884 (F1640):

> Who is it seeks my Pillow Nights –
> With plain inspecting face –
> "Did you" or "Did you not," to ask –
> 'Tis "Conscience" – Childhood's Nurse –
>
> With Martial Hand she strokes the Hair
> Upon my wincing Head –
> "All" Rogues "shall have their part in" what –
> The Phosphorus of God –

As Johnson's gloss for the poem indicates (3: 1100–1101), Dickinson's last line alludes to Revelation 21:8, which describes the punishment in eternity for liars: being burned alive in a lake of liquid fire, or "Phosphorus": "But the fearful, and unbelieving, . . . and all liars, shall have their part in the lake which burneth with fire and brimstone: which is the second death." Despite such dire imagery, Dickinson's poem also poignantly captures the effect wrought upon a child being questioned by a monitoring adult, such as a parent or childhood nurse. This projected figure of authority smooths the hair of a girl going to bed, yet so vigorously as if to inflict punishment, and afterwards, the child's guilty conscience prevents her from sleeping.

An association of rogues with lying also informs the humor of a passage in a letter the poet sent to her brother, Austin, much earlier in her life, on a warm, late-June day in 1851. Joking about the heat, she chides him for his own excessive levity in letters sent home from Boston, saying that although his humor is "worth a score of fans," he should write to his family in a "little more of earnest, and a little less of jest until we are out of August"; after that he can "joke as freely as the Father of Rogues himself, and we will banish care, and daily die a laughing!" (L45). Dickinson's allusion here is to Satan, proprietor of a notably warm subterranean domain and father of lies, as he is identified in John 8:44: "Ye are of your father the devil, and the lusts of your father ye will do. He was a murderer from the beginning, and abode not in the truth, because there is no truth in him. When he speaketh a lie, he speaketh of his own: for he is a liar, and the father of it."

Dickinson's admonishment of her brother is, of course, not meant to be taken seriously, and later in life she persistently associated roguery in men and in women with admirable boldness, and even with attractiveness. Among the last letters she wrote was an acknowledgment of thanks to Charles H. Clark for having sent her a reminiscence connected with the Reverend Charles Wadsworth, who had died in April 1882. In recounting to Clark one of her last interviews with Wadsworth, she wrote of being called to the door of the Homestead, only to encounter Wadsworth unexpectedly standing on the front steps. " 'I stepped from my Pulpit to the Train' was my [i.e., his] simple reply, and when I asked 'how long,' 'Twenty Years' said he with inscrutable roguery." (L1040). In speaking of so famous a preacher as Wadsworth, the poet is, one would assume, not commenting on a tendency to prevaricate; instead, his "roguery" would seem to refer to a mischievous element in his personality to which the poet responded positively, perhaps even passionately.

Less pejorative than "rogue," the term "rascal" is another legally tinged epithet to which Dickinson recurred in her writing, although nearly exclusively in her correspondence. In her verse, the sole instance of her use of a derivative of that word is, however, significant: in F2, the same valentine in which she described insolvency as being *sublime!*," she employs another witty oxymoron, preceding and parallel to her comment about bankruptcy, "Rascality [is] heroic." This literarily minded joke would have resonated with the valentine's probable intended recipient, William Howland, an Amherst College graduate. Paired with a reference to bankruptcy, the line would seem designed to convey a particularly legal emphasis to the reader, who may be an individual, namely Howland, or a dispersed, collective audience. *Bouvier's* defines "rascal" as "An opprobious [*sic*] term, applied to persons of bad character. The law does not presume that a damage has arisen because the defendant has been called a rascal, and therefore no general damages can be recovered for it; if the party has received special damages in consequence of being so called, he can recover a recompense to indemnify him for his loss" (2: 823).[28] Palpably a term of insult, "rascal" skirted the boundaries of libel.

In the poet's later letters, the word acquires connotations almost entirely positive, ironic, and, occasionally, sexual. In a letter drafted in 1882 for Judge Lord, while referring to the Kidder trial over which he was then presiding in Springfield, Dickinson teased her lover by referring to two of his private names, "Phil" and "Papa": "But how can 'Phil' have one opinion and Papa another – I thought the Rascals were inseparable" (L750). Lord may have been familiar with the Dickinson family anecdote in which Samuel Bowles, editor of the *Springfield Republican,* had called the poet a "rascal," perhaps even a "damned rascal." When she refused to come downstairs to meet him on one occasion, Bowles is reputed to have shouted "Emily! Come down here at once, you rascal!" Her witty letter in reply to Bowles (L515) is signed "Your 'Rascal,' " with a postscript: "I washed the Adjective." Plainly, Dickinson enjoyed both the company of "rascals" and being identified as a rascal herself.[29]

In vigorous contrast to these several metaphorical agents of unruliness and disorder stood the figure of Judge Lord, as formidable a voice for the maintenance of law and order as the poet's father once had been. Dickinson evidently enjoyed teasing the judge about the divergence between his reputation for judicial rigor and a predilection for humor and flirtatiousness in his personal life. During their relationship, Dickinson occasionally posed not just as a trespasser, but as a burglar seeking to pillage the deepest recesses of her lover's personality: "Papa has still many Closets that Love has never ransacked. I do – do want you tenderly" (L750). Here, Dickinson's suspense-inducing dash moots the question of whether she wants Lord himself, or the opportunity to rifle his emotions, troped as his belongings, and in this way, the very guardian of civic safety would himself be made a crime victim. Two sentences later, she refers to one of the periodic visits paid by gypsies to Amherst: "The Wanderers came last Night – Austin says they are brown as Berries and as noisy as Chipmunks, and feels his solitude much invaded, as far as I can learn. These dislocations of privacy among the *Privateers* amuse me very much."

Dickinson's train of thought in writing this paragraph would seem to be that the presence of gypsies in Amherst has suggested to mind the danger of burglary, which in turn suggested the figure of herself ransacking the judge's emotional depths. Her wordplay involving "privacy," "Privateers," and "dislocations" conflates the invasion of privacy intrinsic to the crime of burglary performed, potentially, by these alien interlopers, and a positive, disruptive wandering that renews the local social environment by introducing variety, risk, and difference. Austin may complain about the gypsies' noise, but the real underlying threat is not just potential theft, but the intrusion of the unfamiliar. In her letter to Judge Lord, Dickinson, by using humor to distance herself from her brother, suggests that she is to be grouped with the gypsies, rather than with Austin. In doing so, Dickinson is subtly inviting Judge Lord, once again, to associate her with miscreants, mischief-makers, traveling confidence women, and other such societal outliers.

In flirting with Judge Lord, Dickinson evidently emphasized the psychological rewards of theft, as in her reference to "closets" not yet "ransacked." Around 1878, a year after Elizabeth Lord had died, the poet wrote, in a letter to Sue (L580), "The Solaces of Theft are first – Theft – second – Superiority to Detection –," and perhaps only shortly thereafter she composed the following poem (F1482):

> Forbidden Fruit a flavor has
> That lawful Orchards mocks –
> How luscious lies within the Pod
> The Pea that Duty locks –

Dickinson's observation here about forbidden fruits' peculiar deliciousness posits a direct challenge to the stability promised by law and order, and by the rule of law. It is natural, she suggests, for human beings to crave what is forbidden to them by religious proscription, conventional morality, or edicts of law. Yet if the poem is written with Judge Lord in mind, she may also be suggesting that he, as a man sworn to perform his civic duty, should pursue pleasures ordinarily locked up and put away, like valuables concealed from burglars. She herself, she suggests, may be a treasure to be discovered by diligent, perhaps illicit, searching.[30] "Lawful Orchards" exist in a productive opposition to the Garden of Eden, in which certain forms of knowledge were proscribed as well, and conduct between men and women closely monitored.

Dickinson realized that the relationship between lawlessness and law could be reciprocal and mutually reinforcing, and, as spokeswoman for the outlier, the Other, the wanderer and the stranger at the door, she sometimes identified with cultural forces that were disorderly, explosive, and anarchic. Yet her sallies and invasions were not meant to be taken as substantive threats. The law itself presented a model for the attraction of opposites. Even the rigidly militaristic Spartans could send a "kiss" from the site of their destruction at Thermopylae acknowledging their adherence to, and sacrifice for, the law. The law is like love: we must obey it, even lay down our lives for it, because to do otherwise would be tantamount to destroying not only our emotive, affective selves but the entire structure of society on which we depend. For Dickinson, law and love could even be virtually synonymous, in that both bring into high relief the bonds tying individuals to something much larger, and more lasting, than themselves.

NOTES

Introduction

1. Jack Capps writes, "She learned his [Edward Dickinson's] legal terms and used them to such an extent in her poems that we can only conclude she must have occasionally read his law books" (15).
2. For example, in a letter written to Austin in 1853 (L141), Dickinson expressed indignation that a rival attorney in Amherst, Ithamar ("Frank") Conkey, who served as representative to the General Court, should be called the best lawyer in town:

   > George Allen remarked at their table yesterday, that for his part, he hoped Frank Conkey would be chosen representative, for he was a very smart fellow, and the finest Lawyer in Amherst – also that he was said to present his cases in court much finer than any other, and should he himself George Allen, have any difficult business, he should surely entrust it to him!
   >
   > If that is'nt the apex of human impudence, I don't know anything of it. [Susan Gilbert] remarked in her coolest, most unparralled [sic] way, that she wanted to open the door, and poke him out with the poker!

3. Richard Sewall quotes Squire Dickinson's daughter Elizabeth as having said of her father, "His success was so great that it is said 'he *did* more business than *all* the lawyers in Hampshire County" (33n6).
4. In 1851, Dickinson, then twenty-one years old, wrote to Austin, in describing the household atmosphere prevailing since he had left to take a teaching post in Boston, "We dont have many jokes tho' now, it is pretty much all sobriety, and we do not have much poetry, father having made up his mind that its pretty much all real life. Fathers real life and mine sometimes come into collision, but as yet, escape unhurt!" (L65). Significantly, Dickinson's trope would seem to be drawn from reports of the railway accidents that occurred not infrequently during the first half of the century, and, in that frame of reference, it may also refer indirectly to the Amherst & Belchertown Railroad, which Edward Dickinson was laboring to bring to fruition in 1851.
5. See, in Sewall's *Life*, these index entries under "Dickinson traits": "introversion," "home-centeredness," and "rhetoric (hyperbole)" (806).

6. After visiting the poet in Amherst, Thomas Wentworth Higginson wrote a letter to his wife containing his impressions of the Dickinson family: "I shan't sit up tonight to write you all about E.D. dearest but if you had read Mrs. Stoddard's [Elizabeth Drew Stoddard, author of *The Morgesons*] novels you could understand a house where each member runs his or her own selves" (qtd. in Sewall 563).

7. In a letter written to Emily Norcross in 1826 while they were courting, Edward drew a distinction between the arts and business matters: "In looking at life as a scene of action – it is not a fair medium to behold it thro' the glass of the Poet or the Novelist – it is a stage on which all must act a part – each in his proper sphere – & accord[ing] to his talents – it is but a season of preparation for a higher and brighter state of existence – and business is given to men to call their powers into exercise – to strengthen, enlarge & improve them – & better fit them for the employments for which they are destined" (qtd. in Pollak, *A Poet's Parents* 15). Somewhat ironically, Edward, in claiming that poets and novelists do not portray the world of action and the professions accurately, quotes part of Jacques' famously cynical speech in *As You Like It*.

8. William Howard writes, "As far as the words that compose her poetic vocabulary are concerned, they were taken from the living language of her time, the language of the scholar and of the businessman, of the housewife and of the lawyer, of the poet and of the journalist" (248).

9. For an assessment of Dickinson's employment of Latin, see Cuddy.

10. While at Mount Holyoke, the poet also quite likely encountered, with perhaps mixed feelings, the following passage from a sort of civics textbook Lyon recommended to teachers and pupils, attorney William Sullivan's *The Political Class Book; Intended to Instruct the Higher Classes in Schools in the Origin, Nature, and Use of Political Power:* "It is one of the most striking defects in our system of education, that females are so generally uninstructed in the substance and forms of business. Much precious time is devoted, in early life, to some accomplishments, which are neglected and forgotten amidst the cares of married life. It would be far more useful to devote that time to make women intelligent, in those affairs which concern them deeply, as mothers, widows, and guardians, and in the character of executrix and administratrix; and frequently in other employments, which require a familiarity with the forms of business" (98).

11. See, for example, Amherst College ms. A 754, reproduced photostatically in Werner's *Emily Dickinson's Open Folios*. A rough draft of a letter probably intended for Otis Lord is penciled on the back side of what looks to be a legal form setting forth the requirements for the disposal of property.

12. Perry Miller concludes his section pertaining to the development of the legal profession in *The Life of the Mind in America* with this observation: "Among the many respects in which the Civil War brought down upon the American drama a violent curtain, the way in which it terminated a stupendous era of legal thinking is one of its poignant tragedies, if not indeed its most poignant" (265).

13. In *The Legal Mind in America,* Miller says of attorneys during the post-Revolutionary period: "These practitioners found themselves . . . up against the still-prevalent conviction among the dominant Protestant groups, and so of the majority of the population, that lawyers were by the very nature of their profession hypocrites, ready to defend a bad cause as well as a good one for a fee, inherently corrupt and therefore unworthy of the title of American. As was often remarked by observers of the young

Republic, Americans were the most litigious people in the world, as well as the most contemptuous, or at least distrustful, of the lawyers they employed" (17).

14. In *Life of the Mind,* Miller writes, "As a matter of history, one may say that the mania 'for going to law' which European travelers note as a veritable disease among this law-hating people would inevitably have encouraged an increase in the number of practitioners." (111–12).

15. According to Winthrop Dakin, Edward Dickinson had a very respectable record of successes as an attorney: "Of his 33 appealed cases he won 54.5%, and of those he initiated below 47%. As with his father's [legal career] none were criminal cases" (36).

16. The Harvard Law School curriculum in effect while Austin was a student there is described in Lambert 116–23.

17. Sue appreciated Dickinson's mordant wit, which, she wrote in the obituary published in the *Springfield Republican* on May 18, 1886, was a "Damascus blade gleaming, and glancing in the sun."

18. Lambert i–ii. B. J. Smith writes, "Legal images or specific legal language can found in roughly three hundred of her poems" (38).

19. Among the professions, historically, legal practitioners have shown themselves disinclined to hew to generally accepted rules of punctuation and capitalization, preferring to let their mode of expression be dictated by the rhetorical situation. For example, many legal writers used—and use—commas sparingly, preferring to let the syntax of a sentence indicate its underlying grammatical structure. Attorneys remain fond of using capital letters as a tool for emphasis. Bryan Garner, editor in chief of *Black's Law Dictionary,* writes in a widely used legal style manual, *The Redbook,* "In legal writing, there is an unfortunate tendency toward contagious capitalization. It is a reversible condition" (45).

20. It should be kept in mind, however, that in Dickinson's writings the generic boundary between epistle and verse is unusually porous. See Messmer 42.

21. Dickinson likely refers to Genesis 32–33, in which Jacob sends placating gifts to his brother Esau.

22. Late in life, Dickinson particularly enjoyed exchanging such stories with Otis Lord. For example, she retained in her workbox a newspaper clipping on which she had written, "Returned by Judge Lord with approval!" (Bianchi 70):

> NOTICE! My wife Sophia Pickles having left my bed and board without just cause or provocation, I shall not be responsible for bills of her contracting.
>
> *SOLOMON PICKLES*
>
> NOTICE! I take this means of saying that Solomon Pickles has had no bed or board for me to leave for the last two months.
>
> *SOPHIA PICKLES*

Also, during the 1882 Kidder trial in Springfield, with Judge Lord presiding, she enjoyed his account of a juror's apparently discretionary cough which the judge had thought "not pulmonary" (L750).

23. The issuing of a warrant for arrest may ultimately lead to conviction, a situation Dickinson likely alludes to in the fragmentary F1748, which may characterize a dreaded future event that, like a postponed visit from the bailiff, somehow never does come off:

As subtle as tomorrow
That never came,
A warrant, a conviction,
Yet but a name.

The term also appears in F1122, "I cannot meet the Spring unmoved –," in which the narrator speaks of having felt "A Warrant to be fair –," that is, external authorization to adorn herself.

24. Kurzon, building on speech act theories developed by John L. Austin and John Searle, examines the "illocutionary" *enacting* function of legal discourse, especially as deployed by judges. The word "hereby" is particularly representative of legal language's performative function: "The adverb *hereby* . . . is an optional element in a performative. It cannot be used in any other context, however; we may state, therefore, that if this adverb may potentially occur in a given sentence, then we are dealing with an instance of a performative" (6).

25. In F278 Dickinson wrote,

A word is dead when it is said,
some say.
I say it just begins to live
that day.

26. Habegger comments that Edward Dickinson served as signatory witness to his own father's dubious real estate dealings in the months preceding Squire Dickinson's ruin: "He was present at the transactional moment, affixing his name as legal witness" (*My Wars* 19). In Appendix 4 of his biography Habegger also compiles all known instances of Emily Dickinson's signature appearing on legal documents, mostly conveyances of property. Almost all involve sales of the Dickinson family's own holdings in Massachusetts and Michigan. Ironically, his elder daughter provided for Edward Dickinson the same testamentary service he had provided at least two decades earlier for his own father.

27. Habegger writes, "Although it is unlikely that Emily paid close attention to the documents she signed, her signatures do show how much she lived on the periphery of her father's legal business and real estate investments. Again and again she was asked to take notice of transactions in which commitments were made *at that moment*. Such events helped constitute the world as she knew it" (*My Wars* 136–37).

28. While Edward Dickinson was establishing himself as an attorney, appellate courts were coming to rely more and more on the submission of briefs, rather than simply on preliminary oral arguments. Before 1860, Massachusetts courts merely recommended that attorneys file informal lists of "Points and Authorities" they intended to cover during a trial, but after that date state courts began requiring formal written statements, usually very short, of only one or two pages. In writing such executive summaries, attorneys would necessarily need to concentrate on the salient points of their arguments, while keeping their writing concise and to the point. See Cozine.

29. William Sherwood writes of Dickinson: "She was litigious by nature; again and again her poems are concerned with rights, rules, justice, arbitration, redress, evidence, spheres of authority, contracts, settlements, inheritances, and loopholes" (232–33).

30. Despite the prevalence of law in Dickinson's poems and letters, its influence on her writing has received relatively scant scholarly notice. Among the major biographers, Richard Sewall focuses on Edward Dickinson's career as an attorney. Cynthia Wolff,

however, devotes almost no attention to the law's impact on Dickinson's literary life, suggesting that the poet's works reveal "a doubting attitude toward the efficacy of laws" (173). Alfred Habegger's biography provides by far the most thoroughgoing consideration of the law's importance to Dickinson. He supplies valuable concrete information about Edward Dickinson's law business, and about various ethically dubious legal practices indulged in by Edward and by Austin. Among the generalized reference works, Eberwein's *An Emily Dickinson Encyclopedia* includes a useful entry under "Legal Imagery," written by Deborah Dietrich.

The most sustained scholarly consideration of the law's importance to Dickinson's poetry is *Emily Dickinson's Use of Anglo-American Legal Concepts and Vocabulary in Her Poetry: Muse at the Bar,* by Robert Lambert. Himself an attorney, Lambert compiles the various concepts and legal terms without, however, delving very deeply into how the poet deploys them in generating figures of speech. Still, his book is invaluable in elucidating the law's importance for Dickinson. Recently, other scholars have usefully discussed Dickinson's attitude toward class, and to the identification of the legal profession with membership in Amherst's haute bourgeoisie. Groundbreaking work done by Betsy Erkkila and Domhnall Mitchell provides important insights into this dimension of the entire Dickinson family's estimate of themselves. In *Emily Dickinson: Monarch of Perception,* Mitchell furnishes an especially perceptive analysis of the railroad's importance to Edward Dickinson and his daughter.

Among the journal articles, Winthrop Dakin provides insights into the types of cases Edward Dickinson took on, and into the small fraternity of contemporary Amherst attorneys. Joanne Feit Diehl, B. J. Smith, and William Howard integrate considerations of law into analyses of individual poems. I would also refer interested readers to my own work, including various articles treating the poet's concepts of property, trespass, inheritance, and bankruptcy.

1. Delinquent Palaces

1. Samuel Fowler Dickinson's gradual, agonizing descent into insolvency is lucidly explained by Alfred Habegger both in his essay "How the Dickinsons Lost Their Homes" and in his biography of the poet. I am indebted to Habegger for much of the information concerning Squire Dickinson's finances appearing in this chapter.

2. Sewall discusses the Dickinson clan's tendency to be fixated on a family home (38–41). Speaking of the family's predilection as a tribe to cling to hearth and to Amherst, Sewall writes, "Seen against this [family] background, Emily's home-centeredness takes on less the aspect of some deep neurotic fear or psychological compulsion than of a family tendency carried to an extreme" (39).

3. Habegger writes, "Massachusetts did not pass its first insolvency law until 1838, a few years before the 1841 Federal Bankruptcy Act; bankruptcy did not exist in the 1820s and early 1830s as a legal procedure for terminating debt, giving equal treatment to creditors, and starting over" ("How the Dickinsons Lost Their Homes" 164).

4. To buy and sell Amherst properties, Samuel relied heavily on the goodwill of Dickinson relatives, so that the extended family functioned as a sort of informal bank. As Christopher Clark has shown, this practice was commonplace in the Connecticut River Valley. Located far from banking and financial centers in Boston and Hartford, and even Springfield, landowners in western Massachusetts often looked instead to

relatives, in-laws, and friends. Unfortunately, when a businessman failed, he often took down with him a number of his relatives (65).

5. For an account of the tumultuous few years during which Samuel F. Dickinson was employed at Lane Seminary, see Lesick.

6. See Sewall 30 and 42n13.

7. It remains unclear how cognizant Edward was of his father's complicated financial arrangements. Habegger notes that Edward's signature appears as witness on some of the property conveyances his father signed, suggesting that Edward must have understood—especially as a young attorney—the legal significance of the debt burden his father was assuming ("How the Dickinsons Lost Their Homes" 166–67, 173). Nevertheless, Habegger also suggests that Edward was in the dark about much of his father's actual financial condition: "We can fruitfully explore [the] possibility . . . that Edward's knowledge of his father's affairs was limited" (173).

8. Apparently, the partnership of Dickinson and Bowdoin was not always a happy one, and, according to Sewall, the firm was dissolved in 1855 (416)

9. See Habegger: "On almost every New Year's Day from 1850 on, Edward made a written inventory of his productive investments, debts, and dubious assets and then cast the balance" ("How the Dickinsons Lost Their Homes" 174).

10. Habegger, even while suggesting that Samuel Dickinson's insolvency was a "salient element" in "the matrix of conditions that formed Emily Dickinson," implies that the poet, when young, was told little about what had happened: "Dickinson men did not explain legal and financial tangles to Dickinson women" ("How the Dickinsons Lost Their Homes" 165). Yet this supposition that the poet was kept almost entirely in the dark seems unrealistic, especially considering how closely knit the Dickinson family was, the extent of the knowledge of Samuel Fowler's collapse in the small town of Amherst, and the poet's precociousness. Dickinson's awareness of what had happened may have been fragmentary, but it is unlikely that she was entirely ignorant of the affair. Then too, a realization that she was in possession of only some of the facts concerning the matter may have piqued her curiosity.

11. Habegger writes, "The latent fear of being ruined, the relentless quest for perfect security—these elements not only stayed with the father but, in a very different register, shaped the mind of the daughter who would imagine heaven as 'wild prosperity'" ("How the Dickinsons Lost Their Homes" 189).

12. Dickinson was an avid reader of Dickens's novels, including *David Copperfield*. On July 27, 1851, she began a letter to Austin facetiously by quoting Mrs. Micawber: "'I will never desert Micawber' however he may be forgetful of the 'Twins' and me, I promised the Rev Sir to 'cherish' Mr Micawber, and cherish him I will, tho Pope or Principality, endeavor to drive me from it" (L49).

13. According to Habegger, at Amherst Academy Emily Dickinson took three or four years of Latin (*My Wars* 140), a foundation that probably served her well enough to understand much of the legal Latin employed by attorneys. At Dartmouth College, Samuel F. Dickinson had been salutatorian in Latin.

14. No autograph copy of this poem is known to exist, so we may only surmise that the italics were original to Dickinson herself. Conceivably, they may have been added either by Howland or by an editor at the *Republican*. A similarly tacit assumption of in-group familiarity may underlie a thank-you note sent around 1878 to Susan Dickinson: "Where we owe but a little, we pay. Where we owe so much it defies Money, we are blandly insolvent" (L541). Susan could have read this aphoristic

message within the context of her own knowledge of the Dickinson family's finances, for which her friend here makes little excuse. Insolvency may be *bland* when the accusation cannot be publicly refuted; then, Dickinson would seem to say, it is best that the bankrupt stipulate to his improvidence, perhaps even embrace it.

15. Although it is unknown who the valentine's intended recipient was, Howland himself makes an eligible candidate. According to Franklin (1: 53) in later years Howland returned to Amherst often, evidently to visit Lavinia Dickinson, who at some point received a marriage proposal from him. Conceivably, her sister is therefore the "pippin" to which the poet refers, encouraging Howland humorously to press his suit more forcefully.

16. See also F1737:

> When we have ceased to care
> The Gift is given
> For which we gave the Earth
> And mortgaged Heaven
> But so declined in worth
> 'Tis ignominy now
> To look upon –

This short poem, for which no autograph copy is known to exist, emphasizes the status of three properties: Earth, Heaven, and the unexplained, indeterminate "Gift." Implicitly, earth and heaven are properties that had been conveyed as payment to whoever originally possessed the "Gift," although a transfer of ownership has not been effected until long after payment had been subscribed. In a sense, the poem describes a real estate investment that did not pan out, either through bad faith on the part of the owner of the "Gift," or because the value of the "Gift" depreciated so much over time that the speaker realizes she had made a bad bargain. The very word "Gift" is legally inflected, in that Dickinson may be referring to a donor's gift to a family member, a liberality implied both by that word's conflicting with the reciprocity implicit in "Gift" / gave," and with the outright business transaction signified by the phrase "mortgaged Heaven." All in all, the poem would seem to question the sincerity of gift-giving, seeing it as a sort of covert method of exacting payment for questionable goods given for dubious reasons. Although it is impossible to know whether Dickinson wrote this poem in light of an awareness of her grandfather's several feckless investments in property, we may nevertheless discern an association here between mortgages and shame. For an analysis of Dickinson's gift-giving in her correspondence, see Crumbley.

17. Albert Gelpi equates Dickinson's statement here with a bankruptcy more artistic and spiritual than monetary: "These seven lines of an unfinished poem rehearse all the major elements of the Puritan 'vision': the initial harmony of the universe; man's violation of that harmony and his consequent alienation; the possibility of reunion and its fulfillment in visionary instants; the bankruptcy of life without vision" (91).

18. Austin Dickinson wrote a tribute to General Mack that appears in an address written for the 150th anniversary of Amherst's First Congregational Church: "[General Mack was] a man to command attention anywhere, tall, erect, of powerful build, with a fine head finely set, clear, exact, just, a believer in law and penalty for its breach; strong as a lion, pure as a saint, simple as a child, a Puritan of the Puritans: I remember my first sight of him—I was four years old—I thought I had seen God" (qtd. in Sewall 121).

19 Samuel Dickinson's insolvency led to the loss of several houses and properties in addition to the Homestead and the Montague house. According to Habegger, Samuel's

brother-in-law Oliver Smith, who stood surety for many of the Squire's loans, forfeited several properties as a result of his involvement in the Dickinson family's financial debacle, including his own house (*My Wars* 59; "How the Dickinsons Lost Their Homes" 165).

20. The phrase "of the Option" would seem to be synonymous with "at option," that is, an offer or a right that one party in a legal transaction may choose to accept or exercise. In "Paradise is of the Option," Dickinson employs the phrase deliberately to frame the poem as a real estate transaction: potential tenants of paradise may choose to occupy that property now, or later, as they prefer. In other poems she used the phrase "at option" similarly as part of an overall strategy of using the diction of finance and business to satirize and ironize religious orthodoxy. Thus, in an early poem in which she humorously considers the prospect of her own death, "If I should die" (F36), she wrote,

> If I should die,
> And you should live –
> And time sh'd gurgle on –
> And morn sh'd beam –
> And noon should burn –
> As it has usual done –
> If Birds should build as early
> And Bees as bustling go –
> One might depart at option
> From enterprise below!
> 'Tis sweet to know that stocks will stand
> When we with Daisies lie –
> That Commerce will continue –
> And Trades as briskly fly –
> It makes the parting tranquil
> And keeps the soul serene –
> That gentlemen so sprightly
> Conduct the pleasing scene!

Dickinson's somewhat dark humor here is gender-specific in associating the sphere of commerce and trade with men, the "sprightly" "gentlemen" who will go on conducting business as usual after the speaker and her addressee have died. This burst of commercial activity exists in implicit sympathy with the equally "bustling" natural world, in which birds and bees pursue their own goals equally energetically, building as if they too were contractors erecting houses at a frenetic pace. The poet makes a pun on flower "stocks," and perhaps in "fly," as the kinetic business world emulates the airborne bird and bee. The poet's humor here may also be ironical, because in 1858, the year in which she may have written this poem, the country was still recovering from a serious financial panic, and she locates her imagined bourse primarily in nature, and not in the realm of human enterprise. As Vivian Pollak writes, "The stock market crash of 1857 . . . is well on the way to providing the economic vocabulary for [this poem], which speaks of 'enterprise,' 'option,' 'stocks,' 'Commerce,' and 'Trades'" ("'That Fine Prosperity'" 163). Dickinson even depicts death, or a willingness to die, as a business decision that is smoothly integrated with all these other commercial pursuits. Life itself is characterized as an "enterprise" that one may participate in, or not, at will—"at option." Significantly, the putative tranquility or serenity to be experienced by the dying derives not from the comfort of knowing that they will soon enjoy a heavenly reward, but rather from a knowledge that the world will carry on without them. Finally, Dickinson also employs the phrase "at option" in a letter to Elizabeth Holland (L204), in which she jokingly refers to angels as "People with *Wings* at option." Again, Dickinson finds amusement in using the language of business transactions to comment ironically on religious commonplaces.

21. Rhett Frimet writes, "Northern creditors of Southern debtors felt that a national bankruptcy law was probably the only way they would ever see any payment on [Southerners'] accounts as the Northerners could not obtain jurisdiction in civil court over these landed property (cash-poor) debtors. . . . [The 1867 Act] contained both involuntary and voluntary provisions applicable to all persons. The prior Act of 1841 allowed involuntary petitions to be filed against traders only" (12). I have written about Dickinson's interest in involuntary bankruptcy myself, in "Exceeding Legal and Linguistic Limits: Dickinson as 'Involuntary Bankrupt.'"

22. A contrast between owning and renting a house may be drawn in F1718:

> Rather arid delight
> If Contentment accrue
> Make an abstemious Ecstasy
> Not so good as joy –
>
> But Rapture's Expense
> Must not be incurred
> With a tomorrow knocking
> And the Rent unpaid –

In this drily witty commentary, Dickinson opposes quiet contentment to ecstatic joy, characterizing the first, perhaps, as the situation of the renter who, freed from the burden of having to make the larger cash payment required by a mortgage, is able to bank his money, which will "accrue." Outright ownership, on the other hand, is equated with "Rapture," a word that Dickinson may also be using in its alternative sense of signifying the transportation of a person from one place to another, as of someone required to make repeated moves. In the economy of the emotions, joy is expensive, and thus must be indulged in rarely, if at all. A prudent and "abstemious" individual will content herself with "Contentment," despite the knowledge that it is "Not so good" as joy. Yet the first line indicates that this poem is to be read ironically, the arch phrase "Rather arid delight" serving to undercut and impeach the rest of the poem's ostensible praise of thrift and patience. Notably, Dickinson tropes different states of happiness here as shades of difference tied to the stake a renter and an owner have in the properties they occupy.

23. Alternatively, in "Own" Dickinson may be treating a verb as a noun. Cristanne Miller writes: "Using a word of one grammatical class to function as another disguises a complex predication. Juxtaposing words that do not function together in normal usage creates a kind of parataxis, for which the reader must work out the appropriate relationship. To give a simple example: 'The Daily Own – of Love' gives distinct body to a possessiveness, perhaps in reflection of the physical quality of the feeling, and certainly in analogy with the ownership of more mundane and quantifiable possessions. 'The Daily Own – of Love / Depreciate the Vision –' suggests that once love becomes a daily affair (and is in that sense 'owned') it decreases in worth" (60).

24. Vivian Pollak writes: "'I gave myself to Him' . . . describes love as a 'contract,' in which there is 'Mutual – Risk,' especially the risk of satiation. Her lover is the 'great Purchaser,' 'the Merchant' tempted by the spicy cargoes as long as they are remote. She is concerned that daily and total possession of her may 'Depreciate' her worth in his eyes" ("'That Fine Prosperity'" 173).

25. See my article "Exceeding Legal and Linguistic Limits," 95–96. In a letter draft written for Judge Lord, Dickinson created a neologism, "bankrupter," describing her state of expectation while hoping to receive a letter from him: "To beg for the Letter when it is written, is bankrupt enough, but to beg for it when it is'nt, and the dear Donor is sauntering, mindless of it's worth, that is bankrupter" (L561).

26. My noted variants here are drawn from various versions of the poem.

27. See Johnson, *Poems* 2: 717. In appending the word "Aristocrat," the poet may have been seeking to console Sue by flattering her sense of her own family's social standing. Susan's family had known bankruptcy and ignominy in its own right: her father, Thomas Gilbert, had died, according to Lyndall Gordon, "a bankrupt alcoholic" (15).

2. Nor Here nor There

1. Dan Dobbs writes: "The medieval chancellor was a high minister of the king, more closely analogous to a prime minister than to anything else we are familiar with. He was often a Bishop of the church. As a kind of prime minister, the Chancellor did the sort of administrative work ministers do—he was an advisor, negotiator, ambassador, propagandist and stand-in for the king" (58).

2. Perry Miller observes, "No wonder that Tom and Dick [in New England] . . . bethought themselves of their fathers' protests against the Star Chamber or High Commission, and dug in their heels [against the establishment of chancery courts]" (*Life of the Mind* 172).

3. John Selden, a seventeenth-century British judge, commented: "Equity is a roguish thing: for law we have a measure, know what to trust to; equity is according to the conscience of him that is Chancellor, and as that is larger or narrower, so is equity. 'Tis all one as if they should make the standard for the measure we call a foot, a Chancellor's foot; what an uncertain measure would this be? One Chancellor has a long foot, another a short foot, a third an indifferent foot: 'tis the same thing in a Chancellor's conscience" (43–44).

4. Dobbs writes: "[The chancellors said] that they were not speaking law at all; far be it from them to change the law of England. No; the chancellors were keeping the law intact and making personal orders to the defendant. The importance of this was enormous in the later development of equity, both substantively and remedially" (62).

5. Capps cites two letters in which Dickinson also refers to *The Merchant of Venice*, L48 and L958 (184).

6. Kenji Yoshino writes: "For all his urbanity, Shylock is naïve to believe any contract is airtight. When Shakespeare wrote *Merchant,* the severity of bonds was being actively and successfully challenged. Individuals bound by such instruments were appealing to the king through the Court of Chancery. Chancery could not undo the bond, but could enter an order, known as an injunction, that prohibited the collector from enforcing it. By the 1590s, Chancery's interventions were routine" (40).

7. Part of *Bouvier's* definition of "manor" in English law reads: "A tract of land originally

granted by the king to a person of rank, part of which (*terrae tenementales*) was given by the grantee or lord of the manor to his followers. The rest he retained under the name of his demesnes (*terrae dominicales*). That which remained uncultivated was called the lord's waste, and served for public roads, and commons of pasture for the lord and his tenants" (2: 307).

8. Yoshino points out that Portia's subsequent argument that the pound of flesh must be removed without spilling a drop of blood has long been recognized, at least from a legal perspective, as being "absurd" (44). The conclusion to be drawn here is not that lawyers in any era subordinate the saving of a human life to the observance of a legal technicality, but that when *Merchant* was written, a contract such as that drawn up between Shylock and Antonio—while it made for good theater—would have been invalidated anyway by the courts, at least those in Britain.

9. For a thorough discussion of the subgenre of Dickinson's definition poems, see Deppman.

10. On the subjects of reprieves, pardons, and clemency, see, for example, "It came his turn to beg –"; "Tried always and Condemned by thee"; "We talked with each other about each other"; "Joy to have merited the Pain"; "The Heaven vests for Each."

11. Capps points out that Dickinson's historical references in the poem may be confused. Elizabeth's comment refusing forgiveness was made to the countess of Nottingham, not Essex himself (109–10).

12. Andrew Zurcher writes: "'Conscience,' to an early-modern reader, had a range of legal associations, largely bound up with the delivery of equitable judgment through the courts of Chancery and Request. These were courts in which the inflexible rigour of formal common-law process—the key to its knowable security and famed even-handedness—could (at least in theory) be redressed by the intervention of a human conscience" (99).

13. A variant for "merciful," "hazardous" focuses attention on the speculative dimension of placing one's fate in the hands of a single arbiter.

14. Dickinson does refer occasionally in her writings to the Inquisition, most notably, perhaps, in F588:

> The Heart asks Pleasure – first – | Pleasure / Blessing
> And then – Excuse from Pain –
> And then – those little Anodynes
> That deaden suffering –
>
> And then – to go to sleep –
> And then – if it should be
> The will of it's Inquisitor
> The privilege to die –

The tone of this poem comparing the bureaucratic sadism of Inquisitorial courts with a psychological progression from pleasure to pain is coolly detached, as if the narrator were herself gradually adopting a brutally authoritarian viewpoint. It is unclear whether the narrator is speaking dispassionately and generally about the phenomenon of intractable pain, or whether she herself speaks from experience as a sufferer, a deliberate relational confusion that plays into the poem's ostensible design of depicting the dissolution of an individual will. As she tries vainly to bargain with her persecutor, the narrator assumes, like a victim of the Stockholm syndrome, the point of view and language of her tormentor. The haughtily dismissive diction of "those *little* Anodynes / That deaden suffering," the insertion of the euphemism "sleep" for oblivion, and Dickinson's insistently Latinate diction—the neutral vocabulary of an entrenched officialdom—reinforce her portrayal of a consciousness confronted with sanctioned cruelty. The victim's surrender of her own victimhood culminates in her slavish characterization of death as a "privilege" to be requested from her "Inquisitor."

Other Dickinsonian references to the Inquisition are apt to be facetious. In a letter sent to Austin while he was teaching classes composed largely of boys drawn from working-class Irish families, in comparing her willingness to write to him with his dilatoriness in replying, she says, "If I thought you would *care* any I would hold my tongue so tight that Inquisition *itself* should'nt wring a sentence from me – but t'would only punish *me* who would fain get off unpunished, *therefore here I am a'nt* you happy to see me?" (L48).

15. William Howard (240), Judy Jo Small (157), and Jeanne Holland (157) agree with Porter that this poem is probably intended to be read as describing events occurring within a privy.

16. Although this poem has more recently come in for a good deal of critical scrutiny, Porter described it in 1981 as having been theretofore neglected: "A poem anthologists always overlook and to which a reader or two have attached solemn scholarly meditation chronicles, in fact, the visit of a spider to a privy and particularly to an unmentionable part of the occupant's anatomy" (17).

17. A variant for "a visitor," "*the* visitor" [emphasis added] focuses specifically on the *role* of visitor, thereby placing the narrator and the spider more precisely in a binary opposition of host/visitor, which is mirrored negatively in the other implicit binary of owner/trespasser.

18. Adverse possession of a property is sometimes called informally "squatter's rights," a phrase that invites a humorous and scatological interpretation of the underlying plight of the poem's narrator. *Black's* defines the term as "the right to acquire title to real property by adverse possession, or by preemption of public lands" (1439). *Bouvier's* defines "squatter" as "One who settles on the lands of others without any legal authority; this term is applied particularly to persons who settle on the public land" (2: 1026). Could the humor generated by the informal term for the legal doctrine of adverse possession have prompted Dickinson, wholly or in part, to write this poem?

19. See, for example, F513:

> The Spider holds a Silver Ball
> In unperceived Hands –
> And dancing softly to Himself
> His Yarn of Pearl – unwinds –
>
> He plies from Nought to Nought –
> In unsubstantial Trade –
> Supplants our Tapestries with His –
> In half the period –
>
> An Hour to rear supreme
> His Continents of Light –
> Then dangle from the Housewife's Broom –
> His Boundaries – forgot –

Several themes are developed here in common with those in "Alone and in a

Circumstance": the unobtrusiveness of the spider, his industry, and his status as a legitimate alternative occupant, someone capable of establishing entire "Continents" that threaten to supplant the claims of human beings, who come to the competition armed with brooms.

20. At the time of this poem's composition, the definition of "gymnasium" adhered more closely to its ancient sense of a school than to our more modern use of it to designate a large hall dedicated to sports activities. Still, Dickinson would have understood the term to have embraced physical education. Webster's 1828 dictionary defines "gymnasium" as "a place where athletic exercises were performed. Hence, a place of exercise; a school."

21. Variants for "Assiduously" emphasize the impropriety of the spider's intrusion on the narrator, in two regards, social status and sexuality: "deliberately," "determinately," "impertinently."

22. The presence of a variant for "inmates," "Peasants," indicates that Dickinson wrote this poem at least in part as a satire of interclass frictions. The narrator's horrifying discovery that the spiders might consider themselves her heirs, and thus may stand to inherit the *estate* of the privy, makes either extreme of the social spectrum seem ludicrous, not least because they are battling over ownership of a mere privy. Then too, Dickinson's reference to "Peasants" may help solidify the poem's connection to Sand's *Mauprat,* which was also concerned with class conflict (see note 35). The novel's characters Patience and Bernard Mauprat epitomize peasant and aristocratic sensibilities.

23. See, for example, Joel Norcross's reply to a letter from Edward Dickinson: "The cost of Building a house on that or any other lot . . . generally amounts to more than people expect, and *the loss of time and anxiety of mind* is worth something." Qtd. in Habegger, "How the Dickinsons Lost Their Homes" 185; emphasis added.

24. A variant for "take" in line 19, "seize," subtly alters the legal status of the spiders' appropriation of the narrator's property. "Take" is congruent with "larceny," a criminal act, while "seize" suggests that the spiders have some legal pretext for their actions. This ambivalence echoes the legal dilemma confronting the poem's narrator, who argues to a presumably legally empowered audience that the spiders' occupation of the privy is, on its face, criminal, and therefore disqualified from receiving consideration as a legitimate claim.

25. The word "privy" lends itself to the making of various legal witticisms. That word certainly denoted an outhouse during Dickinson's lifetime; Webster defined it in his 1828 dictionary with the polite euphemism "A necessary house." In law, the same word occurs in many contexts, of which but a few examples are "privy token," "privy seal," and "privy verdict." The concept of "privity" in law may also apply specifically to the poem. It is "the mutual or successive relationship to the same rights of property" (*Bouvier's* 2: 758). Someone holding an interest in a property simultaneously with others is, therefore, a *privy* to it, and thus the narrator and the spiders may be considered as privies in a hypothetical joint ownership of the outhouse. The question of whether Dickinson intended her poem to suggest to mind the elided term "privy" cannot, however, be satisfactorily resolved.

26. Virginia Jackson says she discerns no logical continuity of meaning between the text of the poem and the collage it encloses. Jackson provides a rough spatial transcription of the poem, but strangely omits the crucial word "visitor," despite that

word's appearance in the photostatic reproduction of the poem's original text that immediately follows in her book (166–68).

27. See, for example, Johnson's note about letter L137, written to John Graves, on which Dickinson punningly "sketched a grave, with head and foot stones" (267). For a more general discussion of the poet's pairing of impromptu illustrations with texts of her poems, see Martha Nell Smith's "The Poet as Cartoonist."

28. Even some five years after the financial collapse of the Amherst & Belchertown, Dickinson could still write a poem praising the railroad engine, "I like to see it lap the Miles –."

29. Although Holland agrees that the combination of the stamp and two strips of paper is a coded pictorial reference to Edward Dickinson, she interprets the strips anthropomorphically as legs, not tracks (146–47).

30. Another of Edward Dickinson's many civic projects may also undergird the poem's reference to inmates of an asylum. As the *Springfield Republican* noted in May 1859, "Edward Dickinson of Amherst has been appointed by Gov Banks, trustee of the lunatic hospital at Northampton, in place of Dr. Luther V. Bell, resigned." See Leyda 1: 369.

31. Dickinson wrote of her father to Thomas Higginson, "He buys me many Books – but begs me not to read them – because he fears they joggle the Mind" (L261).

32. Because the narrator addresses her listener as "Lord," Otis Lord might seem to provide another eligible candidate for being the poem's intended auditor, but the date of composition, 1870, renders such a conjecture implausible.

33. Domhnall Mitchell describes succinctly the legal and financial fate of the Amherst & Belchertown Railroad Company (30).

34. I respectfully disagree with Thomas Johnson's interpretation of this poem (*Poems* 2: 816).

35. Sand's novel also concludes with a legal drama, as Bernard Mauprat is put on trial for the attempted murder of his cousin Edmée. It is also worth noting that Sand's plot dignifies the peasant values and integrity of the character Patience. Perhaps Dickinson's reference to Sand's novel lends credence to the idea that, in her own fictive legal dispute, the author's sympathies lay with the trespassing spiders.

3. Seals, Signs, and Rings

1. In the play, Antonio may aid Bassanio out of either friendship or family loyalty (they are kinsmen), yet the possibility that Antonio's interest in Bassanio may be erotic, not merely friendly or fraternal, has been explored in many stagings of the play. See, for example, director Michael Radford's 2004 film treatment.

2. Contracts fail too, of course, if one party introduces new conditions to the original offer that the other finds unacceptable. Such is the situation in a comparatively late poem, F1386:

"Faithful to the end" amended
From the Heavenly clause –
Lucrative indeed the offer
But the Heart withdraws –

"I will give", the base Proviso –

Spare your "Crown of Life" –
Thos it fits – too fair to wear it –
Try it on Yourself –

This poem is especially rich in contractual language; as Lambert says, "The clause is clearly contractual, since 'proviso' is also inserted in the poem" (61). From a legal standpoint, the narrator of the poem is rejecting a suggested contract because a "base," or unacceptable, proviso has been added to the original language—here, in Revelation 2:10, "Be thou faithful unto death, and I will give thee a crown of life." Perhaps the speaker comes to distrust an offer that guarantees life only after death, that is, in eternity rather than upon an edenic earth; Capps suggests that she found the offer of eternal life in exchange for unquestioning faith "too businesslike to accept" (57). Interestingly, for a poem criticizing the addition of qualifications to an original document, Dickinson rewrote this poem several times, experimenting with the legal nuances of her words. The addition, or subtraction, of such legally freighted terms as "amended," "clause," "lucrative," "offer," "withdraws," and "Emolument" introduces subtle changes into versions A, B, C, D, and E, although Dickinson's central point would seem to be that constancy cannot, by its very definition, be subject to qualification: "Constancy with a Proviso / Constancy abhors."

3. Dickinson wrote other poems questioning the authenticity of showy displays of kindness. See, for example, "What Soft – Cherubic Creatures –."

4. Capps suggests that Dickinson encountered Sterne's phrase through conversation, rather than by reading *A Sentimental Journey* (73).

5. Contracts could be affected by acts of God in ways both negative and positive. Although contractors accused of failing to deliver what they had promised could defend themselves by saying that events beyond their control had interfered, contracting parties also occasionally enjoyed windfall profits beyond those stipulated in the contract. Such would seem to be the situation in F1217:

I worked for chaff and earning Wheat
Was haughty and betrayed.
What right had Fields to arbitrate
In Matters ratified?

I tasted Wheat and hated Chaff
And thanked the ample friend –
Wisdom is more becoming viewed
At distance than at hand.

During Dickinson's lifetime, the rights of workers, such as the rural laborers in Connecticut Valley fields, waxed and waned during years of crop surpluses and crop failures. Agricultural workers were often bound by contractual relationships with their employers. Here the poem's narrator speaks in the persona of a farm laborer, and the poem's overall subject is, indisputably, I think, the relativism of value, conditioned by experience. Put bluntly, we do not crave that which we do not yet know exists. Acquiring new tastes and new perspectives devalues previous standards of worth, a theme that resonates in many other Dickinson poems. As we saw in "What would I give to see his face?," Dickinson exploited conventional indices of worth, even inverting them to make what was ordinarily considered valuable valueless, and what was most worthless most worthy. The speaker in this poem initially considers her contract with her employer to have been violated because she was not paid what had been promised to her. Yet her impulse turns out to have been naive and ill-considered, for in reality, she realizes (in a double sense) much more than she had bargained for. The windfall she enjoys, represented metonymically by "Fields," is her share in a crop which had turned out to be more bountiful than employer or employee had anticipated, and within Dickinson's legally determined trope, the "Fields" function as an arbiter, that is, a neutral party mediating a legal dispute, particularly a labor dispute. Accordingly, the speaker says that the original agreement between the speaker and her employer had been "ratified": one of the definitions of "ratification" supplied by *Black's* is "rank-and-file approval of a labor union's collective-bargaining agreement with management" (1289). The contract struck between employer and employee may have granted the latter a percentage of the realized profit, which had turned out to be greater than could have been imagined.

6. *Black's,* in defining "breach of promise," states, "Under English common law, an engagement to marry had the nature of a commercial contract, so if one party broke the engagement without justification, the innocent party was entitled to damages" (201).

7. In their reading of *The Pickwick Papers* the Dickinson siblings would have encountered a literary treatment of breach of promise cases arising out of comic romantic entanglements, in the suit Miss Bardle brings against Samuel Pickwick.

8. In my article "Darwinian Dickinson: The Scandalous Rise and Noble Fall of the Common Clover," I suggest that the poet employed the bee/flower metatrope with conscious irony (73–75).

9. Seals also have a long association with aristocratic or even royal prerogative. Thus, for example, "the seal Despair" in "There's a certain Slant of light" is described as "an imperial affliction / Sent us of the Air –."

10. Anson 82. On the same subject, P. S. Atiyah says: "A contract under seal, that is to say a deed, . . . is a written promise or set of promises which derives its validity from the form, and the form alone, of the executing instrument. In point of fact the 'form' of the deed is nowadays surprisingly elastic. The only necessities are that the deed should be intended as such, and should be signed, sealed, and delivered. The sealing, however, has now become largely a fiction, an adhesive wafer simply being attached to the document in place of a genuine seal" (22).

11. In law, "seal," as in the phrase "under seal," also connotes confidentiality and privacy. Thus, for example, in Amherst College ms. A 842, a rough draft fragment of a letter evidently intended for Judge Lord (since part of the text is written on a piece of envelope addressed in Dickinson's hand to "Otis P. Lord / Salem – / Mass. –") the word "seal" may be deployed in several interconnected senses. Dickinson mentions "Apartments in our own minds" which might, presumably, be sealed off against the intrusions of other people. In a visual pun, the poet evidently inscribed that phrase across the envelope's *seal* (Werner 275).

12. Because Dickinson often wrote on sheets of stationery embossed at the top, her poems, copied out below the embossment, may also be thought of as having been written *under* [the] *seal.* The question of whether she herself was conscious of this linguistic coincidence, however, likely remains unanswerable.

13. Rowena Revis Jones points out that within New England's covenantal churches the rite of baptism constituted the "seal" confirming an individual believer's share in the Covenant of Grace.

14. Two versions of this poem exist, one sent to Samuel Bowles, the other to Susan

Dickinson. Susan Dickinson's copy includes an interpolated line after line 11, "In a Day –": "Tri Victory –." Dickinson's intent here would seem to be to emphasize to Susan that conventional women's definitions of the marriage process follow almost parodically the hierarchy of the trinity: "Born – Bridalled – Shrouded –" and Father, Son, Holy Ghost. The word "Victory," particularly, associates women's experience of marrying with the salvation of an individual Christian soul. Yet Dickinson's tone is satirical, not pietistic. She is making fun of women who substitute their own marital histories for Christ's life and tripartite religious significance. More generally, she may be satirizing women for whom marital success is equivalent or superior to their spiritual and religious identities. See Johnson, *Poems* 2: 758–59.

15. To this day, in several states the awarding of an engagement ring remains legally indeterminate, most state courts accepting the giving of an engagement ring as a *pre*-contractual gesture. Notwithstanding that consensus, a good deal of disagreement persists. The predominating view is that the giving of a ring is a conditional gift that may be revoked by the giver if things don't work out. Then the erstwhile fiancée must make restitution to the ring's purchaser.

16. Although relatively common, garnets enjoyed a vogue as gemstones during the nineteenth century. Dickinson's comparison here would seem to be based on a hierarchy of value in which garnets and gold are antitheses.

4. Lands with Locks

1. See, for example, Sprankling: "Suppose B agrees to purchase Blackacre, a house situated on 20 forested acres, from S. What is B buying? S and B would probably characterize the transaction as the purchase of 'land.' But in reality, B is buying *title to the land,* not the *land* itself" (329).

2. In a poem written on the topic of dilatoriness and procrastination (F1279 C), Dickinson discusses "Speculation" in a twofold sense, as conjecture and investment:

> The things we thought that we should do
> We other things have done
> But those peculiar industries
> Have never been begun –
>
> The Lands we thought that we should seek
> When large enough to run
> By Speculation ceded
> To Speculation's Son –
>
> The Heaven in which we hoped to pause | Chivalry / Discipline / Tyranny
> When Chivalry was done | Untenable / Impassable
> Untenable to Logic
> But possibly the one –

That "Lands" have been "ceded" to a "Son" suggests that Dickinson is thinking here about conjecture as a form of intellectual property that may be bequeathed, like real property. She would appear to have had a British model for inheritance in mind: variants for line 10 include "When Chivalry was done" and "When Tyranny was done," both probably alluding to a conventional, nearly stereotypic view of medieval British customs and the monarchy. "Speculation" may refer simultaneously to intellectual curiosity and to financial speculation. The explanation for Dickinson's cultural bias here is, I think, that she wished to emphasize the British practice of primogeniture—"Speculation ceded / To Speculation's Son."

3. Sprankling lists, as examples of "intangible personal property," "stocks, bonds, patents, trademarks, copyrights, trade secrets, debts, franchises, licenses, and other contract rights" (9).

4. In "'Some things that I called mine': Dickinson and the Perils of Property Ownership," I argue that the poet understood the concept of property ownership as being largely illusory (16–22).

5. Provocatively, Robert Lambert suggests that the poem involves three competing claimants—God, Jove, and the mortal narrator: "Thus the poem presents a tripartite rivalry. Essentially, God owns the earth; Dickinson claims the flowers thereon. Jove, the rival claimant of air and rain, has sown the garden with weeds. Far from being a pretty acre, it is a plot gone to haphazard seed" (41). But I disagree with Lambert's essential reading of this poem's legal situation. The narrator, whom Lambert identifies perhaps a little too readily as the poet herself, protests that the garden is being taken from her after she had expended considerable effort to make it "pretty." Although Dickinson's syntax and grammar in the second stanza present formidable interpretive difficulties, the speaker appears to be the person who sowed the garden "with care"—not Jove, as Lambert suggests. Instead, Dickinson is probably employing "Jove" here informally as a synonym for "God."

6. B. J. Smith emphasizes the lawyerly tone of the poem: "The poet asserts ownership from the first, 'The property, MY garden,' and subtly suggests that it is a covetous desire for her well-maintained property that has initiated God's action rather than any real legal claim. These stanzas have a tone not uncommon in a lawyer's use of carefully worded comments that shift blame within a seemingly unbiased statement of the facts" (41).

7. In her essay "Dickinson's 'I had some things that I called mine,'" Jane Eberwein pointed out the family joke on the name *Shaw.*

8. Shaw's most notable decision in favor of business enterprises is *Farwell v. Boston & Worcester Railroad Corporation* (1842), in which the court denied recovery to a railway engineer injured on the job.

9. *Black's:* "Blackacre. A fictitious tract of land used in legal discourse (esp. law-school hypotheticals) to discuss real-property issues" (179).

10. Friedman says, "When, in the 1820s, a movement arose to reform the law, reformers lopped away at doctrines and institutions that seemed positively harmful, then those which, whatever their impact, appeared to be 'tyrannical' or 'feudal.' The urge to modernize was a crucial feature in the important revision of property law carried out in New York in 1827–1828." After primogeniture was discarded, "the fee tail," Friedman says, "was another casualty" (173–74).

11. Sprankling: "Even today, the first-in-time principle is still the basic rule for determining the respective priority of competing title claims to real property" (13).

12. Dickinson's verminous antiheroes do not, it should be admitted, always enjoy successful criminal careers. F1377, a charming poem that is virtually a companion piece to "The Rat is the concisest Tenant" (the two poems were, apparently, composed within perhaps a year of each other) depicts a fitting end for the raffish rat:

A Rat surrendered here
A brief career of Cheer
And Fraud and Fear.

Of Ignominy's due
Let all addicted to
Beware –

The most obliging Trap
It's tendency to snap
Cannot resist –

Temptation is the Friend
Repugnantly resigned
At last.

In common with "The Rat is the concisest Tenant" this piece emphasizes, in its very style, the *conciseness* of the pest, which is, in turn, an attribute of his *smallness*. Here too, as well, the rat's malfeasance is partially mitigated. As a criminal, the rat is depicted as having been led into evil ways by the influence of a false "Friend," here a personified "Temptation," which may be renounced by the rat only, and finally, after death. The death of the felon rodent, convicted in the poem of being a "Fraud," is implicitly represented in the poem as a legal execution, the trap functioning as a sort of guillotine. The second stanza imitates the admonitory language employed in the wake of public executions to instill respect for the law in the populace, whose presence at the execution is adumbrated by the poem's temporal simulation of real time, in the first line's adverbial "here."

13. Helen Vendler writes: "The poem is about the relation of Landlord and Tenant. . . . The Rat is 'concise' (from Latin *concidere,* 'to cut in pieces') because he is usually invisible; he is not the inhabitant of a fixed space. 'You'd hardly know he was there,' as a landlord might say of an unobtrusive tenant. He is also 'concise' because he nowhere appears in the landlord's ledger. Nonetheless, because he lives in the house, the Rat (thinks the landlord) should pay rent (which would formalize a lawful relation between himself and the landlord). But the Rat is not lawful; he spends his whole day intent on schemes that balk our intelligence (our 'Wit')" (460).

14. Paul Ferlazzo says of this poem: "Instead of portraying the rat as scorned by civilization, [Dickinson] presents him as one who scorns civilization because of its reliance upon the laws of property. He is 'concisest,' terse, and succinct toward man, occupying little room for which he will not pay rent. We cannot understand him, nor can we affect him. . . . Although he is beyond our understanding of usefulness and 'Decree,' she affirms that he deserves his part in the scheme of things and remains 'Lawful as Equilibrium'" (122).

15. Alternatively, Jean Mudge suggests that the nearby neighbor Dickinson had in mind while writing this poem may have been either the Sweetsers or the Hills (212).

16. A variant for the line "Embellish all we own –" is "Inebriate our own" (Franklin 3: 1244). In deciding between these alternatives, the poet evidently hesitated between choosing a figure emphasizing beautification or intoxication.

17. In F391 B, "Knows how to forget!," Dickinson also characterizes the ability to forget as a scientific invention:

Is it in a Book?
So, I could buy it –
Is it like a Planet?
Telescopes would know –

If it be invention
It must have a Patent –

18. It had been known since 1856, from a discovery credited to the Swiss anatomist Albert von Kölliker and his German colleague Heinrich Müller, that beating hearts generate electricity.

19. Dickinson's satirizing of advertising language used to pique buyers' interest in new or untested products may also be apparent in F978, "Faith – is the Pierless Bridge." There, faith is described, potentially, as a newfangled bridge that may convey a believer across a gulf of doubt—yet how could a bridge lacking piers retain structural integrity? Suspension bridges, introduced in America during the first half of the nineteenth century, required fewer piers, thus providing a possible context for Dickinson's reference. Dickinson's reference to "Pierless" may also be a play on "peerless," a word familiar to many of her contemporary readers from the language of advertising, and associated as well with technologic innovation, as exemplified by the Hale & Kilburn Company's "Peerless Portable Washstand."

20. Dickinson demonstrates a humorous attitude toward copyright, as well, in a note the poet sent to Susan Dickinson around 1884 (L909):

Dear Sue –

One of the sweetest Messages I ever received, was, "Mrs Dickinson sent you this Cardinal Flower, and told me to tell you she thought of you."

Except for usurping your copyright – I should regive the Message, but each Voice is it's own –

Emily –

21. See also Dickinson's mention of "patent" in relation to patent shoe leather, in "Is bliss, then, such abyss," which I discuss in chapter 6.

22. Inventors' attempts to create locks resistant to lockpickers' efforts generated considerable transatlantic press at midcentury. British visitors to the 1851 Great Exhibition at the Crystal Palace were stunned to witness an American, Alfred C. Hobbs, successfully pick the British-manufactured, state-of-the art "Detector" lock, patented by Jeremiah Chubb of Portsmouth in 1818. Dickinson's interest in inhabiting "Lands with Locks" that she could "pick" may well be rooted in this industrial, technical, and legal context.

5. Has All a Codicil?

1. Dickinson likely alludes to Corinthians 15: "O death, where is thy sting? O grave, where is thy victory?"

2. This letter was discovered within the large envelope containing fragments and drafts pertaining to the correspondence between the poet and Judge Lord. Thomas Johnson concurs with Millicent Todd Bingham's supposition that the letter was sent to Kimball (*Letters* 882). I see no reason to disagree.

3. A strong piece of circumstantial evidence that Judge Lord helped Emily Dickinson and her mother compose their wills is the witnessing signature on those documents of Elizabeth Lord, the judge's wife. See Sewall 657.

4. On the art of dying well, *ars moriendi,* among the Victorians, see St. Armand 59–61.

5. In law, a dying person's words possess special significance. Deathbed confessions have always been regarded as especially trustworthy, on the assumption that a dying person, having nothing to lose, would be more candid than someone hoping to live on. In court, "dying declarations" are, for instance, excepted from rules governing hearsay.

6. In law, gifts given at the point of death, rather than through the instrument of a will, are given *causa mortis:* "done or made in contemplation of one's own death" (*Black's* 233).

7. Daneen Wardrop suggests that the poem's final line expresses "a kind of epistemological nihilism" (192n1).

8. On the devolution of Edward Dickinson's estate to Austin, see Habegger, *My Wars* 564.

9. This poem has a rich compositional history. That Dickinson sent a version of it to T. W. Higginson suggests she came to see the poem as potentially publishable, reworking it several times before she felt satisfied. Here I have taken the liberty of interpolating choices drawn from various drafts. See Franklin 3: 1166–71.

10. In some poems Dickinson enlarged the moments preceding death and their testamentary significance to include not just noxious representatives of natural life such as the fly, as in "I heard a Fly buzz – when I died –," but the entire presence of ephemeral fauna and flora, whose temporary extinction, accomplished annually during New England's first hard frost, emblematized a life lived fully in the brief time allotted to it. A short, and perhaps late, poem, F1746, gestures simultaneously to legal responsibilities that devolved upon the executor or administrator of an estate—the office fulfilled by Benjamin Kimball for Judge Lord—and the courageous tenacity of the living who are dying:

> Those final Creatures, – who they are –
> That faithful to the close,
> Administer her ecstasy,
> But just the Summer knows.

Hallmarks of the estate administrator's position and character we have seen in previous poems are reprised here: the secrecy entailed in administering details of a trust; the fidelity of the appointed fiduciary agent; the finality of the moment, and legal and religious closure. Presumably, the poem describes the crickets and other insects, "Creatures," most of which, unlike birds, do not migrate and so will largely perish during the first onset of freezing temperatures. Insects are avatars and exemplars of "Summer," in the sense that they are coeval with the season, and its administrators, in that they fulfill to the very end of their existence an obligation to continue enacting the "ecstasy" of summer's plenitude of vitality, figured here, perhaps, as a bountiful estate. Because they die, and "Summer" itself also expires, all that the insects leave behind is mystery about the natural cycle. The adjective "faithful" connotes both religious piety and fidelity to professional duty, and "administer" refers simultaneously to the legal responsibilities of a retained attorney and the ceremonial duties of a priest. With the disappearance into the grass of the insects' minute corpses and summer's decline into autumn, no physical evidence of the season's presence remains, thereby preserving the legal and sacerdotal mystery.

11. The anthropomorphized "Grass" is mirrored, I think, in "Nature," in line 17: "Had

Nature any Plated Face." Nature, figured as a family patriarch, possesses a "Face" that may be "Plated," perhaps on a daguerreotype plate.

12. Friedman writes, "Common law dower had once been the chief way to provide for a widow's twilight years. Dower was a peculiar kind of estate. For one thing, it attached to land only. For another, dower was a mere life estate (in one-third of the late husband's real estate). The widow had no right to sell; and she had no rights over the 'remainder,' that is no right to dispose of the land after her death, by will or otherwise. The land remained, in short, in the husband's bloodline" (322).

13. Friedman says that "New York passed its first [married women's property] law in 1848; and by 1850, about seventeen states had granted to married women some legal capacity to deal with their property" (147), and that "married women's property laws . . . were extended, broadened, and generalized after 1850" (373–74). All of Dickinson's poems mentioning dower were written after 1850, when married and unmarried women's rights were undergoing profound legal revisions.

14. Friedman says, "Dower had one rather remarkable feature: a husband could not defeat the right by selling his land or giving it away. Over all land he owned, or had owned, hung the ghostly threat of 'inchoate dower.' This potential claim followed the land through the whole chain of title, until the wife died and extinguished the claim" (322). Friedman goes on to say that dower, although an ancient legal custom in Britain, came to be seen by the American legal community at midcentury as having less and less relevance to estate law: "As a protection device, dower had severe limitations. It perhaps made sense for the landed gentry of England; or for plantation owners. But if the husband's wealth consisted of stocks and bonds, or a business, dower did the wife little good. Dower had another fault, too. It was superior to the claims of the husband's creditors, which was good for wives but bad for the creditors. And dower was an annoying cloud on titles" (322–23). Thus the legal concept of dower inherently put at odds the needs and rights of husbands and wives, sometimes to the detriment of both, and even to that of the estate itself.

15. Lambert, however, says of Dickinson's usage of the word "dower" in her poetry, "There is no stress on the widow's posthumous award of property" (77).

16. The idea of dower being fractional, whether as the bride's investment in the material success of a marriage or as the widow's lawful claim to a portion of her husband's estate, may be present as well in these stanzas from F646:

> 'Tis One by One – the Father counts –
> And then a Tract between
> Set Cypherless – to teach the Eye
> The Value of it's Ten –
>
> Until the peevish Student
> Acquire the Quick of Skill –
> Then Numerals are dowered back –
> Adorning all the Rule –

Understanding that the presence of a "Tract," as if of land, is implied mathematically by gaps between integers depends on an awareness of the existence of fractions. Elementary school students are instructed in the "Value" of the first ten ordinal numbers by teachers who afterward inculcate the principle of breaking whole numbers down into an unlimited number of parts. Enlightened to the concept of divisibility, students find their comprehension of numbers, and of the very concept of *quantity,* enlarged, perhaps infinitely so. In a sense, pupils thereby become cognitively wealthier once they understand that even the number 1 may be viewed as limitless in its own right. Elementary school students learn the skill of "Cypher[ing]," that is, performing arithmetic, before they are taught fractions; later, those students who had become disappointed by the thought of a limited numerical universe are relieved to find their conceptions of infinity have been expanded all over again, as the "Rule" of mathematics becomes "adorn[ed]" by the concept of fractionality.

Dickinson's phrase "*dowered* back" may connote a return on investment made by women entering into matrimony, a sort of legal guarantee that they will not be left destitute by widowhood. Income provided by rents and other sources of profit realized from ownership of real property may be troped here as "Numerals . . . dowered back," or a peculiarly feminine form of an asset's redemption. See also "Doubt Me! My Dim Companion!" (F332), in which a speaker indignantly makes a distinction between that small portion of passion with which even "God, would be content" and the indivisible entirety of her devotion:

> The whole of me – forever –
> What more the woman can
> Say quick, that I may dower thee
> With last Delight I own!

17. Pleasures resulting from delayed gratification constitute a prominent theme in Dickinson's poetry. See Richard Wilbur's seminal essay in Dickinson studies, "Sumptuous Destitution."

18. I examine the phrase "compensated Trust" in "Law, Property, and Provincialism in Dickinson's Poems and Letters to Judge Lord."

19. In most jurisdictions, the administration of trusts pertaining to minors or other dependents, having to do not only with the material support of the beneficiaries or wards but also their education and religious upbringing, fell within the province of equity or chancery.

20. Friedman writes, "Trust litigation was fairly sparse in the early nineteenth century. Except for marriage settlements, living trusts were probably not common. Most trusts were short-term, 'caretaker' trusts, created to protect some weaker member of the family: married women, minors, incompetents" (183).

21. Capps cites references in Dickinson's letters to various short stories and novels by Dickens, including *Bleak House, David Copperfield, The Old Curiosity Shop,* and *Pickwick Papers*—but not *Great Expectations* (95). Nevertheless, it stands to reason that Dickinson would have had at least a cursory knowledge of that novel and its plot, considering her early enthusiasm (in common with much of her generation) for Dickens's fiction.

22. See Andersen: "Good lawyers and fiduciaries know that regular communication with clients and beneficiaries is good business. Communication is also an obligation. Ethics rules require lawyers to keep their clients informed. Probate rules and trust documents regularly require that fiduciaries account to the beneficiaries" (305).

23. Another possible topical frame of reference may be a famous journalistic hoax involving, involuntarily, the younger Herschel, John. In 1835, the *New York Sun* purported to announce observations made by Sir John using a highly advanced telescope that moon "inhabitants" and their settlements could be discerned. But the report was soon revealed to be a fraud, likely contrived by Richard A. Locke, a reporter for the

Sun. In the sense that a journalistic hoax is an "affair," a contretemps perpetrated by a newspaper aiming to boost sales, Dickinson's reference in the poem may generate irony by contrasting sensationalism generated by a very public hoax to the sanctity of attorney–client relations. If so, the speaker in this poem may be approaching the fact of her own identity self-deprecatingly, as if it were a "secret" known to virtually everyone else in town, like an unraveling hoax.

24. This is another poem with several variants, the most striking of which is Dickinson's shift in gender of her initial pronoun. She sent a version beginning with the masculine pronoun to Higginson in August 1877 (Franklin 3: 1270–72).

25. Austin was threatening at the time to decamp to Chicago with Sue to set up a practice there. Edward sought to provide them with a reason for staying in Amherst by building the Evergreens.

26. See Habegger, *My Wars* 344–45, 563.

27. Austin also fell afoul of the rules governing the administration of a trust. According to Winthrop Dakin, "[Austin] too was once a party in an appealed case. The court held that he, as trustee of a certain private trust, had invested an excessive amount in an untried business venture and must personally pay the loss it suffered to the extent of the excess" (38). In his role as trustee, Austin appears to have been found in violation of the "Prudent Man" rule; that is, he committed money to an undertaking too speculative for the investment of trust funds, which courts usually wish to see invested conservatively.

28. Barton Levi St. Armand has harshly criticized the professional conduct of Edward Dickinson in his handling of his nieces' trust, saying that at the very least he played "fast and loose" with the funds (309). Alfred Habegger, on the other hand, says that it is "pointless to charge Edward with criminal peculation," although he does accuse him of "shaving [his] ethics" and turning a "very sweet deal" for himself in his handling of the Newman estate (*My Wars* 346). In any event, Edward Dickinson never was charged in court with self-dealing, as Loring and Albert Norcross had been.

6. Felonies, Trials, and Transcendental Prisons

1. For an extended and dramatic treatment of the Parkman–Webster case, see Simon Schama's *Dead Certainties*.

2. Murray notes the Dickinsons' prejudice against the Irish was typical for the time and for their class (140–44). A friendship between the poet and their servant Maggie Maher evidently softened her view of the Irish.

3. Broadly, the principle that was formulated as a result of the M'Naghten trial held that a lunatic could not be held legally culpable for a crime: "To establish a defense on the ground of insanity, it must be clearly proven that, at the time of committing of the act, the party accused was labouring under such a defective reason, from disease of the mind, as not to know the nature and quality of the act he was doing; or, if he did know it, that he did not know he was doing what was wrong." *M'Naghten's Case,* 10 Clark & F. 199, 203, 210 (1843).

4. Camille Paglia has written about Dickinson's predilection for employing images involving violence and mayhem, labeling the poet "Amherst's Madame de Sade" (623).

5. The Dickinson family had some experience with the subject of criminal insanity. In 1853 Edward Dickinson successfully defended a minister against charges of cruelty and abuse brought by his wife, who was represented by Rufus Choate. Dickinson was able

to persuade the court that the wife was prone to bouts of insanity, and her suit was dismissed. The results of the trial may not redound entirely to Edward Dickinson's credit, yet his besting of Choate, then the attorney general of Massachusetts, would have represented a feather in his legal cap. See Habegger, *My Wars* 288.

6. According to Habegger, Lavinia Dickinson recalled of herself and her sister that "when we were little children we used to spend entire days in the woods hunting for treasures" (*My Wars* 158). Thus, perhaps, the poem's reference to flowers and other woodland souvenirs as "trinkets," that is, merchandise of little value, although irresistible to a child's eye. Later, while at Mount Holyoke, the poet remarked that her fellow students had nearly picked the area around the college clean of wild blooms: "There are not many wild flowers near, for the girls have driven them to a distance." (L23).

7. Dickinson may have changed "Oak" to "Fir" in the final line to achieve congruity between two types of evergreens. She may also have hoped to generate an impression of a family relationship between the two species, perhaps suggesting husband and wife proprietors of a small business.

8. T. W. Higginson declared this poem "the most nearly objective thing she wrote" (qtd. in Bingham 35).

9. Considering Dickinson's careful delineation of the burglars' methods, which involve entering the property through a window, it is ironic that in 1885 the Evergreens was robbed using quite similar methods. The *Amherst Record* reported: "Jewelry to the value of perhaps $100 dollars, beside a small sum of money in Ned's [the son's] pocket-book in a bureau, was taken, and the things in the rooms in the second story were a good deal disturbed. The robbery was thought to have been committed while the family were at their dinner, or between six and seven o'clock, and the robbers entered through a window near the piazza." Times were hard then in New England, and, as Emily Dickinson wrote to her nephew, "Burglaries have become so frequent, is it quite safe to leave the Golden Rule out over night?" (Lombardo 7). Nevertheless, as Habegger writes, "In her later years Dickinson often defended acts of theft and stolen love" (*My Wars* 613).

10. Paul Crumbley usefully approaches Dickinson's polyvocality from a Bakhtinian critical standpoint. In his essay "Dickinson's Dialogic Voice," he recapitulates and contributes to larger critical discussions of the poet's heteroglossia.

11. Cristanne Miller also discerns polyvocality in Dickinson's poems referring to the Civil War: "As a whole, her poems responding to war resemble an amalgam of voices or attitudes taking different emotional and philosophical perspectives, often in the form of dramatic lyrics, more than the crafting of any unified response to the conflict or to war generally" (148).

12. As legal terms, "propound" and "propounder" pertain both to contracts and to estate law. In a letter scrap apparently composed with Judge Lord in mind, Dickinson quoted Jesus's promise made on the cross to the thief, "This Day thou shalt be with me in Paradise" (Luke 23:43), and added, "The Propounder of Paradise must indeed possess it" (L791). For Judge Lord's amusement, she represents Jesus as the purported owner of a piece of property to which, in offering it to the thief, he must prove ownership, as with a title or deed.

13. B. J. Smith makes a similar point about the poem: "The poet evaluates words for proper usage and placement in the poem. The lined-up candidates are not unlike the

scores of possible words in Dickinson's own manuscripts. Lists of possibilities from which the single "right," "legal" word comes [*sic*]. It conveys a comforting image of fruitful, rational activity, within the bounds of the poet's control" (45).

14. As the prominent judge and legal philosopher Jerome Frank once noted, "Only a very foolish lawyer will dare guess the outcome of a jury trial" (186).

15. Robert Meredith points to the definition of "abyss" in Dickinson's "lexicon": "An *Abyss* may be described as 'Bliss' because, as Dickinson's dictionary told her (Noah Webster, 1847), it meant in antiquity a place of 'immense treasures' . . . ; but an abyss is also, according to the same source, a 'bottomless gulf,' a 'deep mass of waters,' here given the light tone on the surface of the poem, a large puddle that the shopper must step in if she is to cross the street to the store" (442).

16. Contrastingly, in the poem "So I pull my Stockings off," the narrator happily overcomes her compunctions about wading through a puddle.

17. Robert Weisbuch writes, "The verdict is a surprise. In the first stanza, the foot represents the usually adventuresome spirit, the boot the usually reticent body. The persona seems ready to risk death to gain bliss, ready to sacrifice the common oxygen for the uncommon lightning—and yet the foot decides in favor of the boot, its antithesis. The point is that too much questioning negates the opportunity, that the will must not abdicate its power of choice. When the foot is allowed to make the choice, it loses its symbolic identity to become a mere part of the comfort-seeking body" (146).

18. Execution, in Dickinson's poems, is more apt to be considered from the perspective of those sympathizing with the condemned than with those personating public order and civility. See, for example, the poet's projected maternal sympathy with an executed felon in "Upon the gallows hung a wretch."

19. Ronald Wallace interprets the poem as being comedic, as exemplified by Dickinson's joke on "matter": "Both the legal matter (the case under consideration) and the physical matter (the poet's body) end in the tranquil and amiable pun" (100).

20. Charles R. Anderson writes of this poem's dialogic narration, "The legal language, concentrated in the first half, not only sets the scene but controls the meaning throughout. Brought up in a family of lawyers, [Dickinson] came by it naturally. But far more important than her precision in handling its terminology is the imaginative fitness with which she puts it to work. The dramatic appeal of a criminal trial comes from the contrast of the lawless emotions involved in the original actions and the ordered procedure by which the court re-enacts them, with the possibility that at any moment the violently human may erupt through the formalism of its jargon. From this situational irony she creates her strategy, giving it a unique twist by having one actor, the masking 'I,' slip successively into all the leading roles—prisoner-in-the-dock, defense counsel, judge, jury, and courtroom spectators" (232).

21. In *Emily Dickinson's Vision*, I discuss the significance of Lord Byron's poem for the poet in the several contexts of her optical illness, Romantic women writers' narratives of confinement, and poetic narrators' searches for an imprisoned Other (69–73).

22. Roger Sedarat, in applying a Lacanian approach to reading this poem, considers the speaker to be prevented from achieving the subjective vision that would permit her to reunite with her "betrothed" by external monitoring that is objectified in distorting "Veils[s]" and "filament[s]" authorized by law: "Here . . . a speaker's individual position in the landscape proves somewhat representative of a legal trend during the

time of this poem's writing. As in other poems . . . she remains subjected to the gaze in nature, in this case at an almost microscopic, underground level" (49).

23. Another poem suggesting the possibility of either sexual union or reunion despite mutual incarceration is "They put Us far apart –," in which the speaker's projected union with the Other is figured as the superimposition of two suns, producing a composite crepuscular disk both can witness, no matter how far removed from each other they may be.

24. "Crease" possesses a second and productive meaning as a synonym for "wrinkle." The fabric of the "Veil" may be wrinkled, but so may a lady's face, especially after long years spent in durance vile. That secondary meaning is reinforced by the way in which the poet deploys "wrinkle" and "crease" in F1264, another piece falling within the subgenre of her poems representing the frost as an attractive assassin. Dickinson gets a good pun from prism/prison, as she refers to the crystalline beauty left by the frost on the flowers it has destroyed.

> Like Time's insidious wrinkle
> On a beloved Face –
> We clutch the Grace the tighter
> Though we resent the Crease
> The Frost himself so comely
> Dishevels every prime
> Asserting from his Prism
> That none can punish him

25. The Dickinsons took an active interest in the reforming of local institutions dedicated to treating the mentally ill. In 1859, the governor of Massachusetts appointed Edward Dickinson one of the trustees for the new Northampton Lunatic Asylum (Longsworth 51). Emily Dickinson mentions madness in at least a half-dozen poems, including "Much Madness is divinest Sense" (F620), written around 1863, where she refers to a possibly insane person being "handled with a Chain."

26. Prison architects have been and continue to be influenced by Jeremy Bentham's Panopticon, a hypothetical structure in which, as Bentham wrote, centralized authority could view prisoners without itself being subject to view. Such a degree of covert surveillance established "a new mode of obtaining power of mind over mind, in a quantity hitherto without example." In *Discipline and Punish*, Michel Foucault writes of such a structure's probable effect on prisoners' psyches: "Hence the major effect of the Panopticon: to induce in the inmate a state of conscious and permanent visibility that assures the automatic functioning of power. So to arrange things that the surveillance is permanent in its effects, even if it is discontinuous in its action; that the perfection of power should tend to render its actual exercise unnecessary; that this architectural apparatus should be a machine for creating and sustaining a power relation independent of the person who exercises it; in short, that the inmates should be caught up in a power situation of which they are themselves the bearers" (201).

27. Brown also suggests that Dix's Calvinistic background predisposed her to favor the "separate" system: "She endorsed the separate system as 'a more direct application and exercise of Christian rule and precepts, than any other mode of prison-government'" (133).

28. Dix said of the Transcendentalists as a group that they were "too wholly destitute

of plausibility to involve danger of harm to even the most credulous" (qtd. in Brown 335).

29. Vivian Pollak says, however: "The search for the perfect society, manifest in the reform enthusiasm of the 1840s and 1850s, never touched [Dickinson]. She was immune to sewing societies and schemes for prison reform" ("That Fine Prosperity" 164).

30. Dickinson consulted a well-known physician in Boston, William Wesselhoeft, for some unidentified complaint as early as 1851.

31. Dickinson's praises of whipping to Austin and to Sue should be understood as being facetious. The poet knew full well that whippings could be administered cruelly, unfairly, and sadistically. In a letter to her brother, Dickinson describes hearing the screams of a servant girl being whipped by her employer: "Has father written you that Edwin Pierce, our neighbor, was arrested last week, for beating a servant girl, tried, and fined two dollars and costs? Vinnie and I heard the whipping, and could have testified, if the Court had called upon us" (L129).

32. For an insightful discussion of the "seclusion of the self of the lyric self in its solitary cell" as a basis for lyric poetry, and of the performative role occupied by readers of Dickinson's carcerative poems, see Jackson 132.

7. A Kiss from Thermopylae

1. On the decline in crime rates see Friedman 449. On the poet's response to civil unrest, David Reynolds writes: "More clearly than any woman writer of her time, Dickinson saw that American popular culture was neither tame nor simplistic. Indeed, when Dickinson wrote poetry about this popular culture, her imagination was inevitably preoccupied with its violent, disorienting elements" (428).

2. In this letter to Elizabeth Dickinson Currier, the poet cites two recent local crimes: "Would Father's youngest Sister believe that in the 'shire Town,' where he and Blackstone went to school, a man was hung in Northampton yesterday for the murder of a man by the name of Dickinson, and that Miss Harriet Merrill was poisoned by a strolling Juggler, and to be tried in the Supreme Court next week?" Her reference to "Blackstone" alludes to her father's reading of law in Northampton, and the letter as a whole appears designed to attribute a local erosion of lawfulness to the death of her father. Her reference to "Supreme Court" must allude to the Supreme Judicial Court of Massachusetts, on which Judge Lord, also deceased at the time of this letter's composition, had once sat.

3. *Black's* provides more modern definitions for "rule of law," as well as example phrases: "1. A substantive legal principle ('under the rule of law known as respondeat superior, the employer is answerable for all wrongs committed by an employee in the course of the employment'). 2. The supremacy of regular as opposed to arbitrary power ('citizens must respect the rule of law'). Also termed *supremacy of law*. 3. The doctrine that every person is subject to the ordinary law within the jurisdiction ('all persons within the United States are within the American rule of law')" (1359).

4. As a body of thought, law in Britain and America has oscillated between a conviction that society benefits from having a set of rules to follow, and a belief that the law needs also to supply a remedy to those for whom the rules prove inadequate. This latter idea was often employed to justify the continued existence of equity as a quasi-independent judicial entity. Lawrence Solum writes, "One important ideal of

Western legal systems is captured by the phrase 'the rule of law.' A common interpretation of this idea is expressed in the proposition that the rule of law requires a law of rules. Another legal ideal is called 'equity.' This second ideal is frequently interpreted as the injunction that legal decision makers sometimes ought to depart from the rules to do justice in particular cases. If these interpretations are correct, the two ideals are in tension" (120).

5. See, for example, Perry Miller's comments quoted in this volume's introduction about changing attitudes toward the practice of law.

6. In an early letter written to Abiah Root when the poet was only fifteen years old, Dickinson mentions approaching comprehensive examinations at school, during which she fears she will have to "recite as precise as the laws of the Medes and Persians" (L7). Dickinson is alluding here to Daniel 6:15, in which the laws of the Persians are described as being immune to alteration or repeal. The phrase was used proverbially to describe a degree of official oversight so exacting as to be oppressive. Although Dickinson was an adolescent at the time of this writing, she seems nevertheless to have been aware already of an essential difference between systems of laws adopted by democratic and dictatorial societies. Her father, and the curriculum at her primary school, would have taught her that the American legal system (and the British, from which it derived), incorporated processes for revising laws, or even rescinding them.

7. In a letter to Higginson, the poet wrote, "For poets – I have Keats and Mr. and Mrs. Browning. For prose – Mr. Ruskin, Sir Thomas Browne, and the Revelations" (L261).

8. For a discussion of the poet's knowledge of classical civilizations, see Cleary.

9. Capps traces the poet's familiarity with the story of Thermopylae to either of two textbooks Dickinson read while at Mount Holyoke: J. E. Worcester's *Elements of History, Ancient and Modern,* or Oliver Goldsmith's *Grecian History.* Worcester's account of the battle emphasizes the famous epitaph reported by Herodotus: "Two only of the Spartans . . . survived the battle. A monument was erected on the spot, bearing this inscription, written by Simonides: 'O stranger! Tell it at Lacedaemon, that we died here in obedience to her laws.' " Capps notes that "the detail of death in obedience to law, omitted by Goldsmith, is included in Worcester's account" (108).

10. The substitution stems from a second version of the couplet, reported in other ancient sources, which has "laws" (*nomimois*) rather than "orders" (*rhēmasi*). See Campbell 399–400.

11. Cristanne Miller also suggests that Dickinson is personifying the law here as Judge Lord (193).

12. Richard Sewall observes of Judge Lord, "While it cannot quite be said that he died in harness, like Edward Dickinson, he kept on nearly to the end" (649).

13. One of the more intriguing plays Dickinson may have made on Judge Lord's name appears in F1575, written perhaps in 1882, while Lord was enduring his final illness. It's a variation on the New England Primer's classic childhood prayer "And now I lay me down to sleep":

> Now I lay thee down to Sleep –
> I pray the Lord thy Dust to keep –
> And if thou live before thou wake –
> I pray the Lord thy Soul to make –

Dickinson's version conflating "Lord" with "the lord" may permit the inference that

Judge Lord, even at the moment of his death, could yet exercise some judicial authority in determining whether he will furnish a soul to be maintained eternally.

14. Lord's career as an attorney was a relatively successful one. Winthrop Dakin writes of him: "Of his 124 appellate court cases he won 48% and of those he initiated below 56%. By comparison with the three Dickinsons [i.e., Samuel, Edward, and Austin] this latter figure indicated in him a more reliable legal judgment as to probable forensic outcome than any of them demonstrated" (38).

15. As biographers have pointed out, however, Dickinson was not alone in regarding Lord as virtually a personification of law. Lyndall Gordon quotes Susan Dickinson: "Susan thought him 'a perfect figure-head for the Supreme Court, from his stiff stock to his toes.' His individuality, she said, was 'so bristling, his conviction that he alone was the embodiment of the law, as given on Sinai, so entire, his suspicion of all but himself, so deeply founded on the rock bed of old conservative Whig tenacities, not to say obstinacies' that he could not 'coalesce' with others at The Evergreens" (161). Alfred Habegger writes, "Whether or not Otis was Edward's best friend, as Emily claimed, it is significant that she saw her lover in that light. Each man was an old-fashioned and unbending Whig lawyer who could be identified with the very idea of law, thus making possible some complicated games involving obedience and defiance. The 'best little girl in Amherst' delighted in setting Lord up as an embodiment of the right to punish, then daring him to become her accomplice in a lawless frolic" (*My Wars* 592).

16. Army troops and the police finally halted rioters near Gramercy Park in lower Manhattan. Many of the rioters were poor Irish immigrant draftees who resented the fact that middle- and upper-class Northerners who had been drafted could afford to pay a bounty for a substitute. Austin Dickinson, for example, paid for a substitute in May 1864.

17. Although the draft riots in New York constituted the largest civil insurrection Americans had seen to that date, other urban disturbances during Dickinson's lifetime also made national headlines: the Astor Place Riot (also called the "Shakespeare Riot") of 1849, the New York City Police Riot of 1857, the New Orleans race riot of 1866, and the Cincinnati Riot of 1884. Riots in European cities during the latter half of the century also seized the attention of Americans, perhaps none so much as those associated with the rising of the Paris Commune, in 1871.

18. Aaron Kramer writes of this poem, "In only thirty-four words [Dickinson] constructs a complete mob narrative from its slow subterranean development 'in a congenial ground' to its unpredictable time and place of explosion, which 'Police cannot suppress'" (208).

19. Dickinson's references to mobs are not always pejorative. Occasionally she used the word ironically and humorously, as in two excerpts from poems written probably during the early 1880s. The first is F1553:

> From all the Jails the Boys and Girls
> Ecstatically leap –
> Beloved only Afternoon
> That Prison does'nt keep
>
> They storm the Earth And stun the Air,
> A Mob of solid Bliss –
> Alas – that Dusk should lie in wait | / Alas – that Frowns should lie in wait
> For such a Sweet as this – |/ For such a Foe as this –

The poet's frame of reference, however, still points toward urban disorder. Children dismissed early from school are compared to escaped prison inmates who "storm the Earth" like sans-culottes assaulting the Bastille. Adults, of course, are implicitly compared to figures of authority determined to put down such civic unrest. In another poem about eerie weather conditions that may precede summer thunderstorms ("There came a Wind like a Bugle –," F1618), the narrator describes shutting up the house just before the deluge strikes, as if the inhabitants were protecting their lives and houses from an insurrection. Groves of trees standing outside during the storm are figured as a desperate "Mob":

> We barred the Windows and the Doors
> As from an Emerald Ghost –
> The Doom's Electric Moccasin
> That very instant passed –
> On a strange Mob of panting Trees
> And Fences fled away
> And Rivers where the Houses ran
> Those looked that lived – that Day –

As if recalling a historic day on which the town had been assaulted by an array of marauding forces including not only the frenzied trees but also the "electric Moccasin" of the lightning (a reminder of western Massachusetts' history of Indian attacks?), the poem's narrator speaks as if describing a narrow escape of civilization itself from various agents of anarchy. Even the fences protecting houses and yards are flattened by the storm, suggesting an implicit attack on personal property. Dickinson derives considerable ironic humor by characterizing a natural and rural event as a scene of urban disorder; also, her adoption of a consciously commemorative tone of voice and somewhat sententious diction parodies modes of address employed by an older generation that had survived the Revolutionary era.

20. B. J. Smith writes of this poem, "Laws are the suburb of content. They are the place of order and peace. . . . [L]aw is represented by the 'Acres' which are a unit of measure universally agreed upon by men. Men live in them and ownership of them is granted by law and the law is binding. Rights to the 'Acres' are enforced by mutual good faith and, if that breaks down, by the law. In these bound and bounded places 'Agony' and 'Affliction' can be avoided even tho [sic] pain and suffering may not because bounded places put limits on extent. . . . In contrast, 'Tremendousness,' 'Boundlessness,' are free of all law, all limits, by their very nature. With them, near them there is no security. . . . Man is safe as long as he stays within the limits of the law, within the society of men, with the 'Acres,' but is in danger of life, sanity and peace if he ventures beyond these limits to the edge of knowing, to God, to the Sublime" (43).

21. Dickinson employed the word "bomb" in her writing generically to mean any explosive device, without specific reference to the bombs anarchists were just beginning to employ for assassination attempts during the late decades of the nineteenth century. The invention of dynamite in 1862 greatly facilitated the use of bombs for political murder. In 1880, Stepan Khalturin used dynamite to blow up part of the Winter Palace in Saint Petersburg, although without succeeding in killing Tsar Alexander II; Benedict Anderson has said of that attempt, "Nobel's invention had now arrived politically" (97). On March 1, 1881, Narodnaya Volya succeeded in killing the tsar

with a bomb. Dickinson's death on May 15, 1886, preceded the Haymarket riot and dynamite bombing in Chicago by a mere two weeks.

22. The image of a bomb in Dickinson's poems would seem to be allied to her other well-known symbolic representations of potential violence, including volcanoes and loaded guns. See Patterson 37.

23. Cristanne Miller, however, suggests that Dickinson's poetic style could have been much less "lawless" than some critics—and the poet herself at times, as in her letter to Higginson—have accused it of being. Miller also points to a fashion for "wildness" in American poetry written at midcentury, saying that Dickinson "was far from unique in bending conventional forms" (20–21).

24. Daniel Lombardo notes the depth of local distrust in Amherst of vagrants during the late nineteenth century: "Amherst had genuine sympathy for residents who suffered from hard times, but not much for those from elsewhere who came to town looking for work" (5).

25. I examine this letter draft at some length in "Heritable Heaven: Erotic Properties in the Dickinson–Lord Correspondence," 203.

26. Wayfaring is also mentioned in Isaiah 33:7–8: "Behold, their valiant ones shall cry without: the ambassadors of peace shall weep bitterly. The highways lie waste, the wayfaring man ceaseth: he hath broken the covenant, he hath despised the cities, he regardeth no man."

27. On a perhaps similar note, Dickinson was apt to describe herself as being "wayward." Others evidently used that term in describing her: in an early letter to T. W. Higginson, the poet wrote, "I think you called me 'Wayward.' Will you help me improve?" (L271). In "Sweet Mountains – Ye tell Me no lie –" (F745) she wrote,

> My Strong Madonnas – Cherish still –
> The Wayward Nun – beneath the Hill –

The word "wayward" is synonymous with being headstrong, and applied most commonly, perhaps, to children and young people. Webster's 1828 dictionary defines the term as "Froward; peevish; perverse; liking his own way." The image conjured up by the term in Dickinson's poem is of someone who has set off stubbornly on his or her own path, such as a novitiate who has left a Catholic order.

28. A roughly analogous term is "scoundrel," similar to "rascal" in having some legal connotations, yet possessing, for those who have been labeled scoundrels, limited legal recourse. *Bouvier's* says of "scoundrel": "An opprobrious title applicable to a person of bad character. General damages will not lie for calling a man a scoundrel, but special damages may be recovered when there has been an actual loss" (2: 962). The word appears only once in Dickinson's extant writings, in a humorous letter sent to her uncle Joel Norcross, in which she rails, "You villain without a rival – unparalleled doer of crimes – scoundrel unheard of before – disturber of public peace – 'creation's blot and blank' – state's prison filler – *magnum bonum* promise maker – harum scarum promise breaker – Oh what can I call you more?" (L29).

29. Dickinson occasionally displaced the figural role of rural vagabond, rogue, and wayfarer onto birds, especially the bobolink, mentioned in five letters and twelve poems. Qualities she associates with the bobolink include artistic talent, a plebian background, and a mischievous lawlessness. In 1883 she wrote to her young niece (L845, emphases added):

I hope you are having superb times, and am sure you are, for I hear your voices, mad and sweet – as a *Mob* of Bobolinks.

I send you my love – which is always new for *Rascals* like you. . . .

Bobolinks serve as figures of lawless creativity in such poems as "The Bobolink is gone – The Rowdy of the Meadow –" (F1620), "No Bobolink – reverse His Singing" (F766), and "The Way to know the Bobolink" (F1348). That last poem's speaker describes the bobolink as a sort of avian sans-culotte:

> Of impudent Habiliment
> Attired to defy,
> Impertinence subordinate
> At times to Majesty –
>
> Of Sentiments seditious
> Amenable to Law –
> As Heresies of Transport
> Or Puck's Apostacy –

30. In another letter draft evidently intended for Judge Lord (L843, Amherst College ms. A 440a), Dickinson referred to herself as an asset that could be stolen by thieves. If so, she says, the best form of security was to enjoy pleasures before they could be taken away: "I feel like wasting my cheek on your hand tonight. Will you accept the squander. Lay up treasures immediately, that's the best anodyne for moth and rust and the thief whom the Bible knew enough of banking to suspect would break in and steal." Part of Dickinson's message to Lord here would seem to be that because their time together is running out, they should capitalize on opportunities immediately. Interestingly, the draft exists in both a preliminary and in a more finished version, indicating that Dickinson took some pains to convey her message clearly.

WORKS CITED

The following abbreviations refer to the writings of Emily Dickinson:

F   *The Poems of Emily Dickinson.* Ed. R. W. Franklin. 3 vols. Cambridge: Harvard University Press, 1998. Citation by poem number; variant is A unless otherwise indicated.

L   *The Letters of Emily Dickinson.* Ed. Thomas H. Johnson and Theodora Ward. 3 vols. Cambridge: Harvard University Press, 1958. Citation by letter number.

Andersen, Roger. *Understanding Trusts and Estates.* 4th ed. San Francisco: Matthew Bender, 2009.

Anderson, Benedict. "In the World-Shadow of Bismarck and Nobel." *New Left Review* 28 (July–August 2004): 85–129.

Anderson, Charles R. *Emily Dickinson's Poetry: The Stairway of Surprise.* New York: Holt, Rinehart & Winston, 1960.

Anson, Sir William Reynell. *Principles of the Law of Contract.* Chicago: Callaghan & Company, 1880.

Atiyah, P. S. *An Introduction to the Law of Contract.* Oxford: Clarendon Press, 1961.

Bianchi, Martha. *The Life and Letters of Emily Dickinson.* Boston: Houghton Mifflin, 1924.

Bingham, Millicent Todd. *Ancestors' Brocades: The Literary Debut of Emily Dickinson.* New York: Harper & Brothers, 1945.

Black's Law Dictionary. 8th ed. Ed. Bryan A. Garner. St. Paul: Thomson West, 2004.

Bouvier's Law Dictionary. 2 vols. Ed. Francis Rawle. Boston: The Boston Book Company, 1897.

Brown, Thomas J. *Dorothea Dix: New England Reformer.* Cambridge: Harvard University Press, 1998.

Campbell, David A. *Greek Lyric Poetry.* Houndsmills, U.K.: Macmillan, 1967.

Capps, Jack L. *Emily Dickinson's Reading, 1836–1886.* Cambridge: Harvard University Press, 1966.

Clark, Christopher. *The Roots of Rural Capitalism: Western Massachusetts, 1780–1860.* Ithaca: Cornell University Press, 1990.

Cleary, Vincent J. "Emily Dickinson's Classical Education." *English Language Notes* 18.2 (December 1980): 119–29.

Coleman, Peter J. *Debtors and Creditors in America: Insolvency, Imprisonment for Debt, and Bankruptcy, 1607–1900.* Frederick, Md.: Beard Books, 1999.

Cozine, R. Kirkland. "The Emergence of Written Appellate Briefs in the Nineteenth-Century United States." *American Journal of Legal History* 38.4 (October 1994): 482–530.

Crumbley, Paul. "Dickinson's Correspondence and the Politics of Gift-Based Circulation." Eberwein and MacKenzie 28–55.

———. "Dickinson's Dialogic Voice." Grabher, Hagenbüchle, and Miller 93–109.

Cuddy, Lois. "The Latin Imprint on Emily Dickinson's Poetry: Theory and Practice." *American Literature: A Journal of Literary History, Criticism, and Bibliography* 50.1 (1978): 74–84.

Dakin, Winthrop. "Lawyers around Emily Dickinson." *Dickinson Studies* 47 (December 1983): 36–40.

Deppman, Jed. " 'I Could Not Have Defined the Change': Rereading Dickinson's Definition Poetry." *Emily Dickinson Journal* 11.1 (2002): 49–80.

De Tocqueville, Alexis. *Democracy in America.* Ed. J. P. Mayer. Garden City, N.Y.: Anchor Books, 1969.

Dickens, Charles. *American Notes.* 1842. Introd. Christopher Hitchens. New York: The Modern Library / Random House, 1996.

Diehl, Joanne Feit. " 'Ransom in a Voice': Language as Defense in Dickinson's Poetry." *Feminist Critics Read Emily Dickinson.* Ed. Suzanne Juhasz. Bloomington: Indiana University Press, 1983. 23–39.

Dietrich, Deborah. "Legal Imagery." *An Emily Dickinson Encyclopedia.* Ed. Jane Eberwein. Westport, Conn.: Greenwood Press, 1998. 172–73.

Dobbs, Dan. *Law of Remedies.* 2nd ed., abridged. St. Paul: West Publishing, 1993.

Eberwein, Jane Donahue. "Dickinson's 'I had some things that I called mine.' " *The Explicator* 42.3 (Spring 1984): 31–33.

Eberwein, Jane Donahue, and Cindy MacKenzie, eds. *Reading Emily Dickinson's Letters: Critical Essays.* Amherst: University of Massachusetts Press, 2009.

Erkkila, Betsy. *The Wicked Sisters: Women Poets, Literary History, and Discord.* New York: Oxford University Press, 1992.

Ferlazzo, Paul J. *Emily Dickinson.* Boston: Twayne, 1976.

Foucault, Michel. *Discipline and Punish: The Birth of the Prison.* Trans. Alan Sheridan. New York: Pantheon Books, 1977. Originally published in Paris by Editions Gallimard, 1975.

Frank, Jerome. *Law and the Modern Mind.* New York: Brentano's, 1930.

Friedman, Lawrence. *A History of American Law.* 3rd ed. New York: Simon & Schuster, 2005.

Frimet, Rhett. "The Birth of Bankruptcy in the United States." *Commercial Law Journal* 96.2 (Summer 1991): 160–88.

Garner, Bryan A. *The Redbook: A Manual on Legal Style.* St. Paul: West Group, 2002.

Gelpi, Albert J. *Emily Dickinson: The Mind of the Poet.* Cambridge: Harvard University Press, 1965.

Gordon, Lyndall. *Lives Like Loaded Guns: Emily Dickinson and Her Family's Feuds.* 1st American ed. New York: Viking, 2010.

Grabher, Gudrun, Roland Hagenbüchle, and Cristanne Miller, eds. *The Emily Dickinson Handbook.* Amherst: University of Massachusetts Press, 1998.

Guthrie, James R. "Darwinian Dickinson: The Scandalous Rise and Noble Fall of the Common Clover." *Emily Dickinson Journal* 16.1 (2007): 73–91.

———. *Emily Dickinson's Vision: Illness and Identity in Her Poetry.* Gainesville: University Press of Florida, 1998.

———. "Exceeding Legal and Linguistic Limits: Dickinson as 'Involuntary Bankrupt.'" *Emily Dickinson Journal* 14.2 (2005): 89–102.

———. "Heritable Heaven: Erotic Properties in the Dickinson–Lord Correspondence." Eberwein and MacKenzie 189–212.

———. "Law, Property, and Provincialism in Dickinson's Poems and Letters to Judge Lord." *Emily Dickinson Journal* 5.1 (1996): 27–44.

———. "'Some things that I called mine': Dickinson and the Perils of Property Ownership." *Emily Dickinson Journal* 9.2 (2000): 16–22.

Habegger, Alfred. "How the Dickinsons Lost Their Homes." *ESQ* 44.3 (1998): 161–97.

———. *My Wars Are Laid Away in Books: The Life of Emily Dickinson.* New York: Random House, 2001.

Holland, Jeanne. "Scraps, Stamps, and Cutouts: Emily Dickinson's Domestic Technologies of Publication." *Cultural Artifacts and the Production of Meaning: The Page, the Image, and the Body.* Ed. Margaret Ezell and Katherine O'Brien O'Keeffe. Ann Arbor: University of Michigan Press, 1994. 139–81.

Horan, Elizabeth Rosa. "Technically Outside the Law: Who Permits, Who Profits, and Why." *Emily Dickinson Journal* 10.1 (2001): 34–54.

Howard, William. "Emily Dickinson's Poetic Vocabulary." *PMLA* 72.1 (March 1957): 225–48.

Jackson, Virginia. *Dickinson's Misery: A Theory of Lyric Reading.* Princeton: Princeton University Press, 2005.

Johnson, Thomas H., ed. *The Poems of Emily Dickinson.* 3 vols. Cambridge: Belknap Press of Harvard University Press, 1955.

Jones, Rowena Revis. "'A Royal Seal': Emily Dickinson's Rite of Baptism." *Religion and Literature* 18.3 (Fall 1986): 29–51.

Kramer, Aaron. *The Prophetic Tradition in American Poetry, 1835–1900.* Rutherford, N.J.: Fairleigh Dickinson University Press, 1968.

Kurzon, Dennis. *It Is Hereby Performed . . . : Explorations in Legal Speech Acts.* Amsterdam: John Benjamins, 1986.

Lambert, Robert. *Emily Dickinson's Use of Anglo-American Legal Concepts and Vocabulary in Her Poetry: Muse at the Bar.* Lewiston, Maine: Edwin Mellen, 1997.

Lesick, Lawrence. *The Lane Rebels: Evangelicalism and Antislavery in Antebellum America.* Metuchen, N.J.: The Scarecrow Press, 1980.

Leyda, Jay, ed. *The Years and Hours of Emily Dickinson.* 2 vols. New Haven: Yale University Press, 1960.

Lombardo, Dan. *A Hedge Away: The Other Side of Emily Dickinson's Amherst.* Northampton, Mass.: Daily Hampshire Gazette, 1997.

Longsworth, Polly. *The World of Emily Dickinson.* New York: Norton, 1990.

MacKenzie, Cynthia. *A Concordance to the Letters of Emily Dickinson.* Boulder: University Press of Colorado, 2000.

Manual of Patent Examining Procedure. 8th ed. U.S. Department of Commerce, 2001.

Meredith, Robert. "Emily Dickinson and the Acquisitive Society." *New England Quarterly* 37.4 (December 1964): 435–52.

Messmer, Marietta. *A Vice for Voices: Reading Emily Dickinson's Correspondences.* Amherst: University of Massachusetts Press, 2001.

Miller, Cristanne. *Emily Dickinson: A Poet's Grammar.* Cambridge: Harvard University Press, 1987.

Miller, Perry, ed. *The American Puritans: Their Prose and Poetry.* Garden City, N.Y.: Anchor Books, 1956.

———, ed. *The Legal Mind in America: From Independence to the Civil War.* Ithaca: Cornell University Press, 1970.

———. *The Life of the Mind in America: From the Revolution to the Civil War: Books One through Three.* New York: Harcourt, Brace & World, 1965.

Mitchell, Domhnall. *Emily Dickinson: Monarch of Perception.* Amherst: University of Massachusetts Press, 2000.

Mudge, Jean McClure. *Emily Dickinson and the Image of Home.* Amherst: University of Massachusetts Press, 1975.

Murray, Aife. *Maid as Muse: How Servants Changed Emily Dickinson's Life and Language.* Concord: University of New Hampshire Press, 2009.

North, Christopher [John Wilson]. "The Greek Anthology. No. V." *Blackwood's Edinburgh Magazine* 34, no. 216 (December 1833): 961–98.

Paglia, Camille. *Sexual Personae: Art and Decadence from Nefertiti to Emily Dickinson.* New Haven: Yale University Press, 1990.

Patterson, Rebecca. *Emily Dickinson's Imagery.* Ed. Margaret H. Freeman. Amherst: University of Massachusetts Press, 1979.

Pollak, Vivian. *A Poet's Parents: The Courtship Letters of Emily Norcross and Edward Dickinson.* Chapel Hill: University of North Carolina Press, 1988.

———. "'That Fine Prosperity': Economic Metaphors in Emily Dickinson's Poetry." *Modern Language Quarterly* 34 (1973): 161–79.

Porter, David. *Dickinson: The Modern Idiom.* Cambridge: Harvard University Press, 1981.

Reynolds, David S. *Beneath the American Renaissance: The Subversive Imagination in the Age of Emerson and Melville.* New York: Knopf, 1988.

Rosenbaum, Stanford. P. *A Concordance to the Poems of Emily Dickinson.* Ithaca: Cornell University Press, 1964.

Ruskin, John. *Modern Painters.* 1873. Ed. David Barrie. London: Pilkington Press, 2000.

Schama, Simon. *Dead Certainties (Unwarranted Speculations).* New York: Knopf, 1991.

Scribner, Charles H. *A Treatise on the Law of Dower.* Philadelphia: J. B. Lippincott, 1864.

Sedarat, Roger. *New England Landscape History in American Poetry: A Lacanian View.* Amherst, N.Y.: Cambria Press, 2011.

Selden, John. *Table-Talk: Being the Discourses of John Selden*. London: E. Smith, 1689.

Sewall, Richard B. *The Life of Emily Dickinson*. New York: Farrar, Straus & Giroux, 1974.

Shakespeare, William. *The Merchant of Venice*. Ed. John Russell Brown. Arden Shakespeare, 2nd ser. London: Thomson Learning, 1955.

Sherwood, William R. *Circumference and Circumstance: Stages in the Mind and Art of Emily Dickinson*. New York: Columbia University Press, 1968.

Small, Judy Jo. *Positive as Sound: Emily Dickinson's Rhyme*. Athens: University of Georgia Press, 1990.

Smith, B. J. "Vicinity to Laws." *Dickinson Studies* 56 (December 1985): 38–52.

Smith, Martha Nell. "The Poet as Cartoonist." *Comic Power in Emily Dickinson*. By Suzanne Juhasz, Cristanne Miller, and Martha Nell Smith. Austin: University of Texas Press, 1993. 63–102.

———. *Rowing in Eden: Rereading Emily Dickinson*. Austin: University of Texas Press, 1992.

Solum, Lawrence. "Equity and the Rule of Law." *The Rule of Law*. Ed. Ian Shapiro. New York: New York University Press, 1994. 120–47.

Sprankling, John G. *Understanding Property Law*. 2nd ed. San Francisco: Matthew Bender, 2008.

St. Armand, Barton Levi. *Emily Dickinson and Her Culture: The Soul's Society*. Cambridge: Cambridge University Press, 1984.

Sullivan, William. *The Political Class Book; Intended to Instruct the Higher Classes in Schools in the Origin, Nature, and Use of Political Power*. Boston: Carter, Hendee & Co, 1834.

Vendler, Helen. *Dickinson: Selected Poems and Commentaries*. Cambridge: Belknap Press of Harvard University Press, 2010.

Wallace, Ronald. *God Be with the Clown: Humor in American Poetry*. Columbia: University of Missouri Press, 1984.

Wardrop, Daneen. *Emily Dickinson's Gothic: Goblin with a Gauge*. Iowa City: University of Iowa Press, 1996.

Weisbuch, Robert. *Emily Dickinson's Poetry*. Chicago: University of Chicago Press, 1975.

Werner, Marta. *Emily Dickinson's Open Folios: Scenes of Reading, Surfaces of Writing*. Ann Arbor: University of Michigan Press, 1995.

Wilbur, Richard. "Sumptuous Destitution." 1960. *Emily Dickinson: A Collection of Critical Essays*. Ed. Judith Farr. Upper Saddle River, N.J.: Prentice-Hall, 1996. 53–61.

Wolff, Cynthia Griffin. *Emily Dickinson*. Reading, Mass.: Addison-Wesley, 1988.

Yoshino, Kenji. *A Thousand Times More Fair: What Shakespeare's Plays Teach Us about Justice*. New York: HarperCollins, 2011.

Zurcher, Andrew. *Shakespeare and Law*. London: Methuen, 2010.

INDEX OF POEMS

INDEX

Adam: fall of, 20, 25, 27, 110, 112;
    intellectual inquiry by, 110–11, 112; in
    "Paradise is of the Option –," 31–32;
    in "Paradise is that old mansion," 30
affidavits, in "The Fact that Earth is
    Heaven –," 15–16
Alexander II (tsar of Russia), assassina-
    tion of, 225n21
"Alone and in a Circumstance,"
    58–70; adverse possession in, 61,
    206n18; Austin Dickinson and,
    66, 70; authority in, 69; autograph
    manuscript of, 66–68, 70; battery
    in, 63; deponent of, 152; Edward
    Dickinson and, 67–68, 208n29;
    equity in, 43, 69, 70; foreclosure in,
    62; gymnasiums in, 61, 207n20; heirs
    in, 62; humor in, 58–60; injury in,
    64, 65; intended audience of, 66, 68,
    70; interclass frictions in, 207n20;
    judicial power in, 69; landlord and
    tenant in, 99; land ownership in, 89;
    larceny in, 64; legal burlesque in,
    59–60, 206n18; legal fact pattern of,
    66; locomotive graphic of, 66–68,
    207n26, 208n29; narrator of, 59,
    60, 61–62, 64, 69, 207n25, 208n32;
    ownership in, 60; powerlessness
    in, 58, 70; privy setting of, 58–59,

206n15, 207n25; property in, 59, 60;
    redress in, 64–65; remedy in, 65–66;
    reticence/residence in, 59–60, 64, 65;
    and Sand's *Mauprat*, 66, 68, 69–70,
    207n22, 208n35; spiders in, 59, 60,
    61–65, 206nn16–17,19, 207nn24–25;
    trespass in, 60, 99; variants in, 70
Amherst (Mass.): attractions for
    Dickinson, 9–10; crime in, 193;
    morality in, 173; outsiders in, 188–89,
    193, 226n24; professional class of,
    1; property owners of, 97–98; rail
    travel to, 150; upper middle class of,
    41, 199n30; xenophobia in, 188–89,
    226n24
Amherst Academy, Dickinson's studies
    at, 3, 200n13
Amherst & Belchertown Railroad:
    Edward Dickinson and, 67, 68,
    195n4, 199n30; failure of, 18, 67,
    208n28; reorganization of, 68–69
Amherst College: Austin Dickinson's
    trusteeship of, 113; Dickinson family
    and, 1, 2, 9; Edward Dickinson's
    trusteeship of, 113; faculty of, 10
anarchy: bombing in, 225n21; law as
    barrier to, 185
Andersen, Roger, 137, 217n22
Anderson, Benedict, 225n21

Anderson, Charles R., 220n20
Andrews, Charles Bartlett, 10
annihilation, in "To lose One's faith –
    surpass," 125–26
anxiety, psychological phenomenon of,
    184
arrest, warrants for, 13, 197n22
ars moriendi, 215n4
assassinations, anarchists', 225n21
"As subtle as tomorrow," warrant in,
    218n2
Atiyah, P. S., 210n10
attorneys: administration of estates,
    113–15; demonstration of intent,
    100; De Toqueville on, 6; ethics of
    communication, 217n22; intellectual
    glamour attached to, 176; of post-
    Revolutionary period, 196nn12–13;
    prose style of, 10, 197n19, 198n28;
    public attitudes toward, 4, 5–6;
    training of, 7–8. *See also* trustees
Auburn system (penal reform), 165, 168;
    abandonment of, 166; silence in, 169
Austin, John L., 198n24
authoritarianism, in Dickinson's
    thought, 17

bailiffs: in "I had some things that I called
    mine," 93; in "A prompt – executive
    Bird is the Jay –," 12–13, 15, 92
Baker, Osmyn, 10
bankruptcy: in antebellum America,
    19–20, 24–26, 32; British tradition
    of, 26; in Dickinson family, 41; in
    Dickinson's works, 16, 26–27, 192,
    204n25; federal law on, 199n3; honor-
    able, 26, 34; involuntary, 36, 203n21;
    in "I think To Love – may be a Bliss,"
    36–38; in Massachusetts, 24, 199n3;
    Samuel Dickinson's, 2, 18–19, 31, 97,
    200nn7,10; sexual, 33; voluntary, 33,
    36
Bankruptcy Act, federal (1800), 19
Bankruptcy Act, federal (1841), 25, 199n3,
    203n21; repeal of, 32
Bankruptcy Act, federal (1867), 32, 33,
    203n21

"The Bat is dun, with wrinkled
    Wings –," 98
battery, in "Alone and in a
    Circumstance," 63
"Because I could not stop for Death –,"
    116
Beecher-Tilton adultery trial (1875), 151
bee/flower metatrope: Dickinson's,
    78–80, 128–29, 171, 210n8; in
    women's poetry, 79
bees, dowry extended to, 129
Bentham, Jeremy: Panopticon of, 221n26
bereavement, financial metaphors for,
    39–40
betrothal: contractual definitions of, 88;
    in Dickinson's poems, 86–87; legal sta-
    tus of, 71, 211n15; marriage and, 86–88;
    rings in, 80; in "Title divine, is mine,"
    87–88. *See also* breach of promise
"The Bible is an antique Volume," 25, 26
Bingham, Millicent Todd, 214n2
Binney, Horace, 133
Black's Law Dictionary: on Blackacre,
    210n9; on breach of promise, 210n6;
    briefs in, 15; on ratification, 210n5;
    right-of-way in, 102; on rule of law,
    222n3
Blackstone's *Commentaries*, 6, 8, 222n2
"The Bobolink is gone – The Rowdy of
    the Meadow –," 227n29
bobolinks, lawlessness of, 226n29
bombs, in Dickinson's poetry, 187–88,
    225n21, 226n22
bonds, legal, 84–85; in *The Merchant of
    Venice*, 85, 204n6
Borden, Lizzie: trial of, 151
Bouvier's Law Dictionary: compensation
    in, 130–31; on jury empanelment, 153;
    on manor, 204n7; on matter, 160; on
    rascals, 192; on rule of law, 174; on
    scoundrels, 226n28; tenements in, 101
Bowdoin, Elbridge, 24, 200n8
Bowles, Samuel, 40, 210n14; Dickinson's
    correspondence with, 192
Bowles, William Lisle, 180
bravery: in death, 179; emotional,
    179–80, 181

breach of contract, 76–78; as act of God, 77, 209n5

breach of promise: in betrothal, 77–78; *Black's* on, 210n6; in Dickens, 210n7; in equity, 78

brides: dowry of, 126, 127; investment in marriage, 216n16. *See also* betrothal

briefs, legal: to appellate courts, 198n28; in "Is Bliss then, such Abyss –," 156, 158; in "A prompt – executive Bird is the Jay –," 15

Brown, Thomas J., 165

Burns, Anthony, 7

Byron, Lord: "The Prisoner of Chillon," 162, 168, 169, 220n21

Calvinism: Dix's, 221n27; Lord's, 182; view of material wealth, 90

capitalism, systems of exchange in, 148

Capps, Jack, 195n1, 204n5, 205n11, 209nn2,4; on Dickinson's reading, 217n21; on Thermopylae, 223n9

chancellors: abuse of authority, 57; clergymen, 44–45; conscience of, 44, 45, 47, 51, 204n3; as idols, 57; injunctions from, 47; judicial authority of, 55; medieval, 204n1; moral authority of, 55, 114; writs of ejectment, 60

chancery courts: in early America, 45; in Massachusetts, 46; resentment of, 45. *See also* equity courts

chancery courts, British, 44; abolition of, 43; appeal to sovereign from, 204n6; capital punishment recommendations, 56–57; in Dickens, 45; ecclesiastical roots of, 44–45, 47; relationship to common-law courts, 46–47

Charles River Bridge v. Warren Bridge, 7

Charlestown state prison (Massachusetts), 165

chattels: legal status of, 91; women's, 117, 118

Cherry Hill (model prison, Philadelphia), 165

Choate, Rufus, 7, 25, 142, 218n5

Christian Examiner, on penal reform, 164, 166

Christianity, eternal life in, 16

Chubb, Jeremiah, 214n22

Clark, Charles H., 191

Clark, Christopher, 199n4

classical civilization, Dickinson's knowledge of, 223n8

Clay, Henry, 134

codicils, 130, 134; in Dickinson's works, 122–24; doubt as, 124; multiple, 125; in "Which is best? Heaven –," 123–24

common law: damages assessed under, 44, 45; and law of physics, 99

common law, English: appeal to sovereign from, 44; foundation of American law in, 6

common-law courts: and equity courts, 44, 45; of Massachusetts, 46

common-law courts, English: relationship to chancery courts, 46–47

confessions, deathbed, 215n5

congregate system (penal reform), 165, 166

Conkey, Ithamar ("Frank"), 122–24, 195n2

Connecticut Valley: British settlers of, 189; frontier of, 94, 96; workers' rights in, 209n5

conscience: of chancellors, 44, 45, 47, 51, 204n3; legal associations of, 205n12; in "Who is it seeks my Pillow Nights –," 190

consciousness, as city, 186

considerations: in contract law, 80–81, 83; in "The Judge is like the Owl," 82; in jurisprudence, 81; in *The Merchant of Venice*, 81; "peppercorn rule" of, 81–82; as performance, 83; tangible, 81, 83–84; in "What would I give to see his face?," 81–82

contract law: consideration in, 80–81, 83; noncommercial transactions in, 71; terms of agreement in, 85

contracts: acts of God affecting, 77, 209n5; agricultural workers', 209n5; in betrothal, 88; breach of, 76–78, 209n5; certification of, 71; in

contracts (*continued*)
Dickinson's poems, 17, 71; enforceability of, 84, 87; failure of, 208n2;
in "'Faithful to the end' amended,"
208n2; of God with humankind,
76–77; in "I gave Myself to Him,"
34–36, 80, 204n24; inviolability
of, 84; in "It always felt to me – a
wrong," 52; in "I worked for chaff
and earning Wheat," 209n5; for land
sales, 82; in lovemaking, 34–36; marriage as, 71, 72, 88; in *The Merchant of
Venice*, 84–85, 205n8; physical tokens
of, 80; ratification of, 210n5; rings in,
71; seals on, 71, 83, 84, 210n10; signs
in, 71; symbols on, 83, 84; in "What
would I give to see his face?," 73, 76;
women in, 71
conveyancing, 95
copyright, 91, 104; Dickinson's view of,
214n19
creativity, Dickinson's, 110, 153–55, 170;
explosiveness of, 187–88; lawlessness
in, 188, 226n23; threats to, 171–72
crime: in Amherst, 193; in Dickinson's
correspondence, 143–44, 222n2; in
"I know some Lonely houses off the
Road," 148; in "I robbed the Woods –,"
147; of love, 162; in "A Rat surrendered here," 213n12; Reconstruction-
era, 173, 222n1; relationship to rail
travel, 150; in "Who robbed the
Woods –," 147–48; witnessing of, 150.
See also rioting, urban
Crumbley, Paul, 151; "Dickinson's
Dialogic Voice," 219n10
curiosity, intellectual benefits of, 111
Currier, Elizabeth Dickinson (aunt of
Emily), 195n3; Dickinson's correspondence with, 222n2
cyphering, education in, 217n16

Dakin, Winthrop, 197n15, 218n27; on
Lord, 224n14
Dartmouth College v. Woodward, 7
death: bravery in, 179; as business
transaction, 202n20; in "I heard a Fly

buzz," 115–17; legal ramifications of,
115; moments preceding, 215n10; of
summer, 119–20, 215n10
"Death is a Dialogue between": courtroom setting of, 131–33; Death as
judge in, 132–33, 134; dialogue of,
132–33; matter/spirit dichotomy in,
132; Spirit as advocate in, 132–33, 134;
topical allusions in, 133, 134; trust in,
132, 133
"Death warrants are supposed to be":
authority in, 57; equity in, 56, 57
debt: imprisonment for, 19–20, 26; of
lovers to beloved, 35
deeds: form of, 84; in "Paradise is of the
Option –," 32. *See also* property; real
property
defendants: indefensible, 98–99; vermin
as, 98
democracies: effect of demographic
change on, 185; mobs in, 185; weakness of, 184
De Toqueville, Alexis: on American
economy, 19; on lawyers, 6
Dickens, Charles: Dickinson's reading
of, 200n12, 217n21; on penal reform,
165. Works: *American Notes*, 165;
Bleak House, 45; *David Copperfield*,
26, 200n12; *Great Expectations*, 135,
136; *Pickwick Papers*, 145, 210n7
Dickinson, Edward (father of Emily):
accounting practices of, 38; and
"Alone and in a Circumstance,"
67–68; on American law, 21–22;
and Amherst & Belchertown
Railroad, 67, 68, 195n4, 199n30; on
the arts, 196n7; breach of promise
case, 78; civic projects of, 208n30;
in Congress, 7; construction of
Evergreens, 138, 140; death of, 4, 118;
Emily Dickinson on, 67–68; estate
of, 118, 215n8; fallibility of, 141; and
father's bankruptcy, 18, 130, 200n7;
financial interest in the Homestead,
23–24, 29; financial inventories of,
200n9; financial responsibility of, 22,
24; illness of, 67; interest in equity,

to Me – She still shall be –," 129;
in "When we have ceased to care,"
201n16
Gilbert, Thomas, 204n27
Girard, Stephen: will of, 133–34
"Given in Marriage unto Thee," 86–87;
rings in, 86; seals in, 86
God: contract with humankind, 76–77;
endorsement of mercy, 49; as fron-
tier, 96; providence of, 119; reclaim-
ing of land, 92; will of, 118–19
Goldsmith, Oliver: *Grecian History*,
223n9
Goodyear, Charles: rubber patent of, 105
Gordon, Lyndall, 204n27, 224n15
"'Go tell it' – What a Message,"
179–81; emotional bravery in, 181;
eroticism of, 179, 181; law in, 179;
nature in, 181; sweetness in, 181, 189;
Thermopylae in, 179, 181
Gould, George, 146; Dickinson's corre-
spondence with, 164
Grant, Ulysses, 32
Graves, John: correspondence with
Dickinson, 208n27
guilt: in "I robbed the Woods –," 147,
148; psychological effects of, 146, 148
Guthrie, James R.: "Darwinian
Dickinson," 210n8; *Emily Dickinson's
Vision*, 163, 220n21; "Heritable
Heaven," 226n25; "'Some things that
I called mine'…," 212n4

Habegger, Alfred, 14, 199n30; on bankruptcy law, 199n3; on Dickinson
family bankruptcy, 41, 200nn10–11,
201n19; "How the Dickinsons Lost
Their Homes," 22, 23, 199n1; on
Lord, 224n15; on Newman trust, 138,
218n28; on witnessing, 198nn25–26
heart: as device, 104; generation of
electricity, 214n18; invention of hope,
105; as tenant, 102, 103
"The Heart asks Pleasure – first –,"
Inquisition in, 205n14
heaven, as mansion, 30
heirs: of estates, 136; fraudulent, 121–22;

in "The Mushroom is the Elf of
Plants," 119–22, 140; responsibilities
of, 136. *See also* estates; inheritance;
trusts
"hereby," in legal language, 13–14
heroism, private, 179–80
Herschel, John, 136; hoax concerning,
217n23
Herschel, William, 136–37
Higginson, Thomas Wentworth: correspondence with Dickinson, 4, 15,
121, 166–67, 169, 178–79, 183, 187,
188, 208n31, 215n9, 218n24, 223n7,
226n27; on Dickinson family, 196n6;
on "I know some Lonely houses off
the Road," 219n8
Hobbs, Alfred C., 214n22
Hoffman, David, 6
Holland, Elizabeth: correspondence with
Dickinson, 11, 167, 203n20; optical
ailment of, 167
Holland, Jeanne, 206n15
Holland, Mrs. Joshua: correspondence
with Dickinson, 11
home: association with hope, 31; loss of,
18, 25, 28, 31–32
the Homestead (Dickinson home), 1;
Edward Dickinson's financial interest
in, 23–24, 29; Edward Dickinson's
repurchase of, 30, 97; loss of, 18, 25,
28; as lost Eden, 25; outsiders at, 189;
return to, 31; right-of-way at, 102;
sale to Mack, 24, 97; sharing with
Mack family, 101
Hoosac Tunnel, Edward Dickinson's
work with, 2
hope: emotional mechanism of, 107;
heart's invention of, 105; psychological phenomenon of, 175; usefulness
of, 106; in "The way Hope builds his
House," 175–76
"Hope is a strange invention –," 105–7;
nonobviousness in, 106; perpetual
motion machines in, 105–6; variants
of, 213n16
Howard, William, 196n8, 199n30,
206n15

Howland, William, 26, 27, 191–92, 200n14, 201n15
"How martial the Apology of Nature!," Thermopylae in, 181–82
"How ruthless are the gentle –," breach of contract in, 76–77
Humphrey, Jane: Dickinson's correspondence with, 145, 164

"I am afraid to own a Body –," 94–97; body/soul binary of, 96, 136; civilizing/decivilizing forces in, 187; "Duke" in, 95, 97; frontier in, 94, 96, 97; inheritance in, 94, 95–96; legal/philosophical ideals in, 95–96; narrator of, 95, 96; property ownership in, 94, 131; risk in, 97; testamentary bequest in, 136
"I cannot meet the Spring unmoved," warrant in, 198n23
"I felt a Funeral, in my Brain," 116; silence in, 168
"If I should die," commerce in, 202n20
"I gave Myself to Him –," 33–36; contractual language of, 34–36, 80, 204n24; parataxis in, 203n23; sexual potential in, 72; speaker of, 34
"I had not minded – Walls –," 221n24; Other in, 163; reunion in, 163, 220n22; solitary confinement in, 162–63
"I had some things that I called mine," 91–93, 134; bailiff figure in, 93; iron in, 93; justice in, 175; land seizure in, 92–93; property in, 152, 175, 212n6; tripartite rivalry in, 212n5
"I heard a Fly buzz – when I died –," 115–18, 215n10; funerary clichés of, 117; legal testimony in, 116–18; narrator of, 116–17, 118; nihilism of, 215n7; portion in, 117
"I know some Lonely houses off the Road," 148–50, 219n8; crime in, 148; witnessing in, 150
"I like to see it lap up the Miles –," 208n27
imagination, as asset, 35

immigration, in nineteenth-century U.S., 185, 224n16
incarceration: in Dickens, 145; in Dickinson's works, 145, 168, 169, 171, 222n32; in "I had not minded – Walls –," 163; in "They put Us far apart –," 221n23; in women's writings, 220n21
indemnity: in "Of so divine a Loss," 40, 41; in "She sped as Petals of a Rose," 39, 40
inheritance: in English law, 94–95, 97; in "I am afraid to own a Body –," 95–96; in "Nature and God – I neither knew," 135; of real property, 94–96; in "To lose One's faith – surpass," 125; by women, 95. See also estates; heirs; trusts
injury, in "Alone and in a Circumstance," 64, 65
Inquisition, in "The Heart asks Pleasure – first –," 205n14
insanity, as legal defense, 144–45, 218n5
insolvency: in Dickinson's works, 26–27, 201n14; emotional, 34
intellectual property, 91; in "'Twas awkward, but it fitted me –," 104; wealth from, 105
inventors, fraudulent, 107. See also patents
inviolability, legal, 84
"I read my sentence – steadily": accused in, 161; criminal trial of, 159–60; legal matter in, 160; polyvocalism of, 159–61; sentence of, 160, 161
"I robbed the Woods –": guilt in, 147, 148; narrator of, 147, 148
"Is Bliss then, such Abyss –," 155–59; abyss of, 156, 220n15; economic considerations in, 157–58; fallen woman trope of, 156; hedonic values of, 157; humor of, 158; legal brief in, 156, 158; narrator of, 155; patents in, 157, 214n21; polyvocalism of, 155, 158, 159; settlement in, 158, 159, 220n17; trial setting of, 155–58, 159
isolation: in Dickinson's works, 162, 163;

in "I tried to think a lonelier Thing,"
168–69
"It always felt to me – a wrong": contracts in, 52; equity in, 51; justice in, 51–52; legal terms in, 50–52; liability in, 52; Mosaic law in, 50–51; narrator of, 50, 51–52; remedy in, 53
"It feels a shame to be Alive –": liberty in, 178; Thermopylae in, 177–78
"I think To Love – may be a Bliss": bankruptcy in, 36–38; bank tropes in, 37–38; emotional solvency in, 38; ordination in, 37
"I tie my Hat – I crease my Shawl –," bomb trope of, 188
"I tried to think a lonelier Thing": isolation in, 168–69; Other in, 169
"I worked for chaff and earning Wheat," contracts in, 209n5

Jackson, Helen Hunt, 10, 11
Jackson, Virginia, 207n26
Johnson, Thomas, 32, 66, 146, 208nn27,34; on nature, 181; on Thermopylae, 179; on wayfaring, 189; on "Who is it seeks my Pillow Nights –," 190
Jones, Rowena Revis, 210n13
"The Judge is like the Owl": consideration in, 82; mutuality in, 82; negotiation in, 83; real property in, 82–83
judiciary, caprice in, 56–57
juries: empanelment of, 153; in "Shall I take thee, the Poet said," 153–54
justice: Dickinson's understanding of, 49–50; in English literary tradition, 49; in "I had some things that I called mine," 175; in "It always felt to me – a wrong," 51–52; in *The Merchant of Venice*, 47–48, 49, 53, 85; miscarriages of, 57; moral, 53; Old/New Testament concepts of, 50–52; and revenge, 53

Kent, James, 6; *Commentaries*, 8; on penal reform, 166
Khalturin, Stepan, 225n21

Kimball, Benjamin: Dickinson's correspondence with, 113–15, 134, 182; executorship of Lord's estate, 113–15, 215n10
"Know how to forget!," 213n17
Know Nothings, 185
Kölliker, Albert von, 214n18
Kramer, Aaron, 224n18
Kurzon, Dennis, 13–14, 198n24

laches (delay), in equity, 62
Lambert, Robert, 10, 126, 209n2; on dower, 216n14; *Emily Dickinson's Use of Anglo-American Legal Concepts*, 199n30; on "I had some things that I called mine," 212n5
land: in American law, 95; frontier, 94, 96–97; in legal "hypos," 93, 212n9; legal ownership of, 89; securing with locks, 111–12; seizure of, 91, 92–93; speculation in, 89, 211n2; titles to, 89, 211n1. *See also* real property
landlords: in Dickinson's poetry, 112; in "The Rat is the conciesest Tenant," 99, 100–101, 213n12; relationship with tenants, 98, 101–4
landlord-tenant law, 90; in Amherst, 97–98; Dickinson's interest in, 97, 101
larceny, in "Alone and in a Circumstance," 64
Latin, Dickinson's knowledge of, 3, 196n9, 200n13
law: affective relations in, 88; attraction of opposites in, 194; as barrier to anarchy, 185; Dickinson's engagement with, 1, 2, 3–5, 11–12, 140–41, 173–75, 194, 198n30, 199n30; emotion and, 88; in "'Go tell it' – What a Message," 179; intellectual glamour of, 176; interpersonal relations in, 151–52, 159; of love, 180; of Medes and Persians, 223n6; Mosaic, 50–51; in preservation of civic order, 173, 174; Puritan distrust of, 45; relationship to equity, 44, 45, 47; relationship to lawlessness, 194; as royal domain, 183; signs in, 85–86; supremacy of,

law: affective relations in (*continued*)
222n3; Thermopylae's embodiment
of, 176, 180, 194; trustees in, 130; in
"The way Hope builds his House,"
175–76. *See also* equity; rule of law
law, American: basis in English
common law, 6; changing attitudes
toward, 223n5; citizen resistance to,
5–6; Edward Dickinson on, 21–22;
equity in, 43–44; Golden Age of, 4;
land ownership in, 95; professionalization of, 7; proliferation of, 5;
revisions to, 223n6
law, English: inheritance in, 94–95, 97;
manor in, 51, 204n7; M'Naghten
rules, 144–45; transfer of property in,
91. *See also* chancery courts, British;
common law, English
lawlessness: of bobolinks, 226n29; in
Dickinson's creativity, 188, 226n23; in
"A nearness to Tremendousness –,"
184–86; relationship to law, 194
legal documents, Dickinson's signature
on, 14, 198nn26–27
legal language: annihilation in, 125;
Dickinson's use of, 11–12, 143, 167,
195n1, 197n18; executory, 13, 14;
illocutionary, 198n24; performative, 13; volitional subjunctive
of, 83
legal thinkers, antebellum American, 6
Leland, John, 23, 24
Leonidas (king of Sparta), 176, 177
lex talionis, 48, 53
Leyda, Jay, 140
liability, in "It always felt to me – a
wrong," 52
liberty, in "It feels a shame to be
Alive –," 178
"Like Time's insidious wrinkle," frost in,
221n24
Lincoln, Abraham: assassination of, 173
litigants, 6; of early Republic, 197nn13–
14; relationships between, 44
Locke, Richard A., 217n23
locks: improvements to, 111, 214n22;
patents for, 111; to secure lands,

111–12; in "What we see we know
somewhat," 111–12
Lombardo, Daniel, 226n24
Lord, Elizabeth: death of, 193; and
Dickinson's will, 115, 215n3
Lord, Otis Philips: association with
Thermopylae, 179–82; Calvinism of,
182; career as attorney, 224n14; correspondence with Dickinson, 11, 31, 33,
56, 123, 183, 189–90, 192–93, 196n11,
197n22, 204n25, 210n11, 214nn1–2,
219n12, 226n25, 227n30; death of,
113, 181, 182, 223n12; in Dickinson's
correspondence, 182; Dickinson's
epitaph for, 180; Dickinson's wordplay on, 183, 192, 223n13; estate of,
113–15, 215n10; final illness of, 180,
223n12; flirtatiousness of, 192; humor
of, 192, 197n22; individuality of,
224n15; judicial power of, 56; judicial
reputation of, 180, 181, 182, 224n15;
in Kidder trial, 192; love affair with
Dickinson, 4–5, 174, 179, 189–90,
192–94; on Massachusetts Supreme
Judicial Court, 222n2, 224n15; morality of, 173; in "Now I lay thee down
to Sleep –," 223n13; personification of
law, 223n11, 224n15; public service of,
182; taste in literature, 5
Lord Chancellor, British: moral function
of, 44–45
loss: in Dickinson's poems, 27–32; nonmaterial, 63–64
"A loss of something ever felt I –,"
27–29; judicial sessions in, 28–29;
legal terms in, 28; prince imagery in,
29, 30; secular fairy tale of, 29, 30
love: as capital, 34; contractual basis
of, 34–36, 204n24; crime of, 162; as
financial risk, 34; laws of, 180
lovers: debt to beloved, 35; power relations between, 55
Lyon, Mary, 3, 196n10

Mack, David, 31; Austin Dickinson's
tribute to, 201n18; purchase of the
Homestead, 24, 97

MacKenzie, Cynthia, 11
madness, in Dickinson's poems, 221n25
manor, in English law, 51, 204n7
marriage: banns, 79; betrothal and,
86–88; as contract, 71, 72, 88; as
financial risk, 34; in "Given in
Marriage unto Thee," 86–87; and
hierarchy of Trinity, 86, 211n14; in
Massachusetts law, 88; women's
contributions to, 129; women's status
in, 87–88, 126, 211n14
Marshall, John, 6
Marvell, Andrew: "A Dialogue Between
the Soul and Body," 131
Massachusetts: bankruptcy law (1838),
24, 199n3; chancery courts of, 46;
common-law courts of, 46; courts
of equity in, 43–44; General Court
of, 46; imprisonment for debt in,
20; Indian attacks in, 225n19; legal
leadership of, 7; marriage law in, 88;
Married Women's Property Act (1855),
127; railway lines of, 67; Supreme
Judicial Court, 222n2, 224n15
Medes and Persians, law of, 223n6
Melville, Herman: "From the House-
Top," 183–84
mens rea (criminal intent), 144–45
Mercury, transit of, 137
mercy: association with equity, 47; deeds
of, 48–49; God's endorsement of,
49; in *The Merchant of Venice*, 47, 52;
natural origin of, 49
Meredith, Robert, 220n15
Merrill, Harriet, 222n2
microscope, in "'Faith' is a fine inven-
tion," 108
Miller, Cristanne, 203n23, 219n10,
226n23; on Lord, 223n11
Miller, Perry, 6, 45, 223n5; *The Life of
the Mind in America*, 196nn12–13,
197n14; on property ownership, 90;
on Star Chamber, 204n2; on *Vidal v.
Philadelphia*, 134
Mitchell, Domnhall, 199n30, 208n33
M'Naghten, Daniel: murder of
Drummond, 145

M'Naghten rules (Britain), 144–45, 218n3
mobs: in democracies, 185; in "From all
the Jails the Boys and Girls," 224n19;
in "The mob within the heart,"
186–87, 224n18; in "There came a
Wind like a Bugle –," 225n19
"The mob within the heart," 224n19;
civic authority in, 186–87; law in,
225n20; ungovernable emotion in,
186–87
"Mortality is fatal" (Dickinson), 26–27,
200n14
Moses, punishment of, 50–52
Mount Holyoke Female Seminary,
Dickinson's studies at, 3, 143, 196n10,
219n6, 223n9
"Much madness is divinest Sense,"
221n25
Mudge, Jean, 213n15
Müller, Heinrich, 214n18
"The Mushroom is the Elf of Plants":
death of summer in, 119–20; drafts
of, 215n9; fraud in, 121–22; frost in,
120; grass as patriarch in, 120, 215n11;
heirs in, 119–22, 140
"Myself was formed – a Carpenter –,"
creative process in, 154

nature: in "'Go tell it' – What a
Message," 181; in "How martial the
Apology of Nature!," 181–82; negotiation with property, 73; sexuality
in, 73; on trial, 99; as trustee, 136; in
"What would I give to see his face?,"
73–75
"Nature and God – I neither knew,"
135–37; inheritance in, 135; narrator
of, 135–36; transit of Mercury in, 137;
trust property in, 135; the unknown
in, 137
"A nearness to Tremendousness –":
affliction in, 185–86; cityscape of,
184–85; lawlessness in, 184–85; rural
landscape in, 185
negotiation: capricious, 85; in "The
Judge is like the Owl," 83; in "What
would I give to see his face?," 73–76

New England: equity courts of, 69; property ownership in, 90; whipping in, 167

Newman, Anna: Edward Dickinson's trusteeship for, 138–40, 218n28; marriage of, 140

Newman, Clara: Edward Dickinson's trusteeship for, 138–40, 218n28; on Emily, 139; marriage of, 140

Newman, Mark: will of, 138

Newman, Mary Dickinson (aunt of Emily), 138

Newton, Benjamin, 183

New York: draft law (1863), 183; draft riots, 183, 224nn16–17; Field Code of, 46; property law in, 212n10, 216n13

Nightingale, Florence, 166

"No Bobolink – reverse His Singing," 227n29

"No Brigadier throughout the Year," jays in, 13

nonobviousness, legal criterion of, 106

Norcross, Albert: administration of father's estate, 139; self-dealing charges against, 218n28

Norcross, Fanny: correspondence with Dickinson, 11

Norcross, Joel, 21, 207n23; correspondence with Dickinson, 144, 145, 162, 226n28

Norcross, Loring, 18; administration of father's estate, 139; self-dealing charges against, 218n28

Norcross, Louise (Loo): correspondence with Dickinson, 11, 67

Norcross, William: estate of, 139

Norcross family, Edward Dickinson's marriage into, 21–22

North American Review, on penal reform, 164

Northampton Lunatic Asylum, Edward Dickinson's trusteeship for, 221n25

"Not One by Heaven defrauded stay –": God's will in, 118–19; restitution in, 119; testamentary wishes in, 118–19; wills in, 140

"Not with a Club, the Heart is broken," whipping in, 167–68

"Now I lay thee down to Sleep –," Lord in, 223n13

numbers, divisibility of, 216n16

obligation: existence as, 131; of property ownership, 94

occupancy: exploitative, 100; in "The Rat is the concisest Tenant," 100–101. *See also* tenancy

"Of Silken Speech and Specious Shoe," 79–80, 86; alliteration in, 80; divorce in, 79–80; sexual terms in, 79

"Of so divine a Loss": indemnity in, 40, 41; ledger tropes of, 40; solvency in, 40

"Of this is Day composed," 65; dower in, 54; remedy in, 54–55

oratory, in American politics, 9

ordination, in "I think To Love – may be a Bliss," 37

originality, value of, 108

Original Sin, redemption from, 20

Other: in Dickinson's works, 161–63, 168, 194; externalized, 161; in "I had not minded – Walls –," 163; in "I tried to think a lonelier Thing," 169; rats as, 99; self and, 162

owls, association with judges, 82–83

Paglia, Camille, 218n4

Panic of 1837, 25

Panopticon, Bentham's, 221n26

paradise, real property imagery of, 30, 202n20. *See also* Eden

"Paradise is of the Option –": Adam in, 31–32, 33; composition of, 32; deeds in, 32; Puritanism in, 201n17; real property in, 33, 202n20; repeal in, 32

"Paradise is that old mansion," 30–31; Adam in, 30

parataxis, Dickinson's use of, 203n23

Parkman, George, 142

Parkman-Webster murder trial (1850), 142–43, 151, 218n1

patent applications, for perpetual motion machines, 106–7

patents, 104; Dickinson on, 109–10; in "'Faith' is a fine invention," 108; infringement of, 109–10; law, 90, 91; legal defense of, 105; for locks, 111; in "What we see we know somewhat," 110

Paul, Saint: martyrdom of, 51, 52

Pearl, Clara Newman, 139

penal reform, antebellum, 143, 144, 164–67, 221n26; Auburn system, 165, 166, 168, 169; congregate system, 165, 166; Dickens on, 165; Dickinson and, 166–67; in New England periodicals, 164; Philadelphia system, 165; silence in, 165, 168; Transcendentalists on, 164. *See also* incarceration; punishment

performance: consideration as, 83; remedy of, 52

perpetual motion machines: in "Hope is a strange invention –," 105–6; patent applications for, 106–7

"Philadelphia lawyer" (phrase), 5–6

Philadelphia system (penal reform), 165

Pierce, Edwin, 222n31

Pierce, Franklin, 7

plaintiffs: in equity courts, 65; nonmaterial loss claims, 63–64

pleasures, deferred, 130

politics, American: oratory in, 9; Edward Dickinson's, 2, 9, 24–25; Whig, 93, 134

Pollak, Vivian, 202n20, 204n24, 222n29; *A Poet's Parents*, 21

polyvocalism: in Dickinson's poems, 151–52, 219nn10–11; of "I read my sentence – steadily," 159–61; in "Is Bliss then, such Abyss –," 155, 158, 159; of "'Twas Love – not me –," 162

popular culture, in Dickinson's works, 222n1

Porter, David, 206n16

possession: adverse, 61, 206n18; by *vi et armis*, 60

power, judicial: in "Alone and in a Circumstance," 69; in Dickinson's works, 56

power relations: in courtrooms, 13; between lovers, 55

"Precious to Me – She still shall be –": bee figure of, 128–29; dower in, 128, 129; fractionality in, 128; gift in, 129

primogeniture, British, 91, 94–95, 212n2; discarding of, 212n10

privity, in law, 207n25

"A prompt – executive Bird is the Jay –": bailiff figure of, 12–13, 15, 92; briefs in, 15; brigadier figure of, 13

property: acts of God affecting, 93; in "Alone and in a Circumstance," 59, 60; analogy with knowledge, 112; chattel, 91, 117, 118; continuous occupation of, 61; conveyance of, 95; in Dickinson's poems, 112; as extension of self, 59; faith as, 125; foreclosure on, 62; in "I had some things that I called mine," 152, 175, 212n6; inheritance of, 94; intangible, 91, 212n3; legal forms of, 90; negotiation with nature, 73; patriarchal dispositions of, 118–19; possession of, 60; in "The Rat is the concisest Tenant," 213n14; seizure of, 119; transfer of, 91; women's, 117, 118, 126–28. *See also* land; real property

property law: British, 95; in Dickinson's poems, 17; English, 90–91; in "The Fact that Earth is Heaven –," 16; reform of, 212n10; reliance of civilization on, 213n14; women's, 216n13

property ownership: in Amherst, 97–98; Dickinson's concerns over, 89–90, 212n4; in New England, 90; obligations of, 94; transcendentalists on, 90

propounding: in Dickinson's works, 219n12; of divorce, 80

"Publication – is the Auction," creative process in, 154

punishment: capital, 144; in Dickinson's works, 143, 144, 162; of rogues, 190; in "'Twas Love – not me –," 168. *See also* penal reform

Puritanism: in "Paradise is of the Option –," 201n17; universal harmony in, 201n17

works, 129–30, 137; misplaced, 130; in "'Remember me' implored the Thief!," 130–31

trustees, 113; accountability of, 217n22; in equity, 132; Jesus as, 131; in law, 130; of minors, 217n18; nature as, 136; standards of conduct for, 137, 138, 215n10. *See also* attorneys

trusts: Austin Dickinson's administration of, 113, 130, 218n27; in Dickens, 135, 136; Dickinson family feuds over, 139–40; dissolution of, 134; durability of, 137; Edward Dickinson's administration of, 113, 130, 138–40; immunity to judicial interference, 133; litigation concerning, 217n20; living, 132, 135, 136; for minors, 217n18; misuse of, 139, 140; in "Nature and God – I neither knew," 135; "Prudent Man" rule in, 218n27; secrecy in, 135, 136; wills and, 129, 130, 135. *See also* estates; heirs; inheritance

Tuckerman, Mrs. Edward: correspondence with Dickinson, 129–30

Twain, Mark: *Huckleberry Finn*, 122

"'Twas awkward, but it fitted me –": emotion and intellect in, 104; eviction in, 104; intellectual property in, 104; landlord-tenant relations in, 103–4

"'Twas Love – not me –": courtroom trope of, 161–62; mistaken identity in, 161–62; polyvocalism of, 162; punishment in, 168

Tyler, John, 32

unruliness, Dickinson's metaphors for, 192

"Upon the gallows hung a wretch," 220n18

U.S. Patent Office, 105; criteria of, 106–7

Vendler, Helen, 213n13

vermin: as defendants, 98; in Dickinson's poetry, 98, 212n12

Vidal v. Philadelphia, estates in, 133–34

violence, Dickinson's images of, 218n4. *See also* crime; rioting, urban

Volya, Narodnaya, 225n21

Wadsworth, Charles, 191

Wallace, Ronald, 220n19

Wardrop, Daneen, 215n7

warrants: for arrest, 13, 197n22; in "Death warrants are supposed to be," 56, 57; in "I cannot meet the Spring unmoved," 198n23

wayfarers: birds as, 226n29; Dickinson as, 189; in Dickinson's poetry, 188; in Isaiah, 226n26

"The way Hope builds his House," law in, 175–76

"The Way to know the Bobolink," 227n29

Webster, Daniel, 25, 93, 142; defense of Goodyear, 105; Edward Dickinson's support for, 9; public admiration for, 6–7; in *Vidal v. Philadelphia*, 133–34

Webster, John: murder trial of, 142–43

Webster, Noah: *American Dictionary of the English Language*, 9–10; definition of "rogue," 190; definition of waywardness, 226n27

Weisbuch, Robert, 220n17

"What Soft – Cherubic Creatures –," kindness in, 209n3

"What we see we know somewhat": dividends in, 110, 111; locks in, 111–12; narrator of, 110; patents in, 110

"What would I give to see his face?," 72–76; bargaining in, 152; bee/flower metatrope of, 78–79; consideration in, 81–82; contracts in, 73, 76; direct address in, 76; fecundity in, 73; financial language of, 74, 75; *The Merchant of Venice* in, 72–76; narrator of, 73–74, 76; nature in, 73–75; negotiation in, 73–76; reproduction in, 75; reunion in, 73–74; sexuality in, 73–74, 75

"When we have ceased to care," gift in, 201n16

"Which is best? Heaven –": afterlife in,

"Which is best? Heaven –" (*continued*)
124; codicils in, 123–24; testamentary
language of, 124
Whig Party: Edward Dickinson and,
2, 24–25, 89; Lemuel Shaw and, 93;
nomination of Clay, 134
whipping: in Dickinson's works, 143, 163,
172, 222n31; in New England domestic life, 167; in "Not with a Club, the
Heart is broken," 167–68
Whitman, Walt: "Song of Myself," 160
"Who is it seeks my Pillow Nights –":
conscience in, 190; rogues in, 190
"Who robbed the Woods –," 219n7;
crime in, 147–48; narrator of, 147,
148
widows, dower of, 126, 127, 129, 216n12
Wilbur, Richard: "Sumptuous
Destitution," 217n17
Williams, Henry W., 169
wills: alternative versions of, 122–23;
codicils to, 122–23, 130, 134; in
Dickinson's poems, 17; in "Not One
by Heaven defrauded stay –," 140;
seals of, 115; secretive, 119; trusts and,
129, 130, 135; women's, 118. *See also*
estates; inheritance; trusts

witnessing: in "I know some Lonely
houses off the Road," 150; of legal
documents, 14, 198nn26–27
Wolff, Cynthia Griffin, 126, 198n30
women: chattels of, 117, 118; in contracts,
71; contributions to marriage, 129;
economic powerlessness of, 75; education in civics, 196n10; emotional
bravery of, 179–80; fallen, 156–57;
gendered poetry of, 188; inheritance
by, 95; interest in estates, 117, 118, 119,
126–27; narratives of confinement,
220n21; property of, 117, 118, 126–28;
reformers, 166; reproductive potential
of, 72, 75–76, 129; self-worth of, 74;
status in marriage, 87–88, 126, 211n14;
widow's third of, 126, 127; wills of,
118. *See also* dower
Worcester, J. E.: *Elements of History*,
223n9
"A word is dead when it is said," 198n25
Wordsworth, William: "Nuns fret not,"
101

Yoshino, Kenji, 204n6, 205n8

Zurcher, Andrew, 205n12

JAMES R. GUTHRIE is a professor of English at Wright State University in Dayton, Ohio. A native of Ann Arbor, Michigan, he attended the University of Michigan, where he received a Hopwood award for his poetry. He then went on to receive an MFA, MA, and PhD in English at SUNY / Buffalo. He is the author of *Emily Dickinson's Vision: Illness and Identity in Her Poetry* (1998) and *Above Time: Emerson's and Thoreau's Temporal Revolutions* (2001). He is the husband of Rebecca A. Cochran, a professor of law at the University of Dayton School of Law, and the father of two sons.